Anonymous

The Brooklyn Council of 1874

Letter-missive, statement and documents, together with an official phonographic

report of the proceedings, and the result of the Council

Anonymous

The Brooklyn Council of 1874
Letter-missive, statement and documents, together with an official phonographic report of the proceedings, and the result of the Council

ISBN/EAN: 9783337301347

Printed in Europe, USA, Canada, Australia, Japan

Cover: Foto ©ninafisch / pixelio.de

More available books at **www.hansebooks.com**

THE

BROOKLYN COUNCIL

OF 1874.

LETTER-MISSIVE, STATEMENT,
AND DOCUMENTS,

TOGETHER WITH

An Official Phonographic Report of the Proceedings,
and the Result of Council.

―――――・―――――

NEW YORK:
WOOLWORTH AND GRAHAM,
1874.

PUBLISHERS' PREFACE.

THE Advisory Council convened in Brooklyn, March 24th, 1874, was so large in numbers, it included so many distinguished men, and was called to consider questions of such substantial and enduring importance to the fraternity of Congregational churches, that, beyond almost any similar body heretofore convened, it attracted public attention; and the more or less full accounts of its proceedings which have been already published have been widely read. In view, however, of the prominence and importance of the Council, a general desire has been expressed to have a more complete report of its discussions than has thus far appeared, presented in a volume for permanent preservation.

Anticipating the probability of this, the committees of the churches calling the Council had made arrangements beforehand for a complete stenographic report of all its public discussions and proceedings, by Mr. Frederick J. Warburton; and that report has been placed at the disposal of the present publishers, and is contained in this volume.

Arrangements had also been made for a similar report of the private deliberations of the Council, if it should seem desirable to the body itself to have such a record made of them. But as the Council preferred, no doubt wisely, to preserve the entirely confidential character of the informal and interlocutory discussions of its private sessions, no report of them exists. The "Result," which was reached by means of them, is their only authentic record and fruit.

That Result is contained in the present volume; as is also the correspondence between the churches, which preceded the calling of the Council, and the final report of the committees to the churches that invited it.

The publishers have spared no pains to make the volume accurate and satisfactory, in its exhibition of all the public words and doings of the Council. They believe that the importance of the subjects discussed will give it a permanent as well as an immediate interest and value, — not only to the Congregational churches of the country, but to the members of other Christian communions, who may wish to know what Congregationalism is, and what power it has to conserve the purity and the faith of the churches.

One of the publishers, having been a member of one of the committees of the inviting churches, desires to add here his testimony to the entire harmony which marked the proceedings of those committees, in regard to the weighty matters entrusted to them, from the time when the first resolutions were passed appointing them to their office, till the time when their final report was made to the churches which had appointed them, and when they were discharged from further service.

He has never seen a company of Christian men more desirous to do fully and faithfully, but to do nothing beyond, what the churches intended ; or more certainly actuated by the spirit of love to the cause and kingdom of the Divine Master. He cannot but believe that such deliberations and action as those of the churches and their committees, and of the Council in which these resulted, will be followed by the blessing of Him who is the Head of the kingdom, and will be found to have been to His honor and praise !

New York, June, 1874.

CONTENTS.

LETTER-MISSIVE.

The Church of the Pilgrims, and the Clinton Avenue Congregational Church, SEND GREETING:

DEAR BRETHREN IN CHRIST:

Since November last we have been in correspondence, through our pastors and special committees, with the Plymouth Church in this city, on certain questions of church-discipline, and of the proper fellowship of Congregational churches.

The occasion of this correspondence, with our letters, and the letters and resolutions of the Plymouth Church in reply, will be found fully spread forth in the documents accompanying this Letter-Missive, and in the explanatory statement prepared, at our request, by our committees.

We have now reached a point where we feel ourselves to need, and at liberty to seek, the aid of the wisdom of other churches ; that we may know how far what we have done is approved by them, and what course we should properly follow in the future.

We have desired, and, as our letters will show, have earnestly sought, that all the questions at issue between us, on the one hand, and the Plymouth Church on the other, should be submitted by that church, as by us, to a Council chosen in common.

We have not been able to obtain from that church a decisive answer, either in the affirmative or in the negative, to this request ; and the further protracting of our correspondence appears to us inexpedient, in view of the delays connected with it, of its comparative fruitlessness hitherto, and of the mutually suspicious and hostile feeling which it has shown itself liable to excite.

We therefore wholly lay aside any effort to secure a Coun-

1

cil which should have it for a part of its function to advise that church, after due inquiry, as to the regularity of its past proceedings, or the proper course to be pursued by it in future ; and we now confine ourselves to asking a Council to advise *us,* in regard to matters which have come before us in connection with this correspondence, and which to us appear of grave importance.

We especially ask the testimony and advice of our sister churches, and of eminent divines, on the points presented in the following Questions, to wit : —

First. Is it in accordance with the order and usage of Congregationalism that a member may terminate his membership in a church by absenting himself from its services and communion? or is a corporate and consenting action on the part of the church necessary to such termination of membership?

Second. During the voluntary absence of a member from the ordinances, if specific charges, of grossly unchristian conduct, are presented against him by a brother in the church, — to which charges he declines to answer, — is it in accordance with the order and usage of Congregationalism that the church shall withhold inquiry as to the alleged wickedness, and, in face of such public assertion of his offenses, shall treat him as if still unaccused, dropping his name from its roll "without reflection upon him"?

Third. When such a member is charged with having "circulated and promoted scandals, derogatory to the Christian integrity of the pastor, and injurious to the reputation of the church," if he be publicly released, by the church which he confronts, without examination of the facts, and without censure, from all further responsibility to it, has the rule of Christ in the eighteenth chapter of Matthew, concerning the treatment of the trespassing brother, as commonly administered in Congregational churches, been maintained? or is it distinctly disregarded, in a case which called for its careful observance?

Fourth. Was the action of the Plymouth Church, in the case of discipline issued by it October 31, 1873, as presented in the published documents, in accordance with the order and usage of Congregational churches? or was it an apparent departure from these, tending, in the circumstances, to injure and offend other churches in fellowship, and warranting apprehension and remonstrance on our part.

Fifth. In view of the aforesaid action of Plymouth Church, and of the fact that this is maintained as in accordance with its customary policy, what is the duty, concerning that church, of the churches calling this Council? Especially, what is their duty in regard to continuing in their fellowship with it?

Sixth. In view of the resolution adopted by the Plymouth Church Dec. 5, 1873, in which its rules are interpreted, publicly, and with authority, "as relieving all other churches from responsibility for the Doctrine, Order, and Discipline of this church, and this church from all responsibility for those of other churches," what is the duty, concerning that church, of the churches calling this Council? Especially, what action, if any, should they take to release themselves from the mutually responsible connection with it, in which they have stood before the Christian public?

Seventh. Have the churches calling this Council acted, in its judgment, in substantial accordance with the principles of Congregationalism, as set forth in our authorized Platforms of Polity, in the remonstrances and requests addressed by them to the Plymouth Church? or in what respect, if in any, have they erred toward that church, and departed from these principles, in the representations which they have made to it?

We ask you, dear Brethren, to meet in Council, by your pastor and delegate, at the Clinton Avenue Church in this city, on the 24th of March, 1874, at 7, p.m., to consider these Questions, or such of them as the Council may deem it wise to consider, and to give us the light of your wisdom upon them.

We purpose to notify the Plymouth Church of our action in the premises, and to convey to them our desire and hope that they will be present with us at the sessions of the Council, by their pastor and a committee, to correct any statements of fact which may seem to them erroneous, and to furnish any further and special information which the Council may request.

But it is to be expressly understood that the Council is called to advise us, and not them ; that we propose no investigation into the truth or falsehood of any charges which have been made against any of their members ; and that, so far as we are concerned, only the public proceedings of that church, concerning which, as matters of fact, there seems room for no doubt, will come within your cognizance.

We wish to know, simply, if our recent action toward that church, when the reasons for it are fully explained, is deemed to have been proper; and how, in the judgment of sister churches, we should order ourselves concerning it hereafter.

And we pray for a Result which may be for the good of all our churches ; admonishing us, if we are deemed to have acted wrongly ; guiding us aright, if we are found in error on the Questions proposed ; but vindicating the polity which is consecrated to us by both memories and hopes, for which we have faithfully labored in the past, which has seemed to us to be intimately connected with the Christian progress of our country, and to which, as understood by us, we continue as ever earnestly attached.

Wishing you grace, mercy, and peace, from God our Father, and from the Lord Jesus Christ, we, are dear Brethren, affectionately yours, in the faith and fellowship of the Gospel :

For the Church of the Pilgrims :

RICHARD S. STORRS, *Pastor,*

RICHARD P. BUCK,
ARCHIBALD BAXTER,
DWIGHT JOHNSON,
JOSHUA M. VAN COTT,   } *Committee.*
ELI MYGATT, JUN.,
WALTER T. HATCH,
LUCIEN BIRDSEYE,

For Clinton Avenue Congregational Church :

WILLIAM IVES BUDINGTON, *Pastor,*

ALFRED S. BARNES,
JAMES W. ELWELL,
HARVEY B. SPELMAN,
THOMAS S. THORP,   } *Committee.*
AUGUSTUS F. LIBBY,
FLAMEN B. CANDLER,
CALVIN C. WOOLWORTH,

*THE CHURCHES AND MINISTERS INVITED TO SIT
IN COUNCIL ARE:*

FROM MAINE:
 BRUNSWICK, FIRST CHURCH.
 PORTLAND, SECOND PARISH CHURCH.
   HIGH STREET CHURCH.
   STATE STREET CHURCH.
 BATH, WINTER STREET CHURCH.
 BANGOR, CENTRAL CHURCH.

  REV. W. M. BARBOUR, D.D., BANGOR.

FROM NEW HAMPSHIRE:
 PORTSMOUTH, FIRST CHURCH.
 CONCORD, SOUTH CHURCH.
 MANCHESTER, FRANKLIN STREET CHURCH.

  REV. ASA D. SMITH, D.D., HANOVER.

FROM VERMONT:
 RUTLAND, FIRST CHURCH.
 BURLINGTON, FIRST CHURCH.
 MONTPELIER, FIRST CHURCH.
 ST. JOHNSBURY, SECOND CHURCH.

FROM MASSACHUSETTS:
 CAMBRIDGE, FIRST CHURCH.
 BOSTON, OLD SOUTH CHURCH.
   UNION CHURCH.
   PHILLIPS CHURCH.
   ELIOT CHURCH.
   CENTRAL CHURCH.
   SHAWMUT CHURCH.
 NORTHAMPTON, FIRST CHURCH.
   EDWARDS CHURCH.
 WESTFIELD, FIRST CHURCH.
 PITTSFIELD, FIRST CHURCH.
 NEW-BEDFORD, NORTH CHURCH.
 WORCESTER, CALVINIST CHURCH.
   UNION CHURCH.
 AMHERST, COLLEGE CHURCH.
 CAMBRIDGEPORT, FIRST CHURCH.

SPRINGFIELD, SOUTH CHURCH.
NORTH CHURCH.
LOWELL, HIGH STREET CHURCH.
ANDOVER, CHURCH IN THEOLOGICAL SEMINARY.

Rev. H. M. DEXTER, D.D., BOSTON.
Rev. S. B. TREAT, BOSTON.
Rev. JOHN PIKE, D.D., ROWLEY.

FROM RHODE ISLAND:
PROVIDENCE, BENEFICENT CHURCH.
CENTRAL CHURCH.
UNION CHURCH.

FROM CONNECTICUT:
HARTFORD, FIRST CHURCH.
PARK CHURCH.
NEW HAVEN, FIRST CHURCH.
NORTH CHURCH.
NEW LONDON, FIRST CHURCH.
SECOND CHURCH.
STAMFORD, FIRST CHURCH.
FAIRFIELD, FIRST CHURCH.
BRIDGEPORT, FIRST CHURCH.
SECOND CHURCH.
NORWICH, SECOND CHURCH.
BROADWAY CHURCH.

Rev. T. D. WOOLSEY, D.D., HEW HAVEN.
Rev. SAMUEL HARRIS, D.D., NEW HAVEN.
Rev. HORACE BUSHNELL, D.D., HARTFORD.
Rev. R. G. VERMILYE, D.D., HARTFORD.

FROM NEW YORK:
NEW YORK CITY, BROADWAY TABERNACLE CHURCH.
FIRST CHURCH IN HARLEM.
ALBANY, FIRST CHURCH.
BROOKLYN, SOUTH CHURCH.
ELM PLACE CHURCH.
CENTRAL CHURCH.
NEW ENGLAND CHURCH, (E.D.)
STATE-STREET CHURCH.
PURITAN CHURCH.
LEE AVENUE CHURCH, (E.D.)

SYRACUSE, PLYMOUTH CHURCH.
BINGHAMTON, FIRST CHURCH.
FAIRPORT, FIRST CHURCH.
HOMER, FIRST CHURCH.

Rev. RAY PALMER, D.D., NEW YORK.
Rev. D. B. COE, D.D., NEW YORK.
REV. E. W. GILMAN, NEW YORK.

FROM NEW JERSEY:
NEWARK FIRST CHURCH.
BELLEVILLE AVENUE CHURCH.
JERSEY CITY, FIRST CHURCH.
ORANGE VALLEY, FIRST CHURCH.
ORANGE, TRINITY CHURCH.
MONTCLAIR, FIRST CHURCH.

FROM DISTRICT OF COLUMBIA:
WASHINGTON, FIRST CHURCH.

FROM OHIO:
COLUMBUS, FIRST CHURCH.
OBERLIN, SECOND CHURCH.

REV. J. H. FAIRCHILD, D.D., OBERLIN.

FROM MICHIGAN:
DETROIT, FIRST CHURCH.
SECOND CHURCH.

FROM ILLINOIS:
CHICAGO, FIRST CHURCH.
PLYMOUTH CHURCH.
NEW ENGLAND CHURCH.
UNION PARK CHURCH.

REV. G. N. BOARDMAN, D.D., CHICAGO.

FROM WISCONSIN:
MILWAUKEE, SPRING STREET CHURCH.

REV. A. L. CHAPIN D.D., BELOIT.
REV. W. E. MERRIMAN, D.D., RIPON.

FROM IOWA:
REV. G. F. MAGOUN, D.D., GRINNELL.

FROM MISSOURI:
ST. LOUIS, FIRST CHURCH.

The Resolutions, providing for the issuing of this Letter-Missive, adopted at special meetings of the Church of the Pilgrims, and the Clinton Avenue Congregational Church, held February 23, 1874, are as follows : —

Resolved, That the Letter-Missive now read be adopted by this church, and that the Council contemplated by it be called, according to its terms.

Resolved, That to the Council be invited such churches, near and more distant, with such eminent ministers of our denomination, as may fully represent the ripe and wise judgment of the Congregational churches on the questions submitted ; and that the pastor and special committee, in connection with the pastor and committee of the Clinton Avenue Church,* be requested to designate, and authorized to invite them, after due consultation, and to sign, on our behalf, the Letter-Missive.

Resolved, That the same committee be requested to send, to the churches and ministers invited, copies of the letters, etc., which have passed between our churches and the Plymouth Church ; with such an explanatory statement, of the history of the case, and of the principles involved, as may seem needful ; and also to prepare and present the case for the consideration of the Council, when convened.

Resolved, That the clerk of the church be instructed to notify the Plymouth Church of the calling of the Council, at least one week before its sessions commence, and to furnish them a copy of the Letter-Missive, with an invitation to be present at the Council, by their pastor and a committee, for the purposes specified in the letter.

       Attest,

LUCIEN BIRDSEYE,

Clerk of the Church of the Pilgrims, pro tem.

FLAMEN B. CANDLER,

Clerk of Clinton Avenue Congregational Church.

BROOKLYN, N.Y., Feb. 23, 1874.

---

* ("Church of the Pilgrims," *as adopted by Clinton Avenue Church.*)

["When difficulties, whether internal or external, threaten the peace and spiritual prosperity of any church, and are not likely to be adjusted without aid, or when any question arises on which the church needs advice, for the guidance and correction, or confirmation, of its own judgment, that church has a right to ask the advice of other churches with which it is in communion." — *Platform of Ecclesiastical Polity*, p. 52.]

STATEMENT.

[The following Statement has been prepared by the Committees of the "Church of the Pilgrims," and the "Clinton Avenue Church," at the request of those churches. It is intended to accompany the documents hereinafter presented, and to give any needful additional information, in regard to the origin and design of these documents, and the principles involved in them. It anticipates, in part, the full presentation of the matters to be brought before the Council, on behalf of these churches, by their committees ; and it is hoped may prepare the way for that, and make it at last more easy and complete.

The careful attention of the pastors and delegates of the churches invited to the Council, is earnestly solicited to it.

BROOKLYN, N.Y., March 2, 1874.]

On the 6th of October last, as is shown by published documents, charges were presented to the Examining Committee of the Plymouth Church in this city, by one of the members of that church, against another, whose name was still upon its roll, although he had withdrawn from its services. These charges alleged, with specifications, that the member accused had "circulated and promoted scandals derogatory to the Christian integrity of the pastor, and injurious to the reputation of the church." No denial of the charges was interposed by the accused ; but, to a special committee, appointed to wait on him, he made answer that he had not been for nearly four years an attendant of Plymouth Church, and did not consider himself a member of it, or amenable to its jurisdiction.

The Examining Committee, however, at a subsequent meeting, in face of this declaration, sent to him another communication, enclosing a copy of the charges, with their specific allegations, and requesting from him an answer to them. In response, he repeated his declaration that he had terminated his connection with the church, was not a member of it, and could not receive the document addressed to him in that capacity.

Thereupon it was recommended by the Committee, without further investigation of the charges, so definitely made, and so recently accepted and forwarded, that since the member accused had abandoned his connection with the church, by prolonged absence from its services and ordinances, therefore his name be dropped from its list. At a meeting of the church, held on the evening of October 31, at which the facts above stated were made known, and at which the member accused was present, it was so voted, by a large majority ; and his name was dropped, as the clerk of the church the next day explained, in a published official note, " without reflection upon him."

The course thus adopted was advocated by the pastor, according to published reports, as being in accordance with the established policy of the Plymouth Church.

These facts becoming public, it appeared to many members of our churches, that, if they were correctly understood, a dangerous error had been committed, whether consciously or not, by a church with which we had been for many years in happy fellowship ; which we had highly honored for its works' sake; with whose pastor ours had been closely allied ; with whose internal affairs we had never, in any case, sought to interfere ; but the preservation of efficient discipline in which, with the unblemished whiteness of its pastor's fame, was important to others as well as to itself, — was important, indeed, to all Christians and churches.

The action taken had been corporate and public, and was not the individual act of one or of many. It had been taken deliberately, after consideration ; and taken in a case so signal and startling, which many circumstances had made so notorious, that the eyes of the whole community were upon it. If, therefore, an instance can ever occur in which neighboring churches, affiliated with another in public fellowship, may properly remonstrate with it against practices adopted, and principles of action publicly applied, this seemed such a case ; and the surpassing importance of the interests involved appeared to leave us no alternative.

It was felt that if the action thus taken was to be regarded as exceptional in its nature, peculiar to the case presented, it could not fail to leave the impression on many minds that the church had departed from its ordinary course, and had shrunk from investigating such serious charges, for reasons personal to the pastor ; through which impression a name long honored in the American churches would inevitably suffer. On the other hand, if the action were to be regarded as *not* exceptional, but representative of a general policy, it appeared yet more dangerous. For then it seemed to exhibit a distinct abandonment by the church of that duty of watchfulness over its members which involves investigation when proof is offered of their unchristian conduct, with such subsequent and remedial church-work as Christian fidelity may suggest, and with the final exclusion, under censure, of those found guilty and unrepentant.

Action like this apparently made void the Covenant of the church ; since those who therein had solemnly promised to " submit to necessary discipline, and avoid all causes of scandal and offense," while the providence of God should continue them in the church, were practically declared at liberty at any time to annul these obligations, by the action of their individual minds, though still enrolled as responsible church-members.

It seemed precisely to contradict the principles which had been avowed and proclaimed by the Plymouth Church, in an elaborate edition of its Manual, published and distributed in 1854, and to show a complete departure from them.

It seemed most dangerous in itself.

It was felt that any member, accused of whatever flagrant wrong-doing, would be authorized and encouraged, by action like this, to avoid all scrutiny and censure by the church, by adding to other misdemeanors the further offense of absenting himself from its services and communion ; and that, in consequence, the conviction of any one, of any offense, however gross, and however capable of absolute proof, must thereafter become impossible.

It was felt that an injury had been done, by the action thus taken, to all the churches in responsible church-communion with the Plymouth Church ; that this action, with the policy apparently declared in it, would cast an undeserved reproach on those whose principles and methods of discipline were wholly diverse from what here were presented ; that they tended directly to injure other more recent churches, in which the example, if continuing unquestioned, might be naturally followed ; that they were wholly opposed to the ancient and honored principles and rules of Congregational churches ; that they were not in accordance with the law of the Master for the treatment of a trespassing brother ; and that they practically dissolved the church, as an organized body, and reduced it to a transient and casual society, without bond or law, from which any one might depart, at any moment, with as little formality as from a street-meeting.

Certainly it was with reluctance and pain that such conclusions were admitted. A public difference with the Plymouth Church was felt by our churches only less an evil than would be silence in the face of such action. It was recognized by them as no light thing to encounter the influence which that church and its pastor had gained for themselves, by many years of eminent service and splendid fame. Our hearts drew back from a collision with those in whose Christian renown we had long had pride, and with whom, only a year before, we had joined in the crowning jubilee of their history.

But so general and strong was the impression among us of the dangerous nature of this action, that the pastors of our churches, with large committees, were at once instructed to communicate with the pastor and members of the Plymouth Church ; to represent to them the impressions made by their action ; to ask for fuller explanations of the policy said to have been adopted by them ; to ask their revisal of this policy, if it should prove to be as reported ; and, if no satisfactory explanation, or action of revision, should be secured, to ask them to unite with our churches in calling a properly representative Council, to consider the subject, and to advise them and us as to their and our duties concerning it.

This office the committees accordingly performed ; addressing to the pastor and members of that church a letter long enough, and earnest enough, to show how strong were the con-

viction and feeling awakened by their action, while not intentionally unkind in its terms ; setting forth, at large, the views
of the matter which were common to our churches, and asking for a private conference, and, if no adjustment of views
were thus secured, for a reference of the whole subject to a
Council, mutually chosen.

This letter was not at first publicly read in our church-
meetings, because it was feared that such a reading of it, before an assembly of many persons, prior to its transmission to
the church addressed, might be held by that church an unfriendly act, equivalent to a premature publication ; by reason of which they would possibly be indisposed to receive the
suggestions, and accept the proposal, conveyed by the letter.
Afterward, however, learning that the meeting of the Plymouth Church was delayed for some weeks, that the letter had
been read in advance to many members of that church and
society, and that its *not* having been read and approved in
our public meetings was made an occasion of objection to it,
it was thus read, November 21, before it had been presented
at the meeting of the Plymouth Church ; and the action of
the committees, in drafting and sending it, was unanimously
approved.

This letter was publicly read to the Plymouth Church on the
evening of November 26 ; and Resolutions were adopted
by that church declining the proposed conference, on the
ground, asserted in the preamble, that we had prejudged the
case, and had threatened the church with a withdrawal of fellowship. At this meeting it was declared by one of the principal speakers, in a long written argument which was afterward published, that the member against whom the charges
had been presented had not been at the time a member of the
church ; that he had before wholly excluded himself from it ;
and that "it has been, from the very beginning, an avowed
principle in the Congregational system that a man can thus
cut himself off from the church, and cease to be a member
of it." "If any thing has deep root in the system of Congregationalism," he added, it is a rule supposed to sanction this
practice.

It was added by the pastor that it was necessary for the

Plymouth Church to maintain the principles involved in its action, in order to have the churches in the neighborhood, and those in the Northwest, "built up on the broadest democratic construction of Congregational church-fellowship ; " and that the basis of that church puts it " on precisely the same relations with Baptist, Methodist, or Presbyterian churches, that it does with Congregational churches." "The Congregational churches," he added, " have no more right to interfere with us than the Presbyterian churches have."

As the Resolutions thus adopted by the Plymouth Church, while refusing the conference which we had asked, did not in express terms decline the Council which had also been sought, in case the conference should bring no satisfaction, a note was addressed to them, asking if they had intended to decline the Council also.

In reply, they requested our committees to state the points which it was desired to submit to a Council ; and at the same meeting, December 5, the following Resolution was unanimously adopted, according to immediate subsequent publication : —

"*Resolved*, That we interpret these principles [contained in rules previously recited] as relieving all other churches from responsibility for the Doctrine, Order, and Discipline of this church, and this church from all responsibility for those of other churches ; and as asserting for this church a right to judge, in every case, what fellowship, advice, or assistance, may, according to the laws of Christ, properly be offered or received."

In responding to their note, the committees presented the points which it seemed desirable to submit to a Council ; and then, as specially directed by our churches, called the attention of the Plymouth Church to the above Resolution, as seeming to affirm for it the position of entire independency of all churches whatever, exterior to itself ; so that its Articles of Faith might be altered or dispensed with, its Rules might require no conditions for admission, its Covenant might be wholly abandoned, without its recognizing any right of remonstrance on the part of other churches. They cited statements from the previous Manual of Plymouth Church, setting forth principles of order and discipline in express opposition to its recent action. They further pointed out the fact, that if such a position as seemed now assumed should be maintained, while we should wish that church all success in its own work, and in its preferred way of doing that work, the special relations of our churches with it, of denominational alliance, and the fellowship which implies reciprocity of duties, would be necessarily suspended.

Though the points needing, in the judgment of our churches, to be submitted to a Council, were explicitly stated in this letter, and the request for such Council was not withdrawn, we did not further urge them to join in it, in view of their preceding Resolution ; since the very act of convening a Council implies a responsibility to other churches which they appeared to have wholly disavowed.

This letter was sent December 15. The answer to it was adopted by the Plymouth Church, January 2. In this answer, that church postponed any discussion of the points presented by us as important in our view to be submitted to a Council, while not declining to join, under any circumstances, in calling one ; and it replied to the other portion of our letter — without any reference to the emphatic statements quoted by us from its former Manual — by affirming that, " Congregationalism is the conduct of the affairs of the church by the whole brotherhood, not embarrassed by the unasked interference of other churches ; " that this has been the view of Plymouth Church from the beginning ; and that this position " is Congregationalism, as we understand it, hold it, and are determined to maintain it." It adds concerning our churches : " If they choose to withdraw from a truly Congregational fellowship, it is their right so to do. But we have not withdrawn, and we will not withdraw."

The letter also declared that no document would thereafter be received from our churches unless accompanied with " proof of the authority of the whole brotherhood, regularly and deliberately conferred ; " nor if it should contain (according to their apprehension) " covert insinuations against the character of any of the members of this church."

Further correspondence with them on the part of our churches was not encouraged by this letter ; as we could scarcely be expected to submit to their inquest the regularity of our meetings, or the proper deliberateness of our church-action ; the signatures of our clerks, even if certified to by the pastors, might not be regarded as giving more " proof " of the authority of the churches than those of our pastors and large committees had previously done. " Covert " is a word of elastic significance ; and it is of course difficult for us to know who are, or are not, members of the Plymouth Church, their connection with it appearing to depend wholly on their individual volitions, of which, at any particular moment, we can hardly hope to be definitely informed.

The letter itself appeared to us, whether correctly or not, evasive and cunning, rather than ingenuous. The tone of it impressed us as angry. Our references to the former utterances of the church, through its authorized Manual, were met by nothing but vehement assertions that the Plymouth Church had always been the same, and was more truly Congregational than were ours. And there were threats in the letter, certainly not covert, for which nothing in our history, so far as we are aware, had given occasion, to which we could hardly bring ourselves to reply, though before them we were conscious of no apprehensions.

It appeared plain enough that a correspondence to be pursued, on either side, in such a spirit, would be of neither credit nor service to any Christian interest. Accordingly, since then, no further letters have been exchanged between our churches. Certain private communications between the pastors, of that church and ours, have since taken place ; but with these neither the churches nor their committees have had any thing to do ; and it is only understood by them that no satisfactory adjustment of the points in discussion, and no agreement on questions to be submitted to a Council, have been attained.

Our churches now find themselves, therefore, in a position in which they urgently need the unbiased counsel of other churches, who can look at the subject with experienced candor, and with minds undisturbed by the local influences which may unconsciously affect our judgments.

Out of the series of facts recited, emerge questions of large extent, and paramount importance ; the early and right decision of which appears indispensable, if Congregational churches are to maintain their place among those which surround them, and to continue to act together in their usual modes of co-operative effort.

It should be distinctly understood what are the questions thus challenging attention.

They are not questions as to the Christian character, or the purity of life, of the pastor of the Plymouth Church. We are not aware that proper charges, impeaching these, have been presented to any church. Certainly, none such have been presented to ours ; and we have none to present to a Council.

They are not questions as to the truth or falsehood of the charges which were made, October 6, against a member of that church, affirming his circulation of injurious scandals against the pastor. These charges, it seems to us, should have been investigated, and a decision upon them rendered, at the time, by the proper authority. That this was not done was the primal occasion of that correspondence out of which has come the calling of this Council ; but the charges themselves, with the evidence for them, it is not our province, or that of the Council, to investigate.

The questions which remain, and which it is vital to the welfare of our churches to have decided, concern the correspondence of the order and usage of the Congregational churches of the country with the action of the Plymouth Church, in the case referred to, and in its subsequent Resolutions and Letters. They are substantially TWO, though naturally distributed into several particulars, — a question of DISCIPLINE, and a question of FELLOWSHIP. Was the action of the Plymouth Church right, according to such order and usage, in the case issued by it October 31, taking that action as presented in the public documents ? Is its position of entire independence, toward all churches exterior to itself, rightly to be maintained, while its public Congregational relations with our churches continue ?

These questions are of controlling importance ; and, in their practical bearings, they have a wide reach, in many directions.

Primarily, and sensibly, they concern our churches ; and we need an answer to them, as speedy as may be given, and carrying all the authority possible. As at present situated, we seem to ourselves entangled in a fellowship which brings the burden of an indefinite obligation without conferring any assured right or privilege. We are responsible without power. We are in the position of a merchant accountable for the debts of partners, upon whose contracts he can put no restraint. We are caught in the meshes of a public fellowship which implicates us in the devious and irregular action of others, while that action may be alien from all our practice, and contrary to our deepest convictions. Even our subsequent protest against it is liable to be resented as an offense, though without such a protest we should appear before the public as abetting a policy which we utterly disapprove.

We cannot sustain such a position. It were, in our judgment, entirely unreasonable to expect it from us.

Even if we could continue to hold it in view of the past, we should feel it indispensable to be extricated from it, in forecast of what may occur in the future. For who can predict what further divergences from the accepted Congregational system may be encouraged by the authorized consciousness in a church of such an entire independence of others as here is affirmed? If the Plymouth Church were at any time hereafter to alter essentially its Articles of Faith, even omitting from among them the Divinity of our Lord, we should plainly be debarred, by its recent Resolution, from any remonstrance against its action, while it still might insist, as emphatically as now, that from "fellowship" with us it would not withdraw.

Such a position is simply insupportable. If this is to be Congregational practice, many churches will certainly prefer to identify themselves with some other communion, in which responsibility is associated with defined and undeniable rights. No church, it seems to us, will be willing to pledge public fellowship to a society which shall afterward be at liberty to do what it pleases in regard to Doctrine, Order, and Discipline, while it claims that the fellowship binds to silence the churches which have pledged it. The isolation of each is the ultimate alternative to the common and recognized rights of all. Instead of a denomination of free but mutually responsible churches, consenting together in essential principles, we shall be irresistibly resolved into a multitude of discordant and suspicious ecclesiastical units, with no more real moral cohesion than belongs to neighboring pebbles on the beach.

This is a result of the principles declared by the Plymouth Church which is not merely special to ourselves, or to other churches in this vicinity, but is common, by its nature, to all Congregational churches in the land.

But beyond this appear grave practical questions, of instant importance, and widest relations.

If it be admitted that a member may at any time terminate his membership in a Congregational church by simply withdrawing from its services, and that all which the church has afterward to do, no matter what charges are brought against him, is to alter its roll in conformity with his will; and if it be further admitted that a church may at any time do what it likes in respect to doctrine, order, and discipline, without responsibility to other churches, and without admitting in them any right of remonstrance, — then the practical question at once arises, whether the churches standing upon the Platform of Polity put forth at Cambridge in 1648, and subsequently amended and re-affirmed by the National Council in 1865, are ready to contribute, of their influence and their means, to propagate and nourish, all over the land, societies like these?

Our own Church-Extension and Aid Committee needs an answer to the radical questions which underlie this, to the further prosecution of its important and promising labors.

Our Home Missionary Societies will find their work in the collection of moneys for the aid of feeble Congregational churches at the West and South limited and hindered, if not arrested, in the absence of a definite settlement of these questions.

So, equally, will the Congregational Union. How many will assist in making up large sums of money to house and help such loosely-compacted and irresponsible societies?

Even the Society for promoting Christian Education, by the aid of students or the endowment of seminaries, will find its constituency crumbling beneath it, if the churches to be served by the men whom it educates are to be at liberty to wholly unloose the bands of discipline, and to hold themselves irresponsible toward others.

Nor can the American Board go forward, as the hearts of its members have urged that it should, as Divine indications have seemed to suggest, in the establishment of churches, substantially Congregational, in foreign lands, if the principles upon which those churches are to be based are left in this intolerable doubt.

In a word, the whole system of co-operative effort, among our Congregational churches, proceeds, in our view, upon the idea that these churches are mutually responsible to each other, in a sense in which they are not responsible to Episcopalians or to Methodists ; and that membership in a church implies something more than a temporary intention which any one may revoke at his will: that if a church, therefore, by corporate action, puts an end within itself to the salutary discipline of the household of Christ, or gives up a principal doctrine of the Faith, it is to be admonished by others ; and, if it shall not heed the admonition, it is to be excluded from fellowship. If these ideas are now to be repudiated, or suffered to lapse as things obsolete, the whole system of co-operative effort based upon them, in our judgment, will rapidly disappear.

We therefore desire and ask the counsel of other churches on the Questions presented in the Letter-Missive with which this Statement will be sent. We have sought to make these as concise as possible, while covering the points concerning which an authentic testimony seems to be needed. If any authority were requisite on our part for making such an appeal for your advice, it would be found in the provision of the Platform which expressly declares (p. 52), in the enumeration of particular occasions for Councils : " When any question arises on which the church needs advice, for the guidance and correction, or confirmation, of its own judgment, that church has a right to ask the advice of other churches with which it is in communion."

We unfeignedly rejoice, that, after the experience — not wholly unlooked-for, but very unwelcome — through which the Lord, during recent months, has called us to pass, we now may have this rightful recourse to a Council so large, so wise, and so impartial, as we hope to convene ; by which we are ready to be admonished and corrected, if to it we shall seem to have done wrong ; to which we gladly remit the questions which to us appear of wide relations, and grave importance ; on whose result the future of Congregationalism in this country may largely depend ; and in which we trust will be plainly revealed that " mind of the Spirit" to which righteousness is dear as the means of true peace, through which the Master still speaks to the world, and in following which is always freedom, safety, joy.

DOCUMENTS.

A.

MR. TILTON'S RELATIONS WITH PLYMOUTH CHURCH.

THE proceedings in Plymouth Church on Friday evening, Oct. 31, concerning Mr. Theodore Tilton and his membership or non-membership in that body, make it proper for "The Golden Age" to give the following documentary particulars : —

The Clerk of the Examining Committee to Mr. Tilton.

BROOKLYN, Oct. 16, 1873.

MR. THEODORE TILTON :

DEAR SIR, — At a meeting of the Examining Committee of Plymouth Church held this evening, the Clerk of the Committee was instructed to forward to you a copy of the complaint and specifications made against you by William F. West, and was requested to notify you that any answer to the charges that you may desire to offer to the Committee, may be sent to the Clerk, on or before Thursday, Oct. 23, 1873.

Enclosed I hand you a copy of the charges and specifications referred to.   Yours very respectfully,

393 BRIDGE STREET.   D. W. TALLMADGE, *Clerk.*

Mr. West's Charge against Mr. Tilton.

I charge Theodore Tilton, a member of this church, with having circulated and promoted scandals derogatory to the Christian integrity of our Pastor, and injurious to the reputation of this church.

["The Golden Age," from motives of proper delicacy, omits to give currency to the specifications.]

23

Mr. Tilton's Reply to the Clerk.

174 LIVINGSTON STREET, BROOKLYN, Oct. 20, 1873.

MR. D. W. TALLMADGE, *Clerk.*

MY DEAR SIR, — I have received from you an official paper addressed to me as a member of Plymouth Church.

Nearly four years ago I terminated my connection with that church, and am not now a member thereof.

Therefore the document addressed to me in that capacity I cannot receive.

To avoid any seeming discourtesy in returning it herewith, I retain it, subject to your direction.

With my best wishes for the prosperity of the church, I remain,

Truly yours,

THEODORE TILTON.

[From the Golden Age (New York), Nov. 8, 1873.]

REPORT OF THE COMMITTEE, AND ACTION OF THE CHURCH.

On the evening of Friday, October 31, a special meeting of Plymouth Church was held, immediately following the stated meeting for voting upon the reception of new members. At that meeting the regular Examining Committee (comprising nine deacons, six deaconesses, and six other members of the church) offered the following report : —

BROOKLYN, Oct. 24, 1873.

At a meeting of the Examining Committee of Plymouth Church, held last evening, the following preambles and resolution were adopted : —

Whereas, Charges were presented to the Committee by William F. West against Theodore Tilton ; and

Whereas, A Special Committee having been appointed by the Committee to wait upon Mr. Tilton with reference to said charges, said Tilton, upon the evening of the 6th of October, made answer to that Special Committee in these words : —

" I have not for nearly four years been an attendant of Plymouth Church, nor have I considered myself a member of it, and I do not now, nor does the pastor of the church consider me a member, and I do not hold myself amenable to its jurisdiction in any manner whatever ; " and

Whereas, Theodore Tilton, in reply to a communication addressed to him by the Clerk of this Committee, which communication, with a copy of the charges preferred against him by William F. West, was put into the hands of said Tilton on the 17th October, inst., and a request made of him that he should answer the same by the twenty-third day of October, inst., says in a letter addressed to the Clerk of the Committee, under date October 22, 1873 : —

"It is about four years since I terminated all connection with the church, and am not now a member thereof ; therefore the document addressed to me in that capacity I cannot receive ;" and

Whereas, It thus appears that Theodore Tilton, a member of this church, has abandoned his connection with the church by prolonged absence from all its services and ordinances ; therefore,

Resolved, That this Committee recommend to the church that the name of Theodore Tilton be dropped from the roll of membership of the church, as provided by rule No. 7 of the Manual.

D. W. Tallmadge,
Clerk Examining Committee.

Some general discussion ensued, in the course of which Mr. Tilton, who was present, having asked and received the privilege of speaking, re-affirmed his declaration of having severed his connection with the church years previously. After remarks by the Pastor and other brethren, and the rejection of divers motions and amendments, the meeting voted that the report of the Committee be accepted, and their recommendation adopted.

[From the Christian Union (New York), Dec. 3, 1873.]

Card of the Clerk of Plymouth Church.

Sir, — Your report of the recent proceedings in Plymouth Church inadvertently speaks of Mr. Tilton's "expulsion." This is an error. Mr. Tilton was not expelled. Having four years ago ceased from his membership, his name, which has hitherto remained on the roll, was last evening, in accordance with the facts, with the rule, and without reflection upon him, taken from the roll.

The rule by which Mr. Tilton's name was dropped from the membership of the church is as follows : —

Rule 7. *Dropping Members.* — Members may be dropped from the roll of the church with or without notice to them, as may be deemed just, by a two-thirds vote of the church, upon the recom mendation of the Examining Committee, either upon their own application, or, in case they have abandoned their connection with the church by prolonged absence or otherwise, upon the application of any other person.   Respectfully,

S. B. HALLIDAY,

Clerk of Plymouth Church.

69 HICKS STREET, BROOKLYN, Nov. 1, 1873.

[From the New York Sun, Nov. 3, 1873.]

B.

Brooklyn, Nov. 8, 1873.

To the Pastor and Members of Plymouth Church, Brooklyn, New York :

Dear Brethren, — For many years we, as Congregational churches, have dwelt in hearty fellowship with you, meeting with you gladly in Conferences and Councils, interchanging members with you, as these have chanced to change their residence, and manifesting in all ways, on whatever opportunity, our cordial Christian confidence and regard.

We have done this in the belief that you, as a church, held and taught the Evangelical faith, and were solicitous with us to honor and maintain, in your internal discipline, the interests and the law of Christian purity.

It is now publicly reported, without contradiction, that, at a meeting of your church, properly convened, and numerously attended, held on the evening of October 31, you voted, by a large majority, to drop from the roll of your membership, without examination, and without censure, a member of the church, present in the meeting, against whom specific and serious charges were known to be pending ; which had been presented by a brother in the church, which had been accepted by the Committee of the church, and of which the accused had been duly notified, — charges vitally affecting the Christian character of the accused, if they should be proven and unexplained, and intimately connected with the good name of your Pastor, if any attempt were made to rebut them by pleading that the statements charged as slanders were justified by facts ; that you did this upon the ground, as stated in your preamble, that the accused member had "abandoned his connection with the church, by prolonged absence from all its services and ordinances ;"—and that your Pastor, in advocating this action, declared in substance, the church acquiescing, that the Plymouth Church "is not, and never has been, like many of the

27

New-England Congregational churches;" that one of its two prominent principles has been, "that the door of entrance to it should be as large as humanity," and the other, "that the door of emission from it should be as large as necessity;" and that the policy adopted by the church has been, when a charge of wrong-doing was made against a member, and the case was thought one which, if pursued, would turn the church from its great Gospel work, for the Examining Committee to go to the accused, and advise him quietly to withdraw from the church.

The policy is here, as we understand it, distinctly avowed, as having been deliberately adopted and pursued, and as therefore proper to be applied to the exciting and prominent case at that moment before the church, of avoiding the thorough investigation of complaints charging members of the church with unchristian conduct, by requesting the accused, if there should seem occasion for the accusation, to withdraw from the church, without censure, in anticipation of such investigation.

This is not a withdrawal of watch and discipline on the part of the church, for the sake of relieving innocent persons, suspected of no moral delinquency, from obligations which to them have come to seem burdensome.

It is not even represented as a hazardous but a seemingly necessary expedient, adopted reluctantly, in some extreme and exceptional case, the prosecution of which might be attended with peculiar embarrassments.

It is announced as a prevailing policy of the church; amounting, with inevitable force, to a definite and permanent abandonment by it of that duty of watchfulness over its members which involves a careful and ample investigation when proof is offered of their unchristian conduct, with such subsequent and remedial church-work as the case may demand, and the Word and the Spirit of God point out.

It seems to us undeniably plain, that such a course, however attractive as avoiding trouble, and giving opportunity to escape such issues as it never is pleasant to encounter, is directly subversive of all true Christian discipline:

That it is unjust to those aggrieved by another's wrong-doing; as denying them the opportunity to make his guilt manifest, and shielding him from the public condemnation which is often to them their only reparation:

That it is injurious even to the person accused; as tending to diminish his sense of his guilt, while withdrawing from him those

Christian processes, of remonstrance, rebuke, and, if he be obdurate, of final excision from the church, under censure, the fruit
of which may be to lead him to repentance :

That it is injurious to the church ; whose Christian wisdom is
developed, whose patience is exercised, whose sense of the beauty
and obligation of righteousness is re-enforced, and whose fair fame
is vindicated, by the careful, considerate, and prayerful exercise of
its power of discipline :

That it is injurious to the world ; which is encouraged, and almost
justified, in deriding the practical morality of the church, and
exalting in contrast its own societies, which at least expel unworthy
members :

That it is, most of all, injurious to Christ ; whose law for the
treatment of the trespassing brother, contained in the eighteenth
chapter of Matthew, it distinctly disregards ; whose spirit it represents as one of fear, not of wisdom, love, and of a sound mind ;
and whose name it dishonors in the house of His f-'ends.

It seems to us to offer opportunity, and positive inducement, to
the flagrant transgressor of whatever rules of morality or religion,
to evade all scrutiny and censure by the church, by simply absenting himself, without reason given, from its services and communion,
— an act which constitutes of itself an offense, instead of operat-
ing to palliate another.

Such a course of action appears to us especially untimely, and
especially dangerous, when the sin alleged is against the good
name of a minister of Christ; in whose undimmed repute for
purity of life the whole church has an interest ; against whom
circumstantial and damaging statements are alleged to have been
made, by the member whom the church thus puts beyond its reach ;
concerning whom suspicion is almost sure to be increased by such
an apparent avoidance of duty ; and where the proper opportunity
to vindicate his name is certainly sacrificed.

But such a course must be always untimely, always dangerous ;
without warrant in the Word, without support of Christian wisdom,
and involving tendencies that can be only prolific of evil.

We are impressed with the conviction that credit cannot properly
be given to the letters dimissory of a church which adopts and avows
such a policy ; that even its unchallenged members will lose the
claim which grows out of their membership, to the confidence of
other Christians and churches, so long as the church with which
they are connected distinctly repudiates its prime obligation to
watch over their purity, to investigate its evidence when it is as-

sailed, and to publicly declare its discovered absence ; that, while injuring itself by such a course, the church brings discredit upon the communion with which it is associated, and does great wrong to the whole Christian brotherhood.

And we feel that we, as related and neighboring Congregational churches, are not at liberty, before our own consciences, or before the Master and Judge of all, to remain silent when a policy is avowed which impresses us as so novel, so unscriptural, so dangerous in its present application, and so demoralizing ; that we cannot continue in unquestioning fellowship with any church which accepts and declares it.

In remembrance, therefore, of the pleasant relations which have so long subsisted between us, in the hope that there may be explanations by you which will cast a new and welcome light on the position which you have assumed, or that you may be moved by our representations to revise your late action, and adopt a course more in harmony with the law of Christ, and with the common usage of our churches, we earnestly invite you, by your Pastor and a committee, to meet with us, in private conference, at your own lecture-room, as speedily as possible, on such a day as you may appoint, that we may more fully ascertain from yourselves the nature and the reason of the action which you have taken, and may more largely present to you the effect of that action, as now understood, on your own church, and on its relations to those hitherto associated with it.

We do this, brethren, not as assuming the slightest authority over you, or seeking in the least to invade the prerogatives which are as dear to us as to you. We do it in the exercise of that fraternal right which always accompanies fraternal obligation, and which is therefore vitally involved in our fellowship with you. We do it in accordance with the evident and perennial principle, essential to Congregationalism, which is correctly and clearly stated in your Church Manual, published by vote of the church in 1854, that Congregational churches " may admonish each other, in case of heresy, lax discipline, or any scandalous offense."

We do it in absolute kindness of spirit, but under the deepest convictions of duty ; believing that you, however unconsciously, are imperiling the name, the influence, and the future of all our churches ; that you are giving the sanction of your large numbers, and prominent position, to measures and a policy which will recoil, with injurious effect, on your own fame and Christian power, and which will work a sure disaster wherever applied ; that you arc leaving a palpable blight on the name of your Pastor, by seeming to shrink from that investigation which the man accused of slanders against him distinctly challenged ; that you are doing essential dishonor to the Lord himself, by representing his kingdom on earth as a promiscuous and casual society, without cohesion or law, out of which any offender may pass, at any moment, whatever his offense, without resistance, and without rebuke.

Brethren, in face of an error so vital and vast, and so threatening in its consequences, we cannot be silent. We are constrained to ask this interview with you. And we must further request, that if no essentially different state of facts from that which now appears, and which has been above recited, shall be presented by your committee, in the conference which we seek, — if your recent action is to remain, as it seems to us, an energetic principle of evil in your own church, and of instant detriment and bad example to every other, — the same committee may be instructed to unite with us, according to the venerable rule of our fathers, in calling a properly representative Council, of the Congregational churches of the country, to which your recent action, with the general policy of discipline involved in it, shall be submitted, and by which you shall be advised on your duty in the matter, and we on our further fellowship with you.

We are, brethren, with affectionate recollections, and earnest prayers for your Christian welfare,

Yours, for the faith and order of the Gospel,

RICHARD S. STORRS, *Pastor,*

> RICHARD P. BUCK,
> ARCHIBALD BAXTER,
> DWIGHT JOHNSON,
> JOSHUA M. VAN COTT,   *Committee of the*
> ELI MYGATT, JUN.,   *Church of the*
> WALTER T. HATCH,   *Pilgrims.*
> LUCIEN BIRDSEYE,

WILLIAM IVES BUDINGTON, *Pastor,*

> ALFRED S. BARNES,
> JAMES W. ELWELL,
> HARVEY B. SPELMAN,   *Committee of*
> THOMAS S. THORP,   *the Clinton*
> AUGUSTUS F. LIBBY,   *Ave. Church.*
> FLAMEN B. CANDLER,
> CALVIN C. WOOLWORTH,

C.

To the Pastor and Members of the Church of the Pilgrims, Brooklyn, New-York:

DEAR BRETHREN, — At a special meeting of Plymouth Church, held in their lecture-room, on Wednesday evening, the 26th instant, called for the purpose of considering a joint letter, bearing date Nov. 8, addressed to it by the pastors and committees of seven brethren each, of the Church of the Pilgrims, and Clinton Avenue Church, and also to consider a communication, *without address or date,* signed "Sidney Sanderson," Assistant Clerk, apparently proceedings of a special business meeting of the Church of the Pilgrims, held Nov. 7, together with a communication from Clinton Avenue Church, bearing date Nov. 22, certified by Flamen B. Candler to be proceedings of the Clinton Avenue Church, at meetings held on the 7th and 21st of November,* after the reading of the several documents, and discussions had thereon, the following preambles and resolutions were passed by the following vote : in the affirmative, 504 ; in the negative, 25.

Whereas, This church has received a letter from the Church of the Pilgrims, and the Clinton Avenue Congregational Church, asking for a conference concerning the alleged lax discipline of this church ; and

Whereas, This letter, confessedly based on public report merely, expresses a settled conviction that this church is in error, "vital and vast ; " that we have done "essential dishonor to the Lord himself ; " that our policy is "unscriptural and demoralizing ; " that such action as the letter accuses us of taking "must be always untimely, always dangerous, without warrant in the Word, without support of Christian wisdom, and involving tendencies that can be only prolific of evil ; " and

---

* The *joint* letter alluded to was received on Saturday, Nov. 8. The two subsequent documents alluded to, came to me just two weeks later, namely, Saturday, Nov. 22.

Whereas, Besides this pre-judgment of the case, this letter distinctly threatens us with a withdrawal of fellowship; therefore,

Resolved, That, while we cherish as sacred the remembrance of many years of harmonious co-operation in Christian work and worship with the Church of the Pilgrims, and the Clinton Avenue Congregational Church, and should look with great pain upon any thing which threatened to disturb the peace and love that have hitherto existed between us, the circumstances recited leave us no alternative but to decline the proposed conference. While this church is, in the words of her Manual (Rule 1), "*an independent ecclesiastical body, and in matters of doctrine, order, and discipline amenable to no other organization,*" she will nevertheless, in the words of the same Manual (Rule 2), "*extend to other evangelical churches, and receive from them, that fellowship, advice, and assistance which the laws of Christ require.*" In accordance with these, her immemorial declarations, Plymouth Church is at all times ready to be advised and admonished by sister churches, according to the ancient, approved, Congregational, Christian method, beginning with proper inquiry into facts, and proceeding through successive steps of mutual explanation and discussion, to the final expression of opinion, including, if need be, admonition or censure. But Plymouth Church is not ready to reverse this order, and submit first to censure, secondly to argument, and afterward to a request for the facts.

Resolved, That the clerk of this church be instructed to send to the Church of the Pilgrims, and the Clinton Avenue Congregational Church, copies of these preambles and resolutions.

S. B. HALLIDAY,
Clerk Plymouth Church.

BROOKLYN, Nov. 28, 1873.

3

D.

BROOKLYN, Dec, 5, 1873.

To the Pastor and Members of Plymouth Church, Brooklyn:

DEAR BRETHREN, — The Resolutions adopted by you, at your meeting on November 26, have been communicated to our respective churches; and certain courses of further action, on the part of these churches, have been adopted by them as probably desirable. This action, however, is in its nature provisional, as being based upon an understanding of your Resolutions which it is felt may possibly not be correct. Therefore, before it is communicated, or any steps are taken to give it effect, it is important that they should know, by an authorized statement, if their understanding of your Resolutions is, concerning one point, the right one.

In their letter of the 8th November, they requested you to unite with them, by your Pastor and a committee, in a private conference, for fuller explanations, and interchange of opinion, on the subject presented in that letter; and, further, in case such conference should lead to no satisfactory result, to unite with them afterward in calling a properly representative Council of Congregational churches, to which the whole subject involved in their correspondence with you might be submitted, and by which you and they might be advised as to your and their duties concerning it.

The invitation to a conference you have, in your Resolutions, distinctly declined; and it has been supposed by our churches that, in declining this, you undoubtedly intended to decline also the invitation to join in a susbequent Council. But, as your Resolutions do not in express terms declare this, it has occurred to them as possible that their impression on this point may be incorrect.

Before taking any further steps, therefore, we desire to ask on their behalf, in a wholly fraternal spirit, and with an earnest desire to follow things which may make for righteousness and peace,

34

whether, in declining to accede to their proposal for a private conference, you intended to be understood as declining also to unite
with them in calling a Council? It is important that they should
be distinctly informed on this point, for the sake of preventing
any possible injury to them or to yourselves, growing out of a misapprehension of each other's position. It is only the more evidently important because their letter, before addressed to you,
seems to have been seriously misunderstood by you, and to have
been taken in a sense, and as manifesting a spirit, which were
not intended, and which, if such a misunderstanding had been
anticipated, would have been distinctly disclaimed.

We are therefore the more solicitous that no future misunderstanding should occur, if prudence may prevent it. And it would
be extremely gratifying to our churches if they should learn, in
answer to this inquiry, that you are ready to unite with them in
asking the advice of an unbiased Council, on matters in which
we have a common interest, and concerning which we may all be
profited by light from others.

Hoping that we may receive an answer to this fraternal inquiry
as soon as it shall be practicable and convenient for you to return
it, and wishing you the best gifts from God our Father, and the
Lord Jesus Christ, we are yours, in the service and kingdom of
God,

(*For the Church of the Pilgrims,*)

RICHARD S. STORRS, *Pastor*,

RICHARD P. BUCK,
ARCHIBALD BAXTER,
DWIGHT JOHNSON,
JOSHUA M. VAN COTT, } *Committee.*
ELI MYGATT, JUN.,
WALTER T. HATCH,
LUCIEN BIRDSEYE,

(*For the Clinton Avenue Church,*)

WILLIAM IVES BUDINGTON, *Pastor*,

ALFRED S. BARNES,
JAMES W. ELWELL,
HARVEY B. SPELMAN,
THOMAS S. THORP, } *Committee.*
AUGUSTUS F. LIBBY,
FLAMEN B. CANDLER,
CALVIN C. WOOLWORTH,

E.

69 Hicks Street, Brooklyn, Dec. 6, 1873.

To the Rev. R. S. Storrs, D.D., William Ives Budington, D.D., and Committees of the Church of the Pilgrims, and Clinton Avenue Congregational Church.

Dear Brethren, — At a regularly called meeting of Plymouth Church, held last evening, it was voted *unanimously*, that the following paper be signed by the Pastor, Moderator of the meeting, and the Clerk, and forwarded to you. Fraternally yours,

S. B. Halliday, *Clerk*
Plymouth Church.

Dear Brethren, — We have received your third letter, dated Dec. 5, 1873 ; and it has been read to the church.

It gives us great pleasure to accept your statements in regard to the spirit and intent of your letter of November 8.

As we do not admit the statement of facts, nor the allegation of principles held by us, contained in your letter of Nov. 8, we are not aware, on our part, of any questions requiring the advice of a Council.

If, however, you desire further light, and will state to us the points to be submitted to a Council, we will promptly inform you of the decision of this church.

We cannot consent to be parties to the calling of a Council, without being definitely informed as to the precise matter which is to be referred to it.

Wishing you Grace, Mercy, and Peace,

E. H. Garbutt, *Moderator,*
S. B. Halliday, *Clerk,*

Henry Ward Beecher,
Pastor Plymouth Church.

Resolutions adopted by Plymouth Church, Dec. 5, 1873.

Whereas, It is desirable that the relations of Plymouth Church with other churches should be clearly understood, — therefore,

Resolved, That this church reiterates the principles declared in Rules 1 and 2 of its Manual, adopted April 17, 1848, as follows : —

This church is an independent ecclesiastical body, and in matters of Doctrine, Order, and Discipline is amenable to no other organization. — This church will extend to other Evangelical churches, and receive from them, that fellowship, advice, and assistance which the laws of Christ require.

Resolved, That we interpret these principles as relieving all other churches from responsibility for the Doctrine, Order, and Discipline of this church, and this church from all responsibility for those of other churches ; and as asserting for this church the right to judge, in every case, what fellowship, advice, or assistance may, according to the laws of Christ, properly be offered or received.

[From the Christian Union (New York), Dec. 10, 1873.]

4

F.

BROOKLYN, Dec. 15, 1873.

To the Pastor and Members of Plymouth Church, Brooklyn, N. Y.:

DEAR BRETHREN,—Your note of the 5th inst. has been received by us, in which you ask us "to state the points to be submitted to the Council," which, on the 8th November, we invited you to join us in calling.

The matter appeared to us to have been stated, with sufficient distinctness, in our letter of that date. We therein asked you "to unite with us in calling a properly representative Council of the Congregational churches of the country, to which your recent action [referred to in the letter], with the general policy of discipline involved in it, shall be submitted, and by which you shall be advised on your duty in the matter, and we on our further fellowship with you."

This request you seemed to some of us to have neither accepted nor declined; though others felt that you had, in intention and in effect, declined it, in declining the conference which we had proposed as antecedent to it. It was to remove all doubt on this point, and avoid any possible misapprehension, that we addressed to you our note of the 5th inst.; and it was a definite answer to this previous request, by an affirmative or negative reply, which we then sought.

As, however, the comprehensive statement, which to us had seemed sufficiently definite, has appeared to you to want exactness, we are quite ready to mention the following as among the points on which we desired, if you should unite with us, to have the testimony and advice of a Council. We put them into the form of Questions, that we may present them more precisely.

First. Is it in accordance with the principles and usages of Congregationalism that a member may terminate his membership in a church by simply absenting himself from its services and communion? or is a corporate and consenting action on the part of the church necessary to such termination of membership?

Second. During the voluntary absence of a member from the

38

ordinances, while the church has not consented by any vote to the termination of his membership, if specific and formal charges, of grossly unchristian conduct, are presented against him, by a brother in the church, — to which charges he declines to answer, — is it in accordance with the principles and usages of Congregationalism that the church shall withhold inquiry as to the alleged wickedness, and, in face of such public assertion of his offenses, shall treat the accused as an innocent absentee, and drop his name from the roll of its membership, "without reflection upon him"?

Third. When such a member is charged with having "circulated and promoted scandals, derogatory to the Christian integrity of the Pastor, and injurious to the reputation of the church," if he be publicly released, by the church which he confronts, without examination of the facts and without censure, from all further responsibility to it, has the rule of Christ in the eighteenth chapter of Matthew, concerning the treatment of the trespassing brother, been honored and maintained? or is it so distinctly disregarded, in a case which called for its careful observance, as to warrant apprehension and earnest remonstrance on the part of other churches?

Fourth. Was the action of the Plymouth Church, in the case of discipline issued by it October 31, in accordance with the principles and usages of Congregational churches, and with the law of Christ as administered by them? or was it an evident departure from these, tending, in the circumstances, to impair the Christian reputation and influence of the church, to leave the name of the Pastor without timely vindication, and to injure and offend other churches in fellowship?

Fifth. In view of the aforesaid action of Plymouth Church, as presented in published documents, and especially of the fact that this has been maintained as in full accordance with its customary policy, what is the duty, toward that church, of the Congregational churches heretofore in public fellowship with it? Especially what is their duty in regard to continuing in this fellowship?

The above questions probably present all the points which we should have wished to submit to the Council, if you had chosen to join us in calling it. Very possibly, after the conference with you which we vainly sought, some of them might have been omitted, or substantially modified. We state them now, as answering your question what points were in our minds, prompting the desire to convene such a Council. They seem to us of sufficient importance to relieve us of any possible appearance of undue importunity, and to explain our repeated application on the subject.

In any event, however, the particular "points" to be submitted would not have been for us alone to determine. You would have determined them, with us, through the careful deliberation of our respective committees. Only the general subject-matter could properly be presented by us, as the ground of our request. And since your note of the 5th inst. expressly declares that you are not aware of *any* questions requiring on your part the advice of a Council, it may have been superfluous in us, even in answer to your request, to specify these. They were all involved, to our apprehension, in our first letter. As that has appeared to you to furnish no ground for uniting with us in asking light from other churches, we shall not be surprised should this equally fail.

But, dear Brethren, at the same time that your note of the 5th was received by us, a Resolution also appeared, published in many newspapers, and published since in that paper which your Pastor controls, as having been unanimously adopted by you at the same meeting which authorized this note; which Resolution seems to us of greater importance, both to you and to ourselves, than does the note, or perhaps any other action of yours recently taken. And on this we desire, if you will allow us, to present to you some considerations. Our desire to do this, kindly and carefully, has been the occasion of delaying this letter. Except for that, it would have been immediately sent, when your note was received.

The Resolution referred to reads as follows : —

" *Resolved*, that we interpret these principles [contained in Rules previously recited] as relieving all other churches from responsibility for the Doctrine, Order, and Discipline of this church, and this church from all responsibility for those of other churches ; and as asserting for this church a right to judge, in every case, what fellowship, advice, or assistance, may, according to the laws of Christ, properly be offered or received."

The above Resolution purports to have been affirmed by you, and pursuantly published, in order "that the relations of Plymouth Church with other churches should be clearly understood." It so forcibly affects the relations heretofore existing between your church and ours, that had it been earlier adopted by you, or known to us, our whole recent history, in relation to each other, would no doubt have been different.

To make our meaning entirely obvious, suffer us to present a rapid recital of what seem to us important and incontestable facts.

In a "Manual of the Plymouth Church," —a large, handsome, authorized Manual, put forth by you in 1854, which bears upon

its front " Published by vote of the church," which was widely circulated, and of which copies were liberally supplied to us,—are
incorporated two chapters, one entitled, " A Brief Account of Congregationalism," the other " Church Discipline." These are not
appended to the Manual, as things accidental and extrinsic. They
are incorporated in it ; made as integral parts of it, so far as appears, as is either of its several divisions. They precede your
lists of " officers " and " members," and appear to present what
those officers and members combine to set forth. If any portion
of that careful " Manual " represents Plymouth Church, as it then
was, certainly these do. And as treating more at large the subjects which they discuss, they seem to show the mind of the church,
in regard to those subjects, more distinctly and fully than does any
thing else within the same covers.

In these important divisions of the Manual, thus prepared,
authorized, and published by you, occur the following statements,
representing the principles of Congregationalism which you then
proclaimed, and no doubt practiced : —

" They [*i.e.* Congregational churches] live in close fraternal
union ; often meet in Councils and Conferences ; ask and receive
advice and assistance from each other ; and may admonish each
other, in case of heresy, lax discipline, or any scandalous offense."

" No member of the church has a *right* to pass over without
notice the dereliction of a fellow-member from Christian duty, on
the plea that the offense is not personal against himself."

" It is proper, therefore, that the church from time to time appoint Committees of Inquiry upon the cases of absentees, or of
members, who, though residing in our vicinity, are supposed to be
living in the neglect of covenant obligations. . . . If, in the
course of their investigations, they find matter worthy of discipline,
they should act precisely as it is proper for church-members to act
in any case where facts requiring the discipline of the church are
brought to their knowledge."

" In all cases of open and scandalous offenses, or of any breach
of morality, or any fundamental error in doctrine, affecting Christian character, when efforts to bring the offender to repentance
prove unavailing, the church should proceed to the act of excommunication or excision, giving the reasons for the same, which
should be publicly announced before the congregation, on the
Lord's Day."

The principles thus cited from your elaborate " Manual " of 1854
are the ancient, approved, and honored principles of the Congre- .

gational order. They are in complete substantial agreement with the principles of the Cambridge Platform, which, surviving the changes of two centuries and a quarter, still retains among our churches its vital authority. They are the principles of the Platform of "Ecclesiastical Polity" put forth by the National Council at Boston, in 1865, of which Council your pastor was a distinguished member. And these principles, which were set forth by you, with this abundant fullness and particular emphasis, in a Manual prepared and published by yourselves, seven years after you were organized as a church, and which must certainly then have represented your existing and previous practice and belief, we have never hitherto supposed to have been annulled or surrendered by you.

Our letter to you of the 8th November was based on the supposition that you still stood, as an organized church, on the foundation of these sound and approved Congregational principles. We should have held it unfriendly on our part to imagine that you had essentially departed, within a period so brief, from the principles which you then so forcibly declared, so clearly, and in a form so permanent, communicated to us, and so widely proclaimed.

Therefore we wrote you as we did, a month since ; intending to write in all brotherly kindness, though with an earnestness proportioned to the vigor of our convictions. We felt then, as we feel now, that if your action, on October 31, was correctly represented in the published reports, you were taking a step, which, for a Congregational church, was novel, unwise, unscriptural, dangerous ; that you had erred seriously, however unconsciously, in dismissing from your membership, without scrutiny or censure, a member of the church, who, though for years withdrawn from your ordinances, was still a member by your own former principles, and who had been specifically and formally charged, according to published documents before us, with having circulated scandals, derogatory to the pastor, and injurious to the church.

Such an act would have seemed to us of doubtful propriety, and of hazardous tendency, if it had been represented by you as wholly exceptional, justified and demanded by extraordinary circumstances ; though we might not, in that case, have been moved to remonstrate. But such an act, when apparently set forth, and sought to be justified, as simply representative of a permanent and governing policy in the church, assumed an aspect far more serious. It seemed then as certain as any moral fact or force could possibly be, not only to bring suspicion upon your Pastor, but to injure your fame and Christian power, to make discipline among you uncertain and difficult, if not to end it altogether, and to cast an undeserved reproach on the churches which were recognized as in special relations of fellowship with you. Their methods of church discipline would be reasonably supposed to be substantially identical with yours, unless they should make a distinct and formal remonstrance and protest.

Therefore we wrote you, frankly, energetically, but with no intentional vehemence or asperity, and asked you, as a church long associated with us, to meet us in private conference on the subject, to present the facts from your own point of view, to hear and consider our impressions ; and afterward, if no adjustment of views were thus secured, to submit the matters involved to a Council.

Brethren : we felt necessity laid upon us to write you thus. What some of you unexpectedly regarded as impertinent intermeddling, appeared to us an imperative duty ; not less imperative because unwelcome. Any action of your individual members would not have been matter of which we should have taken any cognizance. Reported utterances from your pulpit, whether we agreed with them or not, would not have been likely to offer occasion for our remonstrance, so long as your creed remained evangelical. But your deliberate, public action, in open church-meeting, before an intent and watchful community, on a matter so grave, and so intimately and sensibly concerning us all, demanded, we felt, no less at our hands. And we cannot now see, looking back at the subject from the point of view which we then imagined you to occupy, as well as ourselves, how we could have written otherwise, or less, with fidelity to our duty.

It would now appear, however, from your recent action, and from statements made in connection with it, that you have not only wholly omitted the chapters from which we quoted above, in the recent editions of your " Manual," copies of which have not been sent us, but that you have decisively given up the principles themselves, then accepted, honored, and published by you ; and, furthermore, that you no longer regard yourselves as in any special or responsible relations to the Congregational churches around you. You declare to all whom the newspapers reach, that you interpret your still existing " Rules " as " relieving all other churches from responsibility for the DOCTRINE, ORDER, and DISCIPLINE of this church, and this church from all responsibility for those of other churches."

In other words, you seem to us to take henceforth, according to the inevitable force of your words, the position of entire independency of all churches whatever, exterior to your own ; so that your

Articles of Faith might be essentially altered, or wholly dispensed with; your Rules might require no conditions whatever for admission to the church; your Covenant might be entirely abandoned, without your admitting any right of intervention or remonstrance on the part of other churches.

We should not probably be recognized by you as having the right to make any objection to your taking this attitude, if you prefer it, and severing yourselves from the mutually responsible fellowship with us in which we have stood for twenty-six years; and since this is published as your formal, unanimous, corporate action, interpreting your Rules, and declaring the position which you propose hereafter to occupy, we have only to say, that, if you decide to maintain that position, of course our special relations with you, of denominational alliance, and the fellowship which implies reciprocity of duties, will be suspended, agreeably to your desire.

Do not, in any undue sensibility, interpret these temperate words as a threat. They are nothing of the sort. They are simply the indication of what will, of course, inevitably follow, if you insist on such an independence as your Resolution in terms declares. If you are to be in no sense hereafter responsible to us, nor we to you, — if any remonstrance against your action, coming from us, is to be held by you intrusive, — we must, of necessity, be to each other, in coming time, as wholly separate as are Baptists and Methodists, the Episcopalian who would laugh at us if we questioned his canons, the Unitarian who would shut his door in our face if we ventured to remonstrate at his lack of a creed.

This must, we say, be the final result. Before definitive action, however, is taken by us in this direction, we shall wait to be further informed, if we should be, of the exact meaning, and the fully defined relations and extent, of your recent Resolution. In any case, we should be unwilling to take action by ourselves, or unadvisedly, on a matter so grave. As preliminary to it, we would seek the advice of other churches, according to the wholesome custom and rule of our system of government. In what interests all, a fair representation of Pastors and churches should give to all an authorized expression. But pending delay for further light, and the process to secure the needed advice and consenting action, from other churches, while we understand you to maintain this position of entire independence of all other churches, we shall certainly not attempt to intervene in any matter, either of Doctrine, Order, or Discipline, which may engage your attention.

Nor shall we ever do this hereafter, if the relations you seem now to have assumed, toward us and all others, are to be permanent. If you elect to stand hereafter wholly by yourselves, and to relieve all other churches of all responsibility for whatever you may do, and if they who have stood in mutually responsible fellowship with you accept and complete your action in withdrawing, — it will, of course, be no concern of theirs afterward, except as it may be of all citizens and friends, what charges are made against your Pastor, or what you may do with the men who make them. If you should be moved, at any subsequent time, to radically change, or wholly lay aside, your Articles of Belief, while other churches, and ours among them, would no doubt lament such action for your sake, they certainly would not feel authorized to remonstrate. And instead of inviting you to meet with them in Council, we do not see how they could properly take part in a Council with you; since the action of such a Council, if affecting yourselves, will have been vacated in advance, of all just influence and salutary effect, by your declaration of entire irresponsibleness to all other churches.

Brethren, we pause before affirming to ourselves that you have foreseen, and distinctly intended, these consequences of your action, in adopting your recent Resolution; though all these appear to us definitely involved in it. If you have foreseen them, and maintain your position, we can only wish you all the success that you can desire in your own work, and in your preferred way of doing that work, and commend you most heartily, in the separate sphere which you purpose to occupy, to God's guidance and grace.

But, dear Friends of so many years, do not, we beseech you, make the mistake of supposing that yours is the democratic way, ours the aristocratic, of conducting church-affairs. Unless it be deemed aristocratic to guard carefully the reputation of our Pastors from scandalous attacks within our own brotherhood, and while maintaining the rights of church-members to hold them also to their just responsibility, our churches are precisely as democratic as yours. An aristocratic church can only be one in which the authority belonging to all is vested in a few; and that has never been our custom.

We adhere to the early, constant, tried Congregational principles, which change has not shaken, nor age decayed; and you appear to us to have given them up. That expresses precisely our view of the difference between us. Our Manuals remain essentially what they were twenty years ago, and we interpret them now as then; but yours seems since to have been essentially changed. While we intend to be as democratic as were the churches of the New Testament, we are not convinced that irresponsibility is synonymous with democracy. And we find no reason, if you will allow us so to say, in your recent experience, why we should surrender the principles, which, with us, have been vital and organic from the beginning; why our conception of the local church, as a body of associated worshiping believers, watching over each other, mutually responsible, and in responsible church-communion with other such bodies, should be displaced from our minds or manuals, and for it be substituted a changeful assembly of customary attendants on a particular ministry, any one of whom may at any time attack another, or the Pastor, with grossest charges, and be dropped from the roll without trial or censure. We prefer to be so related in the future, as we have been in the past, to neighbor churches, that they may admonish us if to them we seem to do wrong. And we do not desire the irresponsible independence which to us appears to be simply isolation.

It was well said, in the "Manual" which you formerly published, that the principles of church-government from which we have quoted "are in perfect harmony with the principles of our civil government." Unless you regard that as aristocratic, you can hardly so regard the churches which adhere to the principles you then proclaimed, but which you seem since to have discarded and annulled.

With pleasant remembrances of the years of our fellowship, and the prayer that the Word and the Spirit of God may abide with you always in the future, we are,

Your Friends, and Brethren in Christ,

(*For the Church of the Pilgrims,*)

RICHARD S. STORRS, *Pastor,*

RICHARD P. BUCK,
ARCHIBALD BAXTER,
DWIGHT JOHNSON,
JOSHUA M. VAN COTT,　} *Committee.*
ELI MYGATT, JUN.,
WALTER T. HATCH,
LUCIEN BIRDSEYE,

(*For the Clinton Avenue Church,*)

WILLIAM IVES BUDINGTON, *Pastor,*

ALFRED S. BARNES,
JAMES W. ELWELL,
HARVEY B. SPELMAN,
THOMAS S. THORP,　} *Committee.*
AUGUSTUS F. LIBBY,
FLAMEN B. CANDLER,
CALVIN C. WOOLWORTH,

G.

Letter from Plymouth Church, January 2, 1874.

To Rev. Richard S. Storrs, D.D., Rev. William Ives Budington, D.D., and Messrs. Richard P. Buck, Archibald Baxter, Dwight Johnson, Joshua M. Van Cott, Eli Mygatt, jun., Walter T. Hatch, Lucien Birdseye, Alfred S. Barnes, James W. Elwell, Harvey B. Spelman, Thomas S. Thorp, Augustus F. Libby, Flamen B. Candler, Calvin C. Woolworth, Committees:

DEAR BRETHREN,—Your letter of December 15 has been received, and read to this church. It is largely occupied with explicit or implied comparisons between the Congregationalism of Plymouth Church and that of the churches you represent. That there is a difference we admit ; and, since this may be our last reply to you, we feel that the time has arrived for a statement on our part, setting forth the principles which have constituted the inspiration of our history.

Plymouth Church was founded at a time when the domination of ministers in the newly-formed Congregational churches in the city of New York had excited profound indignation ; and its members were determined, from the beginning, to vindicate the rights of the brotherhood.

They refused to allow a Council to organize them, protesting in the midst of the service, and obliging the officiating minister to recognize the fact, that of their own sole right and authority they organized themselves into a church.

They refused to allow their minister to preside, *ex officio*, at any meeting ; and there never has been a formal business meeting of the church at which he has presided, unless elected by vote of the church.

They even went so far, in the earlier years, as to refuse to allow him to preside at the prayer-meeting of the church, lest he might take advantage of that position to call, by virtue of a careless general consent, indifference, or ignorance, irregular business meetings.

47

According to our rules, no business (with a single definite exception) can be conducted at any meeting of the church, of which previous notice has not been given from the pulpit; and in the twenty-six years of our history there has never been a case in which business of importance has been transacted by the Pastor, or any officer, or any committee, except as specifically determined by a vote of a called meeting of the whole church.

It is in view of this history and uniform practice that we declare ourselves to represent the Congregational polity more truly than either of the two churches which have called us to account. It is this history and constitutional policy of our church which should be known by those who would fully understand the steps we have taken since your interference in our domestic affairs. It is this inbred and unalterable spirit of Plymouth Church that is ignored by those who charge us with a change of ground in the interpretation of the rules of our Manual, given at our recent meeting. It is our adherence to this principle, that the authority of the church does not reside in the pastor, or in any standing committee, but in the whole brotherhood itself, which constitutes our peculiar difficulty in dealing with committees professing to represent two churches, our near neighbors.

For it is well known that in neither of these churches has ever been heard the voice of the brotherhood in open and called assembly, pronouncing on the subjects alleged to be at issue between them and us. Your committees are but a pastoral emanation, authenticated by nothing better than a church-meeting, the residuum of a prayer-meeting, gathered without public call or notice.

While the whole spirit and temperament of Plymouth Church resulting from its origin and its management, on principles equally applicable to all Congregational churches, render it averse to interference in its domestic affairs on the part of any other church, yet, had this course been taken kindly and fairly by the whole brotherhood of both or either of the churches to which we have referred, there would have been every disposition on our part to afford them all the light and knowledge that they reasonably could have asked. This we said, in substance, in our first reply, but it seems to have been unnoticed or forgotten. Instead of being thus approached, Plymouth Church has been arraigned, catechised, conditionally judged and threatened, and all the questions of fact, of our independency, of our responsibility, of our relation to Congregationalism, of our competency to join in calling a Council or to take part in one when called, have been determined for our instruction. Under the plea of a desire to be enlightened, a persistent attempt has been made to enlighten us. And this treatment, to which the self-respect of our church and its sense of the influence of its example and testimony would not allow it to submit, has proceeded from a joint committee, which, whether technically irregular as respects both churches represented or not, was at least, in its origin and authority, so foreign to the habits of this church as to render it almost impossible for us to transact business with it.

We do not complain, brethren, of the phraseology of your letters. It is of the substance of the thing covered by that language, that we complain. You have assumed, from the beginning to the end of your correspondence, an unwarrantable attitude toward this church.

We have hitherto waived these considerations and many others, in the hope of an amicable adjustment. We have not used the material in our hands for an offensive warfare, and we hope to be spared the necessity of a course that could not be otherwise than injurious to the peace of the commonwealth of Congregational churches. And we do now again waive all these just and natural scruples in replying to your last letter.

But we wish it now to be distinctly understood that we must hereafter decline to receive, from you, documents which are not accompanied by proof of the authority of the whole brotherhood of your churches, regularly and deliberately conferred ; and that we must decline to receive, in any case, from them or from you, letters containing covert insinuations against the character of any of the members of this church.

With these reservations we now proceed to answer your letter of December 15. In the first part of it you enumerate the points which you would probably have desired to bring before a Mutual Advisory Council. But, after this enumeration, you proceed to say that the most recent declarations of this church have completely altered the whole case, and that, if these declarations are adhered to, you do not see how we could enter any Council. We infer that you mean to withdraw your invitation, and we shall therefore postpone any discussion of its terms until it shall have been renewed by your churches. We do not decline to join in calling a Mutual Council : it is you who seem to us to have first offered an invitation, under dubious authority, and then withdrawn it.

In the second part of your letter you argue that the recent decla-

4

ration of 'this church, quoting and interpreting its ancient and unaltered rules, constitutes a change in its position equivalent to a voluntary disavowal of Congregational fellowship. This is not the case. Congregationalism is the conduct of the affairs of the church by the whole brotherhood, not embarrassed by the unasked interference of other churches. This view of it is at least as old as Plymouth Church. It is as old as many Congregational writers who have expounded the principles which Dexter sums up in the following statement : —

"Christ by his own voice, and through that of his apostles, placed upon the local church the sole and final responsibility of its affairs, under himself" (p. 55).

"Not only did the individual churches, in obedience to apostolic counsel, and under the apostolic eye, perform untrammeled all the functions of their church life, but the sole responsibility of their life and labors was laid and left upon them by Christ and the apostles, who everywhere recognized the right and duty of the brethren to make final decision upon all matters" (p. 57).

This view we also believe to be as old as the apostolic churches. The position of Plymouth Church, deliberately taken at the beginning, and never changed, is Congregationalism, as we understand it, hold it, and are determined to maintain it.

That it does not prevent a church from giving or receiving fellowship, advice, and assistance, is sufficiently proved by the whole history of this church, and of other Congregational churches. That we have not now suddenly invented or discovered or remembered it, may appear from the remarks made in the pulpit of this church last June, on the occasion of a collection for the Congregational Union, a copy of which, as phonographically reported, is appended to this letter.

We have no desire to interfere with the churches you represent in any course they may feel constrained to take. If they choose to withdraw from a truly Congregational fellowship, it is their right so to do. But we have not withdrawn, and we will not withdraw. Nor can we surrender, for their accommodation, the fundamental principle by virtue of which we exist as a church, — the principle of our solemn and sole responsibility to the Master for the management of our own affairs.

Wishing you the enlightenment of the Spirit upon your path of duty, and praying that you may be led to continue in that mutually independent fellowship and mutually voluntary and cordial co-operation which we have for so many years enjoyed, and which we have done nothing to disturb, we are

Yours in Christian liberty and love,

(*For Plymouth Church,*)

HENRY WARD BEECHER, *Pastor,*

F. M. EDGERTON, *Moderator,*

THOMAS G. SHEARMAN, *Clerk.*

Remarks of Mr. Beecher, June 29, 1873, in Plymouth Church, on the occasion of a collection for the Congregational Union.

" Congregationalism is an independency of local churches. It asserts, as its prime idea, that each particular church is a perfect church, and that, so far as discipline and government are concerned, it stands without necessary allegiance or subjection, either to any neighboring church or to any collection of churches. Congregationalism organizes itself just as a family organizes itself, each family standing on its own proper independent basis.

" But then, as all families find themselves strengthened and comforted by instituting a relation of good neighborhood with near families, so Congregational churches enter into alliance with neighboring churches, and accept and render kind voluntary offices.

" There is no ecclesiastical government between church and church. If a church needs counsel, it asks it; if it does not want counsel, it does not ask it. Every church is understood to be competent to the jurisdiction of its own affairs. If it be not, it goes for help where it thinks it can best get it.

" I think the Congregational form is the best, though other forms are good. It is more in accordance with the Anglo-Saxon spirit, and with our political institutions, than any other form. Congregationalism is very much like our household independency.

We Congregationalists, because our churches are independent and separate, need, more than any others, to have voluntary fellowship ; and therefore we call Conventions from time to time. These Conventions, however, have no authority : they simply have influence. We believe in influence, but not in authority, in such matters."

THE BROOKLYN COUNCIL OF 1874.

OPENING SESSION — MARCH 24.

PURSUANT to Letters-Missive from the Church of the Pilgrims and the Clinton Avenue Congregational Church, Brooklyn, N.Y., the Council of pastors and delegates from Congregational churches, called to consider certain questions relating to church discipline and fellowship, was convened at the Clinton Avenue Congregational Church, in the city of Brooklyn, on the twenty-fourth day of March, 1874, at 7, p.m.

The Council was called to order by Rev. Dr. BUDINGTON, pastor of Clinton Avenue Congregational Church, who said, —

BRETHREN OF THE COUNCIL, — I am told that it is proper for me to open the sessions of this Council, by bidding you welcome, as I do most heartily, to the duties that convene you at this time. I am exceedingly happy to recognize so large an attendance, — unexampled, I believe, in the history of such Councils in this country; and I am the more glad to bid you welcome, because I am persuaded that it is an impartial Council; as I am sure it is one which we have endeavored to assemble on the most impartial principles possible. No correspondence has taken place, on our part, with any church here represented; and we are therefore the better pleased to see you here, in the belief that your decisions will be impartial, and that they will be representative of the sentiments of all our churches. We had intended to invite you to a Mutual Council, had that been possible; but our designs in that regard were not accomplished. We have therefore assembled you in accordance with the directions and principles of our polity, to advise us, — the churches who need your advice in

52

the premises; and we ask you, dear brethren, to place yourselves in our place, so far as you can, through the statements that shall be made to you, and then to give us your best advice under the circumstances. And I pray Him whose pleasure it is to be in the midst of his servants, to be in the midst of us, and to imbue your hearts with the spirit of wisdom and of understanding. May this Council be overshadowed by the Holy Spirit, that the results to which it shall come, shall be for the furtherance of the kingdom of our Redeemer, and for the conservation of those principles which we have inherited from our fathers, which we would conserve for generations yet to come. It has been suggested that it will be promotive of business, and the orderly transaction of it, if we first effect a temporary organization; and, if no objection is made to the suggestion, I will wait for the nomination of a temporary Chairman.

Rev. Dr. HENRY M. DEXTER, of Boston, Mass., nominated Rev. Dr. WILLIAM A. STEARNS, of Amherst College, Mass., as temporary Chairman. The nomination, being seconded, was carried.

Rev. Dr. STEARNS, on taking the chair, said, —

I have no objection to serve you, until the Council is organized; but only with the understanding that it is all the service which I shall be called upon to perform in this connection.

Rev. G. B. WILLCOX, of Jersey City, N.J., nominated Rev. Dr. ALONZO H. QUINT, of New Bedford, Mass., as temporary Scribe. The nomination was seconded, and carried. The temporary Scribe read the list of churches which had been invited to send delegates; and forty-eight churches answered to their names.

Rev. Dr. CUSHING, of Boston, Mass., stated that many delegates were upon the train which left Boston at ten o'clock, a.m., who were not present, but who were in the city, and would soon be at the church.

The CHAIRMAN inquired if the list of names should be read over at present, or whether it should be deferred until other members had arrived.

Rev. Dr. LEONARD BACON, of New Haven, Conn.: The question is, whether the Roll of the Council shall be made out now, or after the organization is completed. If it is to be made out now, I think Rev. Dr. QUINT should have the assistance of another Scribe.

The Rev. EDWARD TAYLOR, D.D., of Binghamton, N.Y., moved that the names be now read; which was agreed to.

The SCRIBE requested pastors and delegates to hand in their names; and the following members appeared as present, the Roll of Council being here printed, as finally perfected:—

FROM THE FIRST CHURCH, BRUNSWICK, ME., Rev. E. H. Byington, *Pastor.*

FROM THE SECOND PARISH CHURCH, PORTLAND, ME., Rev. J. M. Palmer, *Delegate.*

FROM HIGH STREET CHURCH, PORTLAND, ME., Bro. J. M. Libby, *Delegate.*

FROM STATE STREET CHURCH, PORTLAND, ME., Rev. E. Y. Hincks, *Pastor;* Bro. T. K. Hayes, *Delegate.*

FROM WINTER STREET CHURCH, BATH, ME., Rev. J. O. Fiske, D.D., *Pastor.*

FROM CENTRAL CHURCH, BANGOR, ME., Bro. J. S. Wheelwright, *Delegate.*

FROM BANGOR, ME., Rev. W. M. Barbour, D.D.

FROM FIRST CHURCH, PORTSMOUTH, N.H., Rev. Carlos Martyn, *Pastor;* Bro. J. S. Rand, *Delegate.*

FROM SOUTH CHURCH, CONCORD, N.H., Rev. S. L. Blake, *Pastor;* Bro. J. McQuestin, *Delegate.*

FROM FRANKLIN STREET CHURCH, MANCHESTER, N.H., Rev. W. J. Tucker, *Pastor;* Bro. A. H. Daniels, *Delegate.*

FROM FIRST CHURCH, RUTLAND, VT., Rev. J. G. Johnson, *Pastor.*

FROM FIRST CHURCH, BURLINGTON, VT., Rev. L. O. Brastow, *Pastor.*

FROM FIRST CHURCH, MONTPELIER, VT., Rev. W. H. Lord, D.D., *Pastor;* Bro. J. C. Emery, *Delegate.*

FROM SECOND CHURCH, ST. JOHNSBURY, VT., Rev. C. M. Southgate, *Pastor;* Bro. C. M. Stone, *Delegate.*

FROM FIRST CHURCH, CAMBRIDGE, MASS., Rev. A. McKenzie, D.D., *Pastor.*

FROM OLD SOUTH CHURCH, BOSTON, MASS., Rev. J. M. Manning, D.D., *Pastor;* Bro. Avery Plummer, *Delegate.*

FROM UNION CHURCH, BOSTON, MASS., Rev. H. M. Parsons, D.D., *Associate Pastor;* Bro. A. Kingman, *Delegate.*

FROM PHILLIPS CHURCH, BOSTON, MASS., Bro. Choate Burnham, *Delegate.*

FROM ELIOT CHURCH, BOSTON, MASS., Rev. A. C. Thompson, D.D., *Senior Pastor;* Bro. J. Russell Bradford, *Delegate.*

FROM CENTRAL CHURCH, BOSTON, MASS., Rev. John De Witt, *Pastor;* Bro. T. H. Russell, *Delegate.*

FROM SHAWMUT CHURCH, BOSTON, MASS., Rev. E. B. Webb, D.D., *Pastor;* Bro. Charles Demond, *Delegate.*

FROM FIRST CHURCH, NORTHAMPTON, MASS., Rev. W. S. Leavitt, *Pastor;* Bro. S. T. Spaulding, *Delegate.*

FROM EDWARDS CHURCH, NORTHAMPTON, MASS., Rev. Gordon Hall, D.D., *Pastor;* Bro. W. H. Stoddard, *Delegate.*

FROM FIRST CHURCH, WESTFIELD, MASS., Rev. A. J. Titsworth, *Pastor.*

FROM FIRST CHURCH, PITTSFIELD, MASS., Rev. E. O. Bartlett, *Pastor;* Bro. Thomas Colt, *Delegate.*

FROM NORTH CHURCH, NEW BEDFORD, MASS., Rev. A. H. Quint, D.D., *Pastor;* Bro. J. Hastings, *Delegate.*

FROM CALVINIST CHURCH, WORCESTER, MASS., Bro. Henry M. Wheeler, *Delegate.*

FROM UNION CHURCH, WORCESTER, MASS., Rev. E. Cutler, D.D., *Pastor;* Bro. P. L. Moen, *Delegate.*

FROM COLLEGE CHURCH, AMHERST, MASS., Rev. W. A. Stearns, D.D., *Pastor;* Rev. W. S. Tyler, D.D., *Delegate.*

FROM FIRST CHURCH, CAMBRIDGEPORT, MASS., Rev. W. S. Karr, *Pastor;* Rev. C. Cushing, D.D., *Delegate.*

FROM SOUTH CHURCH, SPRINGFIELD, MASS., Rev. S. G. Buckingham, D.D., *Pastor;* Bro. D. L. Harris, *Delegate.*

FROM NORTH CHURCH, SPRINGFIELD, MASS., Rev. R. G. Greene, *Pastor;* Bro. T. M. Brown, *Delegate.*

FROM HIGH STREET CHURCH, LOWELL, MASS., Rev. Owen Street, D.D., *Pastor;* Bro. Nathan Crosby, *Delegate.*

FROM CHURCH IN THEOLOGICAL SEMINARY, ANDOVER, MASS., Rev. J. L. Taylor, D.D., *Acting Pastor;* Rev. E. C. Smyth, D.D., *Delegate.*

FROM BOSTON, MASS., Rev. H. M. Dexter, D.D.

FROM ROWLEY, MASS., Rev. John Pike, D.D.

FROM BENEFICENT CHURCH, PROVIDENCE, R.I., Rev. J. G. Vose, *Pastor;* Bro. R. B. Chambers, *Delegate.*

FROM CENTRAL CHURCH, PROVIDENCE, R.I., Rev. George Harris, jun., *Pastor;* Bro. F. W. Carpenter, *Delegate.*

FROM UNION CHURCH, PROVIDENCE, R.I., Rev. K. Twining, *Pastor;* Bro. A. C. Barstow, *Delegate.*

FROM FIRST CHURCH, HARTFORD, CONN., Rev. E. H. Richardson, *Pastor;* Bro. Calvin Day, *Delegate.*

FROM PARK CHURCH, HARTFORD, CONN., Rev. N. J. Burton, D.D., *Pastor;* Bro. T. W. Russell, *Delegate.*

FROM FIRST CHURCH, NEW HAVEN. CONN., Rev. Leonard Bacon, D.D., *Pastor Emeritus;* Bro. H. C. Kingsley, *Delegate.*

FROM NORTH CHURCH, NEW HAVEN, CONN., Rev. Edward Hawes, D.D., *Pastor;* Bro. H. N. Day, *Delegate.*

FROM FIRST CHURCH, NEW LONDON, CONN., Rev. T. P. Field, D.D., *Pastor;* Bro. Samuel Dennis, *Delegate.*

FROM SECOND CHURCH, NEW LONDON CONN., Rev. O. E. Daggett, D.D., *Pastor.*

FROM FIRST CHURCH, FAIRFIELD, CONN., Rev. E. E. Rankin, D.D., *Pastor;* Bro. H. F. Curtis, *Delegate.*

FROM FIRST CHURCH, BRIDGEPORT, CONN. Rev. C. R. Palmer, *Pastor;* Bro. D. F. Atwater, *Delegate.*

FROM SECOND CHURCH, BRIDGEPORT, CONN., Rev. Edwin Johnson, *Pastor;* Bro. E. Sterling, *Delegate.*

FROM BROADWAY CHURCH, NORWICH, CONN., Rev. D. Merriman, *Pastor;* Bro. A. S. Bolles, *Delegate.*

FROM NEW HAVEN, CONN., Rev. Samuel Harris, D.D.

FROM FIRST CHURCH, HOMER, N.Y., Rev. W. A. Robinson, *Pastor;* Bro. M. Hobart, *Delegate.*

FROM FIRST CHURCH, FAIRPORT, N.Y., Rev. J. Butler, *Acting Pastor.*

FROM FIRST CHURCH, BINGHAMTON, N.Y., Rev. E. Taylor, D.D., *Pastor;* Bro. W. B. Edwards, *Delegate.*

FROM BROADWAY TABERNACLE CHURCH, NEW YORK CITY, Rev. W. M. Taylor, D.D., *Pastor;* Bro. W. H. Smith, *Delegate.*

FROM HARLEM CHURCH, NEW YORK CITY, Rev. S. H. Virgin, *Pastor;* Bro. E. F. Brown, *Delegate.*

FROM FIRST CHURCH, ALBANY, N.Y., Rev. W. S. Smart, D.D., *Pastor;* Bro. Bradford R. Wood, *Delegate.*

FROM SOUTH CHURCH, BROOKLYN, N.Y., Rev. A. J. Lyman, *Acting Pastor;* Rev. H. M. Storrs, D.D., *Delegate.*

FROM ELM PLACE CHURCH, BROOKLYN, N.Y., Rev. Isaac Clark, *Pastor;* Bro. H. H. Van Dyke, *Delegate.*

FROM CENTRAL CHURCH. BROOKLYN. N.Y., Rev. H. M. Scudder, D.D., *Pastor;* Bro. D. M. Stone, *Delegate.*

FROM NEW ENGLAND CHURCH, BROOKLYN, N.Y., (E. D.), Rev. J. H. Lockwood, *Pastor;* Rev. S. S. Jocelyn, *Delegate.*

FROM STATE STREET CHURCH, BROOKLYN, N.Y., Rev. I. C. Meserve, *Pastor;* Bro. L. L. Robbins, *Delegate.*

FROM PURITAN CHURCH, BROOKLYN, N.Y., Rev. C. H. Everest, *Pastor;* Bro. S. B. Terry, *Delegate.*

FROM LEE AVENUE CHURCH, BROOKLYN, N.Y., (E. D.), Rev. T. J. Holmes, *Pastor;* Bro. H. C. Hodgdon, *Delegate.*

FROM PLYMOUTH CHURCH, SYRACUSE, N.Y., Rev. A. F. Beard, *Pastor;* Bro. Peter Burns, *Delegate.*

FROM NEW YORK CITY, Rev. Ray Palmer, D.D.

FROM NEW YORK CITY, Rev. D. B. Coe, D.D.

FROM FIRST CHURCH, NEWARK, N.J., Rev. W. B. Brown, D.D., *Pastor;* Rev. George Brown, *Delegate.*

FROM BELLEVILLE AVENUE CHURCH, NEWARK, N.J., Rev. G. M. Boynton, *Pastor;* Bro. J. H. Denison, *Delegate.*

FROM FIRST CHURCH, JERSEY CITY, N.J., Rev. G. B. Willcox, *Pastor;* Bro. J. Dixon, *Delegate.*

FROM FIRST CHURCH, ORANGE VALLEY, N.J., Bro. John Wiley, *Delegate.*

FROM TRINITY CHURCH, ORANGE, N.J., Rev. G. E. Adams, D.D., *Acting Pastor.*

FROM FIRST CHURCH, MONTCLAIR, N.J., Rev. A. H. Bradford, *Pastor;* Rev. H. Q. Butterfield, D.D., *Delegate.*

FROM FIRST CHURCH, WASHINGTON, D.C., Rev. J. E. Rankin, D.D., *Pastor;* Bro. A. L. Barber, *Delegate.*

FROM FIRST CHURCH, COLUMBUS, O., Rev. R. G. Hutchins, *Pastor;* Bro. B. D. Hills, *Delegate.*

FROM SECOND CHURCH, OBERLIN, O., Rev. Hiram Mead, D.D., *Acting Pastor;* Rev. Henry Cowles, D.D., *Delegate.*

FROM OBERLIN, O., Rev. J. H. Fairchild, D.D.

FROM FIRST CHURCH, DETROIT, MICH., Bro. C. I. Walker, *Delegate.*

FROM SECOND CHURCH, DETROIT, MICH., Rev. S. M. Freeland, *Pastor;* Bro. E. Palmer, *Delegate.*

FROM FIRST CHURCH, CHICAGO, ILL., Rev. E. P. Goodwin, D.D., *Pastor;* Rev. W. W. Patton, D.D., *Delegate.*

FROM NEW ENGLAND CHURCH, CHICAGO, ILL., Bro. C. G. Hammond, *Delegate.*

FROM CHICAGO, ILL., Rev. G. N. Boardman, D.D.

FROM SPRING STREET CHURCH, MILWAUKEE, WIS., Rev. George
    T. Ladd, *Pastor.*
FROM BELOIT, WIS., Rev. A. L. Chapin, D.D.
FROM RIPON, WIS., Rev. W. E. Merriman, D.D.
FROM FIRST CHURCH, ST. LOUIS, MO., Rev. T. M. Post, D.D.,
    Pastor.

The SCRIBE reported that the Orange Valley Church, in
New Jersey, had sent two delegates, the pastor not being able
to attend.

Rev. Dr. J. M. MANNING, of Boston, Mass. : That does not
seem to be in accordance with the Letter-Missive, which
says, "pastor and delegate."

Rev. Dr. GEORGE E. ADAMS of Orange, N.J. : I hope the
question will be cleared up, and settled, whether a church is at
liberty to send, two delegates, in the absence of the pastor,
or when the pastor is not able to attend. It is a practical
question to a number of us. There are several of us, here,
whose names have been read as pastors, who are really acting-pastors. If it is settled that such a church may send two
delegates, as I trust it will be, in accordance with common
sense, then those who are acting-pastors will know how they
can be provided for ; for in these cases the church can send
their acting-pastor and a lay brother as a delegate ; for I
conceive that "delegate" means "layman." I perceive that
we Congregationalists do not understand, apparently, that
pastors represent churches, and are delegates from churches,
and nothing else. "Delegate" means "representative," — one
deputed to act in behalf of another.

At the suggestion of the temporary SCRIBE, the question
was reserved, until after the reading of the Letter-Missive.

The CHAIRMAN requested members to prepare their ballots
for a Permanent Moderator.

Rev. N. J. BURTON, D.D., Hartford, Conn. : In order that we
may focus ourselves, a little, when we come to cast our ballots,
I beg leave to nominate, as Moderator of this organization,
Rev. Dr. LEONARD BACON, of New Haven, Connecticut.

Hon. CHARLES I. WALKER, of Detroit, Mich., nominated
President FAIRCHILD, of Oberlin College, Ohio.

Rev. Dr. MANNING, of Boston, nominated the Hon. LAFAY-
ETTE S. FOSTER, of Connecticut.

Rev. HENRY M. DEXTER, D.D., of Boston: I move that
the Council choose two Moderators. The Council is very
large, and the sessions may be very arduous; and as, in olden
time, it was customary in the large Councils of New England
to have more than one Moderator, I would suggest that we
can divide the honors between the East and West, the clergy
and the laity; in that way having two Moderators, as in the
Boston Council in 1865, who can relieve each other during
the sessions.

The motion was seconded by the Rev. Dr. BACON, and
was agreed to.

Rev. Dr. JOHN O. FISKE, of Bath, Me., nominated Hon.
BRADFORD R. WOOD, of Albany, New York, as one of the
Moderators.

Rev. GEORGE HARRIS, junior, of Providence, R.I., and Rev.
CHARLES R. PALMER, of Bridgeport, Conn., were appointed
tellers to collect and count the ballots; and they subsequently
reported as follows:—

Whole number of votes cast	119;
Necessary to a choice	60;
Rev. Dr. LEONARD BACON, of New Haven, Conn., has	60.

He was therefore declared elected Permanent Moderator.

Rev. Dr. BACON, on taking the chair, said: If I wanted to
sway this body by personal influence, or by speech, I should
ask you to excuse me entirely from this place; but, inasmuch
as I rejoice in the opportunity of being relieved from responsibility in regard to the action and decision of this Council, I
thank you for placing me here.

Hon. CHARLES I. WALKER: I renew the nomination of
President FAIRCHILD, of Oberlin, Ohio, for the Second Moderator.

Rev. Dr. PARSONS, of Boston, Mass.: The suggestion has
been made, that the Associate Moderator should be from the
laity, and also be from the West. I beg leave, therefore, to
nominate Hon. CHARLES I. WALKER, of Detroit, Mich., for that
office.

Rev. Dr. FISKE, of Bath, Me.: I would renew the nomination of Hon. BRADFORD R. WOOD, of Albany, New York.

The tellers, having collected the ballots, reported as follows: —

Whole number of votes cast	119;
Necessary to a choice	60;
For Hon. CHARLES I. WALKER	81.

He was accordingly declared to be elected Associate Moderator.

The Council proceeded to the election of a Permanent Scribe.

Rev. WILLIAM B. BROWN, D.D., of Newark, N.J., nominated Rev. Dr. ALONZO H. QUINT, of New Bedford, Mass.

The nomination was seconded by Rev. Dr. FISKE, of Bath, Me., and was unanimously agreed to.

Rev. E. C. SMYTH, D.D., of Andover, Mass., nominated Rev. I. C. MESERVE, of the State Street Congregational Church of Brooklyn, N.Y., as Assistant Scribe.

The nomination was seconded, and was agreed to.

The MODERATOR announced that the first business in order would be the reading of the Letter-Missive, after which the meeting would be opened with prayer.

Rev. Dr. W. H. LORD, of Montpelier, Vt., moved that the reading of the Letter-Missive be dispensed with.

The motion was agreed to.

The MODERATOR then led the Council in prayer; after which Hon. AMOS BARSTOW, of Providence, R.I., said: I have not seen the Letter-Missive, and I should be glad to hear so much of the Letter read, as names the points on which the churches are requested to act; and, also, such other parts as may open the door to make this a Mutual Council.

The MODERATOR: You hear the suggestion. One of our brethren is not satisfied with undertaking to proceed to business, without having a statement of what the business is. I never knew a Council, before, to take the responsibility of refusing to hear the Letter read by which it was convened, and which was the charter of its existence. (Applause.)

I beg leave to say that this Council is not to be influenced, nor to be disturbed, by any indications of approval or disapproval on the part of the audience ; and I shall demand protection, on behalf of the Council, against all such interference.

Mr. DIXON, of Jersey City, N.J., moved that the Letter-Missive be read.

The SCRIBE stated that a motion had already been agreed to, that its reading be dispensed with.

Mr. DIXON moved that that vote be reconsidered.

The motion to reconsider was agreed to ; and the motion to dispense with the reading was rejected.

On motion of Mr. DIXON, the Letter-Missive was then ordered to be read, and was read by the Scribe, as it appears on pages 1–4 of this volume.

Professor E. C. SMYTH, D.D., of Andover, Mass : I suppose, as we have come up to this Council, from different parts of the land, there has been one question uppermost in all our minds ; and that is, — What is the relation which this Council is to sustain, in its action, to one of the churches in this city, prominent in the discussions that have taken place, but which is not represented here to-night ?   As the Letter-Missive has been read, I suppose every one of us has been impressed anew with the distinctness of the statement of that Letter, that this Council is called to advise the churches summoning it, and not the Plymouth Church ; and I suppose, that as we have heard those specific, definite statements, contained in what the Moderator has so distinctly and emphatically stated to be the charter of this Council, the question has arisen, — What, under such a Letter, can we do, to express the feelings of our hearts towards the Plymouth Church ? and especially, our desire, that, in this discussion, there should be the utmost manifestation of the spirit of charity and of kindness toward that church, and of our desire, above all things, to be magnanimous and fair, from the beginning to the end ?

Now, in reading the Letter, and considering how we can carry out such a purpose as that, we are, of course, in the first place, governed — I suppose we should all admit — strictly, by the terms of the Letter-Missive. The whole question that comes before us is, then, what we can accomplish under this Letter.   It has seemed to me, that we might properly and fairly, without going over in the least, the boundaries fixed by the Letter, invite that church to sustain a relation to this Council, equivalent, substantially, to the relation sustained by the churches that have called it ; while, at the same time, we avoid technical embarrassments, which at once arise if we consider this as an *ex parte* Council, and proceed to make overtures to the Plymouth Church to unite with us in a technical Mutual Council.

We are not called to advise them, as we should do immediately, and directly, if we sought to transform this Council into a Mutual Council ; but we are called to consider a great principle, in which, as a matter of fact, there are parties : and, if an *ex parte* Council means, simply, that we have to do with questions in respect to which there are parties, there will be no difference of opinion among us. But we have to do with a controversy to which there are parties, on the basis of a Letter which summons us to advise one of the parties, and not the other. There is precisely where we stand.

Now, I have been in consultation with a few brethren since I have come in, simply that I might not come forward as an individual, to express the thoughts of my own mind and heart ; and I have here, in writing, a Resolution, which I should like to propose for the consideration of the Council, and which seems to me to accomplish precisely the object, as to substance, which we must all desire, of gaining all the light which we could have as a Mutual Council, while it avoids the embarrassments to which I have referred. With the permission of the Council, I will read this Resolution, and it may then be submitted, without further remarks of mine.

" *Resolved*, That the Plymouth Church be invited, with the consent of the committees of the churches [the churches, of course, calling this Council], to present its views, orally, before the Council, on the questions presented in the Letter-Missive, by its pastor and such committee as it may appoint ; and, by the same committee [of course including the pastor], to furnish such information concerning the action referred to in these questions, as the Council may request."

The substance of this Resolution is not hastily entertained or submitted. The object is, that we may, in the beginning of our discussion, put ourselves in a relation to that church,

through which they may appear here, to make their statements, in the same way as the brethren who have called this
Council will appear to make their statements ; so that we may
thereafter come to a result with all the light which can be shed
on the questions before us.

Rev. CARLOS MARTYN, of Portsmouth, N.H. : I rise to a
point of order, which touches a question prior to the question
raised in the Resolution. I hold in my hand a work by our
honored brother, Dr. Dexter, on Congregationalism. Opening
at page 64, under the head of *Councils*, I find these words : —

"A Mutual Council is one, in the calling of which, all parties to the difficulty or perplexity concerning which relief is
sought, unite. An *ex parte* Council is one which is called by
one of those parties after every proper effort to induce all interested to call a Mutual Council has failed ; and no *ex parte*
Council has a right to proceed to the consideration of the case
before it, until it has satisfied itself that every reasonable endeavor to secure a Mutual Council has been tried and failed,
and until it has offered itself as a Mutual Council to all parties, and has been rejected as such."

I also hold in my hand, a Resolution passed on Friday evening, in Plymouth Church, to this effect : —

"*Resolved*, That the calling of this *ex parte* Council, to consider the
affairs of a church which has not declined a Mutual Council, is the
consummation of a course," &c.

My point of order is, as to whether we have any right to proceed, at all, until we are satisfied that Plymouth Church has
declined a Mutual Council. Upon that point I, for one, am not
clear, and I ask for further light.

Rev. Dr. N. J. BURTON, of Hartford, Conn., suggested that
after the word "orally," in Prof. Smyth's resolution, the words
"or otherwise" be inserted.

The MODERATOR : The point of order was suggested by Rev.
Mr. Martyn, whether the Council can proceed to do any thing,
without first disposing of the question whether this is an *ex
parte* Council ; and whether all reasonable efforts have been
made to induce Plymouth Church to unite in calling it. That
seems to me to be a question of fact, rather than a question of

order. It opens large inquiries, and I do not feel myself competent to decide it.

Rev. Mr. DE WITT, of Boston, Mass.: I rise to submit to Brother Burton, whether his object would not be attained if the word "orally" were stricken out from the Resolution.

Dr. BURTON: Yes.

Rev. Prof. SMYTH: A word of explanation. The object is, that the representatives of Plymouth Church may be here, in the same way in which the representatives of the churches which have convened the Council, are present. We want to see these brethren; we want to learn from them, not simply what may be present to their minds, and may be conveyed by writing, but we may wish to obtain information also by our own questions. What I wish, is, that all these churches may be here, in that respect, in precisely the same way. That seems to me the fair way to bring the subject fully before us; and, therefore, the word "orally" is important, as regards the object in view.

Rev. Mr. TWINING, of Providence, R.I.: I would like to inquire whether the character of this Council, as an *ex parte* Council, or as a Mutual Council, is indelibly fixed upon it by the Letter-Missive? I wish to inquire whether there is not a body of Congregational precedent, and of common law, which would, in a measure, dictate the proceedings of the Council, and the principles by which we are to proceed; and whether those principles do not require us, in case we are summoned under a Letter which looks toward an *ex parte* Council, to use all means, in our power, to make it a Mutual Council; and whether, according to the proceedings of past centuries, an *ex parte* Council is not regarded as a misfortune, which is to be averted by every means in our power; and whether, after our assembling, we have not the right to do all that we can to put the Council on another basis? And I desire, furthermore, to state that it has seemed to me, after a perusal and examination of this Letter-Missive, that all pains were taken by its authors to avoid giving this Council the character of an *ex parte* Council; and I expressly and particularly wish to call attention to some words on the last page. After the seventh point which is to be laid before the Council, occur these words: —

"We ask you, dear brethren, to meet in Council, by your pastor and delegate, at the Clinton Avenue Church in this city, on the 24th of March, 1874, at 7, p.m., to consider these questions, *or such of them as the Council may deem it wise to consider*, and to give us the light of your wisdom upon them."

Now, I beg leave to submit that that clause, of itself, gives the Council a certain liberty. And, if there were no such thing as a Congregational common law to give us this right, I beg leave to submit, that, in my understanding of the document itself, we should get it there. And with this view, until I can see the matter in a different light, I shall certainly oppose the resolution of Prof. Smyth ; because, although I think the *animus* of it is right, — though I think it is dictated by a desire to bring the Plymouth brethren in, — I think it would fix upon this Council, from the start, a character which it is very unfortunate for it to bear ; and that it would preclude us from taking those steps which, heretofore, *ex parte* Councils have always taken, and which, I believe, always ought to be taken.

The MODERATOR : On the point of order raised, I desire to say, that an *ex parte* Council is a Council called by a party in a church. There is no other *ex parte* Council. This is a Council called by a church ; not by a church only, but by two churches ; to advise *them :* and it is a misnomer to call it an *ex parte* Council, in the technical sense of that word. All the rules and precedents about *ex parte* Councils are rules and precedents which will apply to a Council called by a party in a church, which is not itself a church.

Rev. Dr. BROWN, of Newark, N.J., inquired whether our standards recognized any other than either Mutual Councils or *ex parte* Councils.

The MODERATOR : Yes ; they do.

Rev. Dr. BROWN : I should like to see that in our books.

The MODERATOR : Were you ever ordained by a Council, brother ?

Rev. Dr. RANKIN, of Washington, D.C., moved to amend the Resolution offered by Professor Smyth, by substituting the following : —

5

Whereas, This Council, convened at the instance of two of our most important and influential churches, presided over by two of our ablest, wisest, and most respected pastors, though technically *ex parte*, is in no proper sense partisan ; and, —

Whereas, The questions to be submitted to its decision relate to the administration of discipline in another of our churches, no less important and influential, and presided over by a pastor whose reputation and influence are dear to all the churches, and to true Christians the world over ; and, —

Whereas, The Council is desirous of discovering some method of removing all misunderstanding and prejudice between our brethren, as well as correcting errors in discipline, if such exist ; therefore, —

Resolved, That we cordially invite the pastor and members of the Plymouth Church to accept the Council now convened, as Mutual, and to submit all differences between themselves and the Clinton Avenue Church, and the Church of the Pilgrims, of this city, to its advice and determination ; promising, so far as possible, to extend to them all the rights and privileges of original parties in the calling of this Council ; also, —

Resolved, That a committee of five be appointed to convey these resolutions to the Plymouth Church, and to kindly urge the acceptance of the same ; and that, when the Council adjourns, it be to eleven o'clock to-morrow morning, to await the report of the committee.

Rev. Dr. RANKIN said : I do not know that this is wise ; but in thinking the matter over, with a great deal of solicitude, and conversing with some of the brethren, on the cars, respecting it, it seemed to me that this was the first step for us to take. I do not know which of these venerable and noble men I love most or best. I love them, — all these pastors ; and I feel that I have at heart the interests of all these churches. It seems to me there are misunderstandings between these pastors and churches, which may be adjusted ; and it certainly is evident, from the little I have seen of the correspondence between the pastors, that we ought to have something more than we are likely to have submitted to us ; that we ought to have something more from the pastor of the Plymouth Church, or the church itself ; and, therefore, I move this substitute.

The motion was seconded.

It was stated that the question was upon the adoption of the substitute, offered by Rev. Dr. RANKIN.

Mr. DIXON, of Jersey City, N.J.: It seems to me that this

Preamble and Resolution are, in their expressions, directly in the teeth of the ruling of the Moderator, in reference to the character of this Council. The preamble to this Resolution declares the Council to be technically *ex parte*. I understand the ruling of the Moderator to be that it is not an *ex parte* Council, but a Mutual Council, in the sense that it is called to advise the churches that have called it.

The MODERATOR: No, sir; not a Mutual Council, but simply an Advisory Council, called by two churches. Not Mutual, not technically *ex parte*.

The SCRIBE: Are we to understand that the Moderator's ruling has any binding force upon the Council, or is it simply his opinion in regard to the case?

The MODERATOR: It has not. It is my opinion.

Mr. DIXON: I supposed it was a ruling, on a question of order raised, and would be binding on the Council, until appealed from in a regular way, and reversed; and therefore, as yet, it stands binding upon the Council, in reference to that question of order. It struck me, too, that there was a great deal of force in the suggestion that this is not an *ex parte* Council, even technically. We are called, it is true, by parties who are, to some extent, parties to what seems to be a controversy; but we are called to advise the churches that call us, and the Letter-Missive expressly repudiates the idea that this Council is summoned for the purpose of advising Plymouth Church; and, therefore, it seems to me, that, as we are only to advise the churches that have called us, it is not *ex parte*, in the sense in which Councils are called *ex parte*. It strikes me, further, that the Resolutions which are proposed as a substitute for the Resolution offered by Professor Smyth are of such a character that this Council cannot properly adopt them. The charter of this Council, as I understand it, and as it has been stated by the Moderator, is its Letter-Missive. Is it competent for this Council, when convened, to change its character from the character indicated by the Letter-Missive, and to become another sort of a Council, which shall be summoned, not by the two churches that have summoned it, but by those churches in conjunction with another church? Have we the power to give to Plymouth Church the exact position, on this floor, that it would have had, in case it had joined in the call ? It seems to me, that, if the Letter-Missive be the charter of the Council, we have not the authority to do that thing. We are a Council called by these two churches ; and that sort of a Council we must remain.

I shall oppose the substitution of these Preambles and Resolutions, also, because of the phraseology of a portion of the Preamble in reference to the character of the churches and pastors concerned. It seems to me that we ought not to cast such a reflection upon the other churches belonging to the Congregational denomination, as to undertake to compliment, in any such terms, the churches which have called this Council. We stand on the same footing. We are none ablest, none wisest. They have called us to advise them. I can see clearly that it is a part of the province of this Council to ask Plymouth Church to give us light. We are asked to consider questions ; and it is one of the very first principles in the consideration of any question, — "*audi alteram partem,*" — " hear both sides." And if there be possibly any sides to this controversy, it will be proper, and necessary perhaps, that we should have the Plymouth Church represented on the floor of this Council, just as fully as it is possible to have it ; and therefore I am in favor of the Resolution, as proposed by Professor Smyth. Perhaps I would make it a little broader. My own notion would be to invite Plymouth Church to stand upon the floor of this Council, by its pastor and delegates, just as the delegates who are here stand, except in the right to vote ; so that upon all questions that may arise they may be heard, in reference to their own views. But it seems to me that the Resolution of Professor Smyth sufficiently meets that ; and therefore I shall favor his Resolution, and oppose the substitute. I therefore move to lay the substitute upon the table.

The MODERATOR stated that that motion would carry the original Resolution with it.

Mr. DIXON then withdrew his motion.

Rev. Dr. R. S. STORRS, pastor of the Church of The Pilgrims, Brooklyn, N.Y.: I wish to say a very few words in regard to this subject, as to the impression under which the Letter-Missive was prepared and sent out. We under-

stand that there are four kinds of Councils recognized in
the Platform : — a Mutual Council, where two parties, having a
difference, agree to refer the whole subject to a Council, as a
common tribunal ; an *ex parte* Council, where one of the parties in the controversy, the other party having refused to
unite in such a reference, refers the same subject to a Council called by itself alone. In that case, the same questions
must be presented to the *ex parte* which it had been proposed
to present to the Mutual Council. An *ex parte* Council has
no right to exist until a Mutual Council has been distinctly
declined. A third Council is what is called, in a specific
sense, an Ecclesiastical Council ; convened simply for the performance of some public ecclesiastical action, such as the
ordaining of a minister, the installing of a minister, the institution of a church, or the recognition of it. An Advisory
Council is a different Council from either. It is a Council
with which we are very familiar, here. A church wishes help,
advice, counsel, in regard to pecuniary affairs ; in regard to
the removal of its church edifice ; in regard to any questions
which have arisen within it, upon which it needs the guidance, the correction, or the confirmation of its judgment, —
to employ the terms which the Platform expressly uses. We
intended to call this not as a Mutual Council, not as an *ex parte*
Council, not as a specific Ecclesiastical Council, for common
ecclesiastical action, but, precisely as we style it, and have
styled it always, as an Advisory Council ; to advise us, as to
whether what we have done in the past is proper, and as to
how we should order our affairs in time to come. And we have
said expressly, in the Letter-Missive, that after you have heard
our statements, and have got all the light you can, if there
are any of these questions on which you cannot give us your
advice, you are at liberty to be silent. We lay the matters
before you ; we tell you our difficulties ; we give you all the
information, and all the conceptions of principles, which we
have ; and then you will, by yourselves, after the full discussion of the subject, give us the benefit of your wisdom, we hope,
on all the questions, — on every one. But, if you find, when
you come to consider the matters laid before you, that, in your
judgment, the answer to any question impinges upon another

church, more sharply than you are willing to have it, it is in
your discretion to decline to give us there any advice. But
we desire your advice, and ask for it ; and we need it, on all
the questions.

This is an Advisory Council, or it is no Council at all. If it
is an *ex parte* Council, it has no existence. For we have expressly said in the statement accompanying our Letter-Missive,
that we have obtained no decisive answer to our requests for
a Mutual Council ; and we are not so young in our Congregationalism as not to know that before we call an *ex parte* Council we have got to have a precedent declinature of a Mutual
Council. Therefore we called no *ex parte* Council.

Therefore the Questions submitted to you are not the same
Questions which were submitted to the Plymouth Church, on
which we desired a Mutual Council. They are distinctly different. We asked them, for example, to join in calling a Mutual
Council to decide whether their action — not as presented in
public documents merely, but as obtained from an investigation of their records, as obtained from oral testimony — was
not injurious to the Christian reputation and influence of that
church, and did not involve a failure to give timely vindication to the name of the pastor. We have asked you no such
question. Our questions to you are thus not the same which we
proposed to them, as furnishing the occasion for a Mutual
Council ; but all these questions concern ourselves, — the past
action, and the future action, of these churches. Of course
they concern ourselves in regard to another church ; and we
appreciate and feel, with you, all the delicacy of the situation.
But suppose we had been in fellowship with another church
which had omitted from its Articles of Faith the doctrine of
the inspiration of the Scriptures, or the doctrine of the divinity of our Lord, and we had said to them : " Will you join us
in a Mutual Council to consider whether this is proper, in the
relations we sustain to each other, and whether our fellowship
should continue ? " and we had got no answer to that question :
would it not be our right to ask our neighbor churches to
come in and advise us, as to whether we ought to continue in
that fellowship ? Are we to be forever debarred from seeking
the advice of sister churches when a church, concerning

which we wish advice, as to *our* action toward it, not as to
its action, by delay, or by failure to reply positively either one
way or the other, leaves us without any proper resort to an
ex parte Council?

Our conception of the thing is this, — let me sum it up in
a word : This is not a Mutual Council, not an *ex parte* Council,
not a specific Ecclesiastical Council, for the performance of
common and public ecclesiastical functions ; but it is strictly
and absolutely an Advisory Council: called under that provision
in the Platform which says, in so many words, that when a
church needs advice for the guidance or correction or confirmation of its own judgment, it has a right to ask the advice
of its sister churches. And we adhere to that Letter-Missive.
We desire that you shall have all the light you can get, from
every quarter. We have not the least disposition in the
world to shut out a ray, a gleam, a glimmer, but we would
gather all the light we can, from every side ; and we welcome,
— I speak for myself, and have no doubt that I speak for the
entire committees, — we welcome *any* opportunity that you
may give to the Plymouth Church to represent its views here,
on the floor of this Council, by its pastor and committee ;
giving it precisely as much opportunity to do that as we have
ourselves, in all your public sessions. But we do not want you
to change the Letter-Missive, and we do not want you to say
that this is an *ex parte* Council ; for then it is not a Council
at all. It is an Advisory Council, as we meant it to be, as we
have expressly called it from the beginning. And if, after you
have heard all our views, and gathered all the light you can
from every side, there are any questions which you do not feel
like giving us an opinion about, let them alone.

Judge C. I. WALKER of Detroit, Mich : This question of jurisdiction is a preliminary one, and one of very great importance ;
and for myself, little versed in law of this sort, I desire all
the light I can obtain. I have listened to the suggestions
that have been made, and especially to the very clear and able
presentation, by Dr. Storrs, of the questions presented to the
Council ; but I have one trouble in my mind in relation to the
character of this Council. And first I will say, in relation to
an *ex parte* Council, Is it true that there can be no *ex parte*

Council until the adversary party has absolutely refused to join in a Mutual Council? I do not know but it is. I have no learning upon that subject. That is an inquiry I desire to make. If we all agree with what Dr. Storrs has said upon that subject, that there must be an absolute refusal before there can be an *ex parte* Council, then, of course, this cannot be considered an *ex parte* Council. But suppose there is evasion; suppose there is neglect; suppose there is unreasonable delay; may not then the aggrieved party then call an *ex parte* Council? That is a question for those learned in this law to determine: I cannot determine it. If we all agree with Dr. Storrs, then, of course, this cannot be an *ex parte* Council.

Unquestionably there are Ecclesiastical Councils. I don't know so much about this question of Advisory Councils. Unquestionably they exist in the church; but is it possible that they can relate to a trouble between two churches, where the church implicated is not brought before the Council? Is not the proceeding, in its nature, adversary? Can you pass upon such questions without passing upon the conduct of the church that is complained of? Are there any such Councils known to the Congregational body? If that is so, that there are Councils that may consider matters which, in their very nature, are controversial, then it is well to have it settled. These questions that are presented here, if passed upon in a certain way, do necessarily implicate another church. Have we a right to pass upon their conduct by a mere Advisory Council? I make these inquiries because I am unlearned on the subject. It seems to me there ought to be no such Councils. It seems to me that a church ought not to be condemned, without having an opportunity to be heard. That, as a common-law lawyer, seems to me their just right. But is it true that this may *not* be virtually, if not technically, an *ex parte* Council? That is a question of fact, to be considered. If it belongs in this fourth class, and it is true that we may thus pass upon the doings of a church that is not before us, that is not invited before us, as a party to the proceedings, if there is such a class of Councils, then, of course, we may go on as an Advisory Council. These are questions upon which I desire light. I submit that the Resolution offered by Professor Smyth is one that seems to cover the ground. But whether this is technically an *ex parte* Council or not it seems to me, in its nature, to be an *ex parte* Council, and that we may go forward and invite the other party whose conduct is implicated, the other church, into this Council, to be heard as we hear these churches that have called this Council. It is hardly worth while that we should waste a great deal of time on a mere technicality; but can we act as an Advisory Council, thus implicating a party that is in no way before us?

Rev. CARLOS MARTYN: The great trouble in inviting Plymouth Church before us is, that if Plymouth Church has not been invited to unite in the call for a Mutual Council, or if, that call having been given, it has been withdrawn, then to ask Plymouth Church to unite with us, on the basis of a Mutual Council, is to ask Plymouth Church to unite with us without having had any voice in saying who shall constitute that Mutual Council; which to me seems to be exceedingly unfair. Moreover, on our dear brother Storrs' showing, I cannot conceive how there can be any difference whatever between an *ex parte* Council and an Advisory Council. Whenever it becomes essential, or seemingly necessary, that a church should deny that it is calling an *ex parte* Council, it may hide its action under the admirable and convenient phrase of an Advisory Council, and so avoid all stigma.

Rev. Dr. RANKIN: I did not introduce the epithets by way of complimenting any church, but to state the truth with regard to the churches. The presumption is, that, having been called by these churches, there is some ground for the call. But then, on the other hand, this church that is also involved, indirectly, is a very important church; and we cannot do any thing to injure that church, or its pastor, with our eyes closed. We want to know the facts of the case. I have no preference for the Resolutions which I presented; but it did not seem to me that the Resolution of Professor Smyth was quite broad enough in the invitation which it extended, and perhaps not quite warm enough; and for that reason I moved the substitute.

The MODERATOR: You will observe that there is no dissenting voice, in the debate, about the propriety of inviting the Plymouth Church to be present here, to be heard on all the questions submitted to this Council. There is no debate on that point. And the only question is on substituting Dr. Rankin's Resolutions for the Resolution proposed by Professor Smyth. Are you ready for that question?

Rev. Dr. Rankin withdrew his Resolutions.

Rev. Dr. H. M. Storrs, of Brooklyn, N.Y.: I will move the adoption of a Resolution, most of the language of which will be found in the Letter-Missive, on page 3* : —

Resolved, That a committee be appointed to notify the Plymouth Church of our assembling, and to convey to them our desire and hope that they will be present with us, at the sessions of the Council, by their pastor and a committee, to correct any statements of fact which may seem to them erroneous, and to furnish any further information or statements which may be of use to the Council in reaching its decision.

This invitation was communicated by these two churches which have called the Council. It was not communicated by the Council itself. The force of the invitation lies in the person that gives it, in the party that proposes it, more than it does in the language which conveys it. I take it that that is an accepted fact : the same words, precisely, from two different persons or parties, affect us very differently. It has been stated through the public press, that Plymouth Church, at least some portions of it, very highly respect this Council. We have seen that statement in the public press. I choose this language, thinking that it is the language which will most adequately express the sentiments of the committees of the churches, who had drafted this Letter-Missive and sent it forth. They said, we purpose to do a certain thing. I take it they have done it. Suppose Plymouth Church has declined that invitation, — I don't know whether it has ; but suppose that it has declined that invitation, as addressed to it by these two churches. We want to address to that church an invitation. This language is certainly broad enough, as I have presented it, — it seems so at least to some gentlemen sitting by me, — broad enough to cover what may be desired on the part of Plymouth Church. It is courteous to these churches that have called us, and it is courteous to that church ; it will express cordially the sentiments of this Council, in language that seems fitly chosen to convey such an invitation ; and therefore I offer it, desiring to combine in the invitation, in language which has evidently been chosen with care, the cordial desire of this Council to greet that church here, and to receive such aid and information as it can give.

There are two or three points of difference between the two Resolutions : one of them I think, is in the closing phrase of the Resolution of Professor Smyth, — "such information as the Council may request." It seemed to me unadvisable that, if they wished to say any thing, they should first be called upon to get a request from the Council that they should say it. They might feel hampered, by such a phrase as that. As I understand from our brother who addressed us a few minutes ago, it is the desire of these committees, who are present, that that church should be represented, and should take as free a part in stating matters here as themselves. Then, let us put it a little broader, and not say merely "such information as the Council may request."

The MODERATOR : Let me read the first part of the original Resolution, — "to present its views, orally, before the Council on the questions presented in the Letter-Missive, by its pastor and such committee as it may appoint." By that they are to come, and tell their own story, and give their own views ; and, after giving such a statement, they are to "furnish such information concerning the action referred to in these questions as the Council may request."

Mr. DIXON : Perhaps "presenting their views," may possibly not include a statement of the facts. And I therefore would move to amend the Resolution of Professor Smyth by adding, at the close of it, the words, "or as may seem advisable to Plymouth Church," — that is, such information as the Council may request, or as may seem advisable to them.

Hon. BRADFORD R. WOOD, of Albany, renewed his motion to strike out the word "orally," saying : They may choose to present their case, here, not orally ; and, as the object is to give them perfect liberty to present the case as they please, I move that the word be stricken out.

Rev. Dr. R. S. Storrs: If you will allow me, I would ask if the Council would be content in our case, in the case of our Committees, with our sending in to them written statements, which might be read, in their hearing, without the presence of the Committees? In the course of the statements which we have to make, there will be some things referred to, as a matter of course, concerning which the Council may wish to ask us questions, — concerning which they may wish to have evidence particularly presented by us. We shall make affirmations of fact, which we expect to be questioned about, — for which we expect to furnish our evidence, if it is required. We desire that the Plymouth Church shall have every right and privilege, with regard to the expression of its views, which we ourselves have ; but we should like, unless that seems objectionable for some reason not apparent to the Committees, that the Plymouth Church Committee should be here precisely as we expect to be here ; so that their declarations of fact may be inquired about, and evidence may be requested from them, if any thing is doubted ; and that there may not be extended statements sent in by parties to whom no question can be addressed in regard to the meaning or the evidence of those statements. Not that I mean to imply that they would affirm any thing with intentional untruth, — not in the least : but that as facts are viewed from different points, they wear different aspects. And as we expect to be here, to be questioned, we should like to have the Committee of Plymouth Church on the ground also, to present their statements as we present ours, and to be subjected to the same inquiries from the Council, to which we expect, and are ready, to be subjected.

Hon. Mr. Wood : It has been stated, here, that there is a strong desire to give this church the opportunity to place itself upon the record, as they wish to be placed on the record. Now, it is perfectly evident to every one that a written statement cannot be misrepresented, whereas a verbal one may be ; and that is the reason why I move to place this church, in the situation in which it may choose to be placed, and not in that in which we may choose to place it.

The Moderator : The word "orally" does not exclude a

written statement. Most of the ministers in this Council
preach "orally," though they read every word they preach.
"Oral" means that they shall not send us a letter through
the post-office. It means that they shall not send a letter
which our Scribe is to read ; it means that they shall come, if
they come at all, and be heard, by the hearing of the ear, on
their views. I take it that that is the meaning of the word.

Mr. KINGSLEY, of New Haven, Conn. : I desire to second the
motion of the Honorable Mr. WOOD, to strike out the word
"orally," for the following reason : We are invited here to
answer questions relating to the action of Plymouth Church.

Rev. Mr. TWINING raised the point of order, that there was
another question before the house, — the question upon the
substitute.

Mr. WOOD withdrew his amendment.

Rev. Dr. LEAVITT, of Northampton, Mass. : I am not prepared to vote upon either of these Resolutions to-night. I
hope that the vote will be postponed until to-morrow morning ; and I therefore move that we adjourn until to-morrow
morning.

SEVERAL MEMBERS : No ! no !

The motion to adjourn was not seconded.

Rev. Dr. FISKE : It was suggested by Rev. Dr. STORRS that
there will be private sessions, to which these Committees are
not to be invited ; and if we should move to go into a private
session, and should invite the Plymouth Church to act with
the Council, without qualifying it by introducing the word
"public," they would go with us into private session.

Rev. Dr. H. M. STORRS modified his Resolution, by introducing the word "open."

The question was stated to be upon substituting the resolution offered by Rev. Dr. H. M. Storrs, for that offered by Professor Smyth.

Mr. KINGSLEY : I am opposed to the resolution of Rev. Dr.
STORRS, for the following reason : We are invited here to
answer certain questions relating to the action of Plymouth
Church ; and, in reading the letters upon this subject, I find
a great difference between the action of Plymouth Church and
the statements of the members of that church. I prefer, there-

fore, to take the action of the church which we are called to consider, as the basis of our action, rather than the statements of the church, or of any committee of the church. Furthermore, I find in the documents which have been placed in our hands, that Plymouth Church claims to act as a democracy, and not by a Committee. Therefore I think it better that we should ask them to make such representations, to us, as they choose, in the way that they choose, in accordance with the motion made by Professor Smyth, amended by Rev. Dr. Burton.

The question was taken upon the substitute offered by Rev. Dr. H. M. Storrs ; and it was rejected.

The question recurred upon the adoption of the Resolution offered by Prof. Smyth.

Rev. Dr. George E. Adams moved to strike out the words "with the consent of the Committees of the churches," and said : —

We come here from New York, Chicago, and other places, without asking leave of Plymouth Church.

Rev. Dr. R. S. Storrs : Is it not just to the Committees, if the Committees consent, as they do, that they should appear to consent ? Ought it to be recorded as if it were an action of the Council, overriding the wish of the Committees, when these Committees have expressed their entire assent, in the strongest terms possible ? It cannot invalidate the action, to recognize the fact that we welcome it. It cannot operate as a bar, to make the action ineffectual. Why not, then, retain the language ?

Dr. Adams : I feel a difficulty about that, that the language implies that we are to ask leave.

The Moderator : It does not imply that.

Mr. David M. Stone, of Brooklyn, N.Y. : I was about to make the same motion. We all desire to see Plymouth Church here, represented in its own way, and to express its own views. The Committees had already invited it. We knew the Committees favored their coming. Their offer was declined ; and I thought that the expression in the invitation, that they were to come by consent of the Committees, might possibly be offensive. I therefore arose to make the same motion.

Rev. Isaac Clark, Brooklyn, N.Y., suggested the substitution of the phrase, "the Committees having freely con-‸ sented."

A Delegate : Might it not be amended further, making it a little more truthful, recognizing the fact that the Committees have extended the invitation, and have repeated the expression of their desire here.

Rev. Dr. Adams: I would not twit the Plymouth Church with that.

Rev. Dr. Boardman, of Chicago, Ill. : The Letter-Missive records that the Committees asked the Plymouth Church to be represented, and we are informed that they have been invited. Why should we re-enact what is a necessary part of the platform on which we stand ? I think it is desirable that it should be understood that we assent to, and cordially approve of, the action of the Committees in what they did.

The question was taken on the amendment ; and it was rejected.

Mr. Dixon moved to amend by adding to the Resolution the words, "or, as may seem to the Committee advisable ;" so that they may not be hampered in their statement of facts, or by the request for facts, but may state such facts as they may desire.

The Moderator : That is all covered by the anterior part of the Resolution.

Mr. Dixon : The anterior part of the Resolution, as I understand it, covers a simple statement of their views. That seems to be rather an expression of opinions, and not a statement of facts. If it be covered by that, the latter part of the Resolution is entirely unnecessary.

The Moderator : The former part of the Resolution proposes that they should come and tell us what they think and know, and the latter part that they should submit answers to our questions.

Rev. Mr. Twining moved to strike out the word " orally."

The motion was not agreed to.

The question was stated to be upon the amendment to add the words, " as to them may seem advisable."

The amendment was rejected.

The question recurred upon the adoption of the Resolution offered by Professor SMYTH.

Hon. NATHAN CROSBY, of Lowell, Mass.: As I propose to vote against that Resolution, I wish to make a single remark with regard to it. We come here to act under a charter. These churches have invited us to come and advise them, in certain particulars. I hold that we are bound by the charter, and cannot go out of it ; that we must confine ourselves, out of respect to the churches which have called us, to the questions put to us, and we cannot dictate others ; that we cannot ask them to change this, or to make a new Letter-Missive for us, but we are to go by the Letter-Missive which we have received, and which we are here to answer. They say to us that they have asked the Plymouth Church, by their Committee, to come here : they were satisfied to do that. They notify us that they asked them ; and I contend that, in due respect to the Committees that have called us, in due respect to ourselves, we should simply send a Committee to the Plymouth Church, and say that this Council is now ready to hear any thing which they have to say in answer to the invitation of the churches calling us here, and not put ourselves before them to be snubbed, if you will allow me to use that expression, for I know it is not a dignified one. Suppose they say, "Who are you? We don't acknowledge you." The Committees calling us here, have told us that they have invited them. I hope this Council will only send a Committee to them to say : "Gentlemen, we are now ready to hear you, if you have any thing to say, under the request made by the churches which have called us here."

The question was taken on the resolution offered by Professor SMYTH, and it was agreed to.

Rev. HENRY M. DEXTER, D.D., of Boston, offered the following Resolution, which was seconded, with the understanding that it lie upon the table, to be taken up, the first thing in the morning : —

Resolved, That it is the opinion and judgment of this body that this is neither an *ex parte* Council, nor a Mutual Council, but a Council for advice, only ; called regularly, according to the provisions of the Boston Platform of 1865, and in the exact line of Congregational principle and precedent ; and as such, we are ready to proceed to the hearing, on the questions presented before us in the Letter-Missive.

Hon. C. I. WALKER moved that Professor SMYTH, together with the Scribe of the Council, Rev. Dr. A. H. QUINT, be a committee to present the Resolution of Professor SMYTH, adopted by the Council, at the earliest opportunity, to the Plymouth Church.

The motion was agreed to.

After an announcement by Rev. Dr. BUDINGTON, with regard to the entertainment of members, the Council adjourned to 9 a.m., Wednesday, March 25.

COUNCIL convened at 9.30, a.m., the Moderator in the Chair, and was opened by singing. Rev. Dr. J. L. TAYLOR, of Andover, Mass., led the Council in prayer; after which Rev. Dr. BUDINGTON said: Would it be improper that I should make a suggestion at this moment? It occurs to me, that, in sympathy with the prayer in which we have just united for the blessing of God upon us, we should ask, Mr. Moderator, some brother to continue our supplications, with especial reference to the request authorized last evening by the Council, and being presented just now, by two of our brethren, to Plymouth Church, that it would please God so to guide that church in answer to the request, that the issue of this Council shall be for the glory of our common Lord, and for the honor of his visible Kingdom upon earth. I express, in this remark, my own feelings, awakened by the tender prayer of our brother; and I think I may presume enough to say, that, in making this suggestion, I speak in behalf of the committees of the churches that convened this Council.

By request of the MODERATOR, Rev. Dr. COWLES, of Oberlin, Ohio, followed in prayer; and then the Moderator announced that the minutes of the meeting of March 24th not being present (the Scribe being absent with the committee appointed on that day), the Roll of members would be read by the Assistant Scribe.

The Roll was accordingly read.

The MODERATOR: Probably there are delegates and pastors present who have arrived since the close of the last evening's session. They are requested to communicate their names and credentials to the Scribes, that they may be entered upon the Roll.

I will observe that the Scribe has made a pretty liberal use of academic titles in making out the Roll; but I recognize some cases where the title was due, but not duly credited. That is a matter of little consequence, but I make the remark because I shall be liable to make the same mistake myself; and I hope no offense will be taken by any brother who happens to be a Professor or a Doctor, should these dignities be overlooked.

The Rev. Mr. TWINING, of Providence, R.I.: I should like to ask a question in regard to that Roll. Last evening I understood that there were some points of regularity brought up, with regard to certain names. I should like to know how those questions have been settled. It seems to me that it would be well to have the credentials examined by a committee ; and I move that a committee of two be appointed to act with the Scribes, to examine the question of credentials.

The MODERATOR: There are two questions involved. One is : Whether anybody shall be recognized as a pastor who is known not to have been placed in that office by the consent of the neighboring churches and a Council ; in other words, whether a man who comes here and calls himself acting-pastor shall be installed by this Council ? And the other is : Whether a church not represented by a pastor may be represented by two delegates ? Those will be the two questions that I understood Mr. Twining wants to have considered. The question is on the appointment of such a committee.

Hon. Mr. BARSTOW of Providence : I will ask whether there may not be another question : Whether it is proper for the individuals invited by these two churches to have places in the Council ?

The MODERATOR: The Hon. Mr. BARSTOW raises the question whether individuals invited by the inviting churches have a right to places in the Council. I will give a ruling officially on that question, which the Council will of course overrule if it sees fit. It is, that the churches inviting this Council having invited these individual brethren, and the churches sending their messengers to the Council having recognized the fact that those individual brethren were to sit

in the Council, this Council has no right to consider the
question at all, since it has been settled by the action of
the churches that sent us hither. They said to us " Go,
and sit with Dr. Harris, with President Merriman, with
President Fairchild of Oberlin, with each and all of these
individuals, — go, and sit as our representatives." We have
no right, being thus sent, to alter the basis on which we were
sent.

The motion of Rev. Mr. TWINING was agreed to ; and Rev.
Mr. TWINING, of Providence, and Rev. Dr. LORD, of Montpelier, Vt., were nominated and appointed as the committee
to act with the Scribes.

The question was stated to be upon the Resolution offered
by the Rev. Dr. DEXTER, of Boston, Mass.

Rev. Dr. DEXTER suggested that it would be well, first, to
fix the hours of meeting, for the convenience of the families
by whose hospitalities members were entertained.

Rev. Dr. BUDINGTON stated that that convenience would
probably be best subserved by an adjournment for dinner or
lunch, between one and three, p.m. ; the final adjournment for
the day to take place at five or six o'clock, unless it should be
concluded to have an evening session.

It was thereupon ordered that a recess should be taken at
one o'clock.

The resolution offered by Rev. Dr. DEXTER was read, as
follows : —

Resolved, That, in the judgment of this body, this is neither an
ex parte Council nor a Mutual Council, but an Advisory Council,
regularly called, in accordance with the Platform of the Boston
Council of 1865, and in the exact line of Congregational law and
precedent ; and as such is legally competent for, and is now ready
to proceed with, the work which is presented to it in the provisions
of the Letter-Missive.

Rev. Dr. DEXTER then spoke to the Resolution as follows : —

THE objection has been taken in advance against this Council that it is *ex parte;* and being such has been improperly called, and cannot, therefore, under the Congregational system, be fairly competent to the functions to which it has been summoned. It surely becomes, then, Mr. Moderator, our first duty, whether we regard the clearing for ourselves of our own path toward right action, or the pre-establishment in the public mind, and particularly in that portion of the public mind which is reasonably familiar with Congregational principles, and equitably disposed toward them, of such a substratum of general confidence in our right to be and to act as must be indispensable to that moral effect to be desired for our decision, whatever it may prove, — it becomes, I say, our first duty to settle this matter for now and for ever, that we may know, and that those who have disfavored the assembling of this Council may know, and that the whole world may know, whether we are rightfully assembled, and Congregationally competent to our work, or illegitimately, and so ineffectually, here.

For one, Mr. Moderator, I am certainly disposed to look with utmost leniency upon the confusion of thought which has prevailed in regard to this matter, and which has afflicted with incertitude some minds usually clear-sighted in such studies, on the ground that the precise point involved happens to be, perhaps, the only one practical to the working of our polity which has never been thought out, and — speaking of legislation in the Congregational sense — legislated through, to its last and completest issues. That polity, as I have no need to remind the experts whom I address, has been of gradual growth. That is to say, starting with a few rational and scriptural principles, it has from time to time applied them more and more widely to the exigencies of ecclesiastical life, as occasion has presented itself. Thus its law is largely a law of precedents, having force, not in themselves, and because our honored fathers took the views which they took, but because our fundamental Biblical principles are unchangeable, and the first good men who were called upon to apply them to any particular condition of affairs were presumably led under the guidance of the Holy Spirit to a right decision ; and there is necessarily a strong probability, that whenever other good men are called, under the same guidance, to apply those identical principles to a similar condition of affairs, they ought to reach, and will reach, substantially the same results.

It is a part of the law of such gradual growth as this, that new checks and balancings and equipoisings shall from time to time suggest themselves, until, by their combined action and counteraction, if not ideal perfection, at least practical excellence, has been reached.

The *ex parte* Council was one of the later expedients Providentially suggested as needed to round out Congregationalism to its necessary fullness ; and the time — I think I may accurately say — has before this never come to demand final judgment upon all that it is and is not, and as to what are the exact limits within which it may properly act. And, Mr. Moderator, if this Council were to do nothing else than to apply the great force of its calm and deliberate judgment to the settlement of this matter, I think we could all agree that it would not have been summoned over these long distances, from the East and from the West, in vain.

Now, then, sir, I respectfully ask the attention of the Council to this proposition, which, with permission, I shall undertake to prove, viz. : —

A Congregational Council ex parte is always, and of the fixed necessity of its own being, a Council called within the local church, growing out of conflicts of opinion there arising, and consequent processes of judgment therein ultimated, from whose conclusiveness there is provided no other appeal ; and the very philosophy which underlies and justifies such a Council, when such final action within a local church has become to any member morally insupportable, condemns the notion of its existence outside the local church, and between such churches, as an absurdity and an impossibility.

We may, perhaps, approach the subject most intelligently from its historic side.

We shall get no light, however, upon it from our excellent brethren over sea. The Congregationalism of the mother country, after living at a disadvantage without them for two hundred and fifty years, is just now bestirring itself determinately in the direction of something like our Ecclesiastical Councils, — if haply it may feel after them and find them.

The first suggestion of any thing like the *ex parte* Council in our New England history appears to have been in connection with a difficulty arising in the Church of Weymouth, in the year 1646. A woman had been cast out "for some distempered speeches," by a major party (the ruling elder and a minor party being unsatisfied therein), whereupon complaint was made to the elders of the neighboring churches, and request that they would come to Weymouth, and mediate a reconciliation. Those elders laid it before their churches. Some " scrupled the warrantableness of the course, seeing the major party of the church did not send to the churches for advice. It was answered that it was not expected that the major party would complain of their own act ; and if the minor party, or the party grieved, should not be heard, then God should have left no means of redress in such a case ; which could not be " [Winthrop, ii. 277]. Some of the churches approved of their elders going ; the rest permitted it. So they went, and all ended happily in the Weymouth church's consenting to make the Council mutual ; whereupon some failing was found in both parties, and confession and right action on both sides followed.

We get one or two glimpses only of the recognition of the principle which here seems to have found its first enunciation, — that, " if the grieved party should not be heard, then God should have left no means of redress in such a case; which could not be," — in the next twenty-three years (notably in an *ex parte* council at Barnstable, June 4, 1662), — when, in 1669, we reach the most celebrated, and perhaps the most influential, *ex parte* Council ever held in New England ; which at once gave distinctness of form, if not something of respectability, to an expedient which up to that time had been clearly little known, — that Council which authorized and aided in the formation of the Old South Church in Boston. A considerable number of members of the First Church, dissatisfied with the settlement

of John Davenport in the place of John Norton, had asked
for "an amicable dismission in order to the propagation of
another church ; " but the church, though advised to do so by
a Mutual Council, to whom the question was submitted, per-
sistently declined to accede to their request.   The disaffected
brethren called an *ex parte* Council, among others inviting
the church in Salem.   The Salem Church inquired of the
First Church whether they consented to the measure ; and
got for answer that they would have nothing to do with it
whatever.   The Salem Church then put on record their judgment, " That there was, and ought to be, relief against miscar-
riages in particular churches in the Congregational way," and,
hazily discerning that such relief might possibly come
through this new expedient, cautiously sent their elder and a
messenger, "not as members of the Council, and to vote therein,
but to be present, and do what good they could " [Judge
White's New Eng. Cong., p. 76]. Fourteen churches were represented, besides this qualified presence from Salem ; and the
aged and illustrious Richard Mather, then in his last month
of life, — in fact, going straight from the Moderator's chair to
his death-bed in Dorchester, — gave to the body the weighty
sanction of his presence and presidency.   The First Church
continued obdurate ; rudely shut indeed (on the ground of
declining to hold intercourse with a body so " irregular ") the
door of their meeting-house in the face of the venerable Moderator himself, when, with sundry others, he sought to wait
upon them as a committee of persuasion ; so, after days of
debate, they advised the dissenting brethren that " they might
take their liberty seasonably to be a church of themselves, as
if they had had a formal dismission " to that end ; which was
done.

   During the half century that followed, the *ex parte* Council
appears to have been in occasional use, but to have encoun-
tered the not unnatural fear that it would tend to unsettle
church government, and weaken the rightful force of all
council decisions, by putting it always into the power of the
dissatisfied party to obtain a new hearing.   Cotton Mather,
in his *Ratio Disciplinæ* (in 1726), after describing the *ex
parte* Council, adds a further suggestion in the same line,

clearly intended to provide a less hazardous manner of reaching the same end : " It has been thought an aggrieved party is allowed by the New-English Platform, to apply unto one single church in the vicinity ; who by their delegates may, after due preliminaries, come to the church complained of, and ask some account of their proceedings. And if they cannot put into joint what was out of it, this church which had been applied unto may then pray a competent number of other churches to unite their delegates with them in a larger Council, to use further endeavors for the rectifying of what is out of order" (p. 162). And when, twelve years later (1738), Cotton Mather's son Samuel published his " Apology for the Liberties of the Churches in New England," he sets forth this last without so much as mentioning the other : " If this disciplinary method be not carefully observed, these churches have no remedy at all against maladministrations in particular churches ; for I cannot find, that, by the constitution of these churches, the power of calling Councils belongs to any particular persons in them, but to the churches themselves. So that, according to this constitution, if there be maladministration in any particular church, the aggrieved members of it may not convoke such assemblies. But they should desire the advice and assistance of a neighbor church ; and unless one particular church interfere in this state of things, and inquire into the case, in the way of communion by admonition, particular churches may remain at eternal variance within themselves, without showing our dislike of their proceedings. For there is no other process that we know of in the published order of our churches by which we can testify against them, but in this disciplinary method " (p. 130).

Time and experience, however, gradually demonstrated that it must always practically prove very difficult for a single aggrieved person to succeed in interesting even the working majority of a neighboring church in his grievance sufficiently to overcome its natural inertia, and persuade it to enter upon ungracious action on his behalf. So that, in point of fact, the good sense of New England Congregationalism gradually settled back upon the *ex parte* Council, as being, on the whole, the best expedient to meet the occasional need in that direction. Not,

indeed, without much hesitancy and many protests was this
done. A venerable Council at Hopkinton, in 1735 (19th Septem-
ber), censured such Councils as "a way, we think, not agreeable
to the Congregational constitution" ["Congregational Quar-
terly," 1863, p. 344]. And nearly all those Congregationalists
who appear to have been fore-ordained from before the foundation of things to be Presbyterians, but who got somehow
mixed, if not misplaced, to the frustration of the divine decree,
when they came into the ecclesiastical world, have nearly
always had many fears concerning them ; have often declined to
take part in them, and have generally done what they could to
discountenance them.   Nevertheless, Councils *ex parte* have
sturdily held their own ; have fought their way into the manuals, and into the law-books of the courts ; and now hold, upon
the Boston Platform of 1865, as legitimate and honorable a
place — for their own peculiar use — as any other form of
Council whatsoever.

But what are the fundamental ideas which experience has
developed as their root-principles ? They are simply these
two, viz. : —

1. There must be proper ground for calling such a Council.
That is (1), the subject matter to which it relates must be
within the legitimate sphere of consideration and advice by a
Council ; and (2) ultimate action must have been reached upon
it by the church, so that no possibility is apparent of getting
what is felt to be wrong righted, without such external help.
Thus the Boston Platform of 1865 says distinctly [Part III.
Chap. ii. Sec. 7 (4)] : "A refusal on the part of a church to
call a Council *before trial* does not give any occasion for an
ex parte Council." This is because, until the normal processes
of church action have been carried as far as they can be carried, and its last possible stage has been reached, and an
authoritative decision pronounced, there can be no certainty
that justice will not be done ; it ought, in Christian charity,
to be presumed that justice will be done, in whatever action
remains ; in which case no Council will be needful : and no
Council can have legitimate life except as an expedient of absolute necessity. *Nec concilium intersit, nisi dignus vindice
nodus inciderit.*

2. The matter involved being suitable to the advice of a Council, and final action having been taken in regard to it by the normal tribunal, with the result to leave one party in what it conceives to be a condition of wrong and of oppression, for which no relief can be hoped from any other source than a review of the procedure by Council, it is further necessary to the legitimacy of an *ex parte* Council, that a Mutual Council, reasonably requested, shall have been unreasonably refused. It must be reasonably requested; that is, deliberately, distinctly, and, to use the apt language of a Massachusetts judge in the case of Thompson *vs.* Rehoboth [7 Pickering, 159], "substantially set forth," so that the party appealed to "may exercise his judgment whether to unite in a Council or not." And it must be unreasonably refused; that is, unreasonably in the judgment of the aggrieved, fortified by that of candid and impartial third persons — inasmuch as the party refusing is not to be expected to stultify itself by conceding its own unreason, and so no unanimous judgment of that character can rightly be demanded.

On the basis of these two conditions, if fairly called, of impartial churches, an *ex parte* Council has now a recognized and reputable right to be. But on no other. So declares the Boston Platform. So say all our approved manuals.

In other words, our denomination has settled down upon the judgment that the only possible basis on which an *ex parte* Council can be Congregationally called together, is that of a difference between parties in a local church, finally decided by that church as against one of them, where this ultimate decision of the normal tribunal is felt by that party to be intolerable; in which case, to add another safeguard against unjust feeling and unchristian action, this particular method of review, unconstitutional under all other circumstances whatsoever, becomes legitimate; because without it "God should have left no means of redress in such a case; which could not be!"

It follows from all this, especially, that there can be no such thing as an *ex parte* Council where there is no supreme tribunal holding ultimate jurisdiction; which, acting according to its legitimate function, but, in the judgment of aggrieved parties, reaching wrong and oppressive results in so doing, has come to a decision which must be final, unless this opportunity of revision be afforded.

Bear in mind the express language of the Boston Platform already cited, that a refusal on the part of a church to call a Council before trial does not give any occasion for an *ex parte* Council, and it will be seen to follow inevitably, that the very idea of an *ex parte* Council between churches, under any circumstances, or for any reason whatsoever, becomes impossible and absurd ; because there is, and there can be, no Congregational tribunal over churches, which, though associated, are independent, before which trial can be had, and by which final judgment can be rendered, in any such manner as to furnish what we have seen to be the one indispensable pre-requisite to the legitimacy of an *ex parte* Council.

Let us illustrate this. Here is a church which includes a member, A B, who is in good and regular, but by no means high standing ; concerning whom nothing is really known which makes against his Christian character, but who has come somehow to be unfavorably regarded. A business difficulty arises between him and an influential member, C D, which gets to be notorious and scandalous. Both are good quarrelers. The church directs a committee to see the parties, and endeavor to heal the breach. That committee, after some labor had with both, at an ordinary church-meeting, when no previous notice has been given that the subject is to come up, and from which A B is absent, declare that they have looked into the subject, and think both are to be blamed ; but recommend that A B be hereby suspended from church privileges for the space of six months, closing their written report with a Resolution to that effect. The church at once adopt that report, with its rider, and the clerk the next day notifies brother A B that he has been suspended for one-half year ! He is naturally surprised and indignant, and at the next meeting protests against such a summary process, without citation, charge, or hearing, and asks that the vote be reconsidered, and that they at least give him a fair trial. The church respond by passing another vote that he be excommunicated on the spot!

He beseeches them to right this greater wrong, in vain. His friends plead with them ; they answer that they don't like him ; and that even if he be not guilty of any thing worthy of stripes in this particular case, they are convinced that he is generally unworthy and discreditable, and deserves all that he has got. He asks for a Mutual Council, and it is refused. What shall he do ? Here he is summarily and peremptorily put outside of that church, and of all churches ; denied everywhere Christian ordinances ; a heathen man and a publican. He thinks he don't deserve it ; and he knows he don't like it ; and he knows, too, that the grossest injustice — an injustice impossible to any secular tribunal in the civilized world — has been done to him in his summary exclusion. There can be no possible doubt, that, under these circumstances, he has the right to call an *ex parte* Council, and that that Council would have the right and the duty — the church continuing obdurate — to do him the service of at least certifying that nothing has been proved against his Christian character ; that rude violence has been done him ; and that, so far as those votes of suspension and excommunication are concerned, they were Congregationally so illegal in their origin and process as to be void, and therefore to justify sister churches in regarding and treating him as still uncensured, and, as of right, in as regular standing as he had been before their passage. Such a result puts a new face upon his affairs. Its moral weight may work him redress in his own community ; at any rate, it will enable him to sit down at the table of the Lord with some other church, and so it gains him a redress impossible to be gained in any other manner. Punchard well styles *ex parte* Councils, in this view of their use, "courts of errors, to which the humblest member of a Congregational church may appeal" [View, p. 124].

Suppose another case. Here are two Congregational churches, side by side, in the same community. Like in faith, they are unlike in spirit and works. One is conservative and respectable ; the other radical and plebeian. The tide of incongeniality at length rises so high as to float them into collision ; and the one refuses to dismiss members to the other, and indulges in various kindred unfraternal acts, ending in general charges of heresy and infidelity. Correspondence follows, making bad matters worse. All ends, at last, in the endeavor on the part of the grieved church to get the whole subject of their differences referred to a Council. But the regnant spirit which inflicted the wound prompts to keeping the surgeon at a distance, and all effort in that direction fails. What is to be done here? Things are unpleasant, — that is clear; they are disgracefully damaging to the cause of Christ, — that is even more sadly clear. But is there a case for an *ex parte* Council? Clearly not. There is no such irremediable hardship as to justify that. These people are not without regular ordinances. They are not without their own fraternity. They are as really a church as the other. There is no judicatory over them which has passed snap judgment upon them, leaving them helpless until some friendly hand be stretched out to their relief. The only tribunal which is above them, lower than the throne of God and the Lamb, is that of the general judgment of their fellows of the church and of the world; and that has not yet been ultimated — cannot be, until all the elements which are bound up in events yet partly future shall have been made apparent. So, then, there is no similarity between the two cases whatsoever. The vital element which legitimated an *ex parte* Council in the case between the church and the aggrieved individual, comes into that between church and church to render an *ex parte* Council inapt and irrational.

Nor ought we to forget, in this connection, the obvious fact, that — if I may be pardoned a metaphor from our plain-spoken fathers — the plaster of an *ex parte* Council could never cover the sore of a difficulty between churches: so that, as it may not in such cases lawfully be held, it could not offer healing even if it were held. Rightly called, as in the matter of the unjustly excommunicated man to whom I have just referred, such a Council offers two things: (1.) Access, with some moral authority, to the public ear, as an individual cannot enjoy it. (2.) The practical restoration in some degree of forfeited rights, in furnishing a ground on which other churches may lawfully restore such an one to church privileges. But where two churches are at variance, were an *ex parte* Council a possible alternative to one of them, its result could scarcely give to the church any appreciable heightening of the moral authority with which, as a church, it was, without it, able to appeal to the general moral sense; while there has been no forfeiting of rights, no loss of ordinances, and no rupture of any sort in the regular ongoing of that church's affairs, which such a result could offer itself to repair.

A church situated as I have supposed may do well to call a Council in the interests of light and peace ; but it would not be technically a Mutual Council if the other church were to consent to join in it, as it cannot be an *ex parte* Council if it continue to decline. In either case, and in any case, such a Council, arising outside of the local church, and relating to questions of comity and fellowship between local churches, is a third thing, — a totally different species of the same genus ; the kind of Council which Thomas Hooker had in mind, whose function is, as he says, "to discover and determine of doubtful cases, either in doctrine or practise, according to the truth" [Survey, Part IV., p. 45], or, to take the good old phrase of the fathers, called "for light and peace."

So, then, we Congregationalists have *within* the local churches two kinds of Councils, — mutual, or *ex parte*, as the case may be ; and we have *outside* of the churches a species of Council neither mutual nor *ex parte*, but an Advisory Council, as the Boston Platform calls it [Part III., chap. 2, sec. 7 (3)] : that is a simple calling together of churches, by their messengers, to consult for light and peace.

In order partly to reach the simplest analysis, but mainly for the purpose of emphasizing the never-to-be-forgotten fact, that the only power which can be reached in the case of the result of any Council is that it is advisory, and " hath so much force as there be force in the reason of it," I class together the last two forms of Council referred to last evening by my learned and eloquent brother, the pastor of the Church of the Pilgrims, as (his third form) " ecclesiastical," — for settling pastors, &c., — and (his fourth form) " advisory " Councils. I call them all Councils for advice, with the two subdivisions : 1. Councils on questions of fellowship ; 2. Councils on questions of light and peace.

Perhaps a body of believers propose to confederate into a church estate, and desire the approval in so doing of sister churches ; perhaps some one church, under stress of adverse providences, feels its need of advice from those who have the common cause at heart, and can impartially survey the ground, whether it should remove or disband ; perhaps some question of fellowship with another church is agitating one or many churches of a neighborhood ;— whatever the exigency, or its cause, need of fraternal counsel and sympathy being felt, the church, or the churches, feeling it, can call a Council to the end of obtaining it, and will be quite right in doing so. There are no two parties in the case ; or, if there be, the distinctions and terms appropriate concerning Councils called inside the local church will not apply. Such a Council will be neither mutual nor *ex parte*, but a Council, simply. The authorities recognize and emphasize this general classification, not as distinctly as I have tried to do, indeed, because, as I have suggested, the exigency never arose before to demand it. Upham [Ratio Dis., pp. 179–204] treats first of Councils, and the obligations of churches sometimes to seek advice through them ; second, of Mutual Councils, " called only in case of doubt and difficulty ;" and *ex parte* Councils " called in doubt and difficulty by one of the parties, without the concurrent action of the other." The Maine Manual divides Councils into three classes, — mutual, *ex parte*, and " those called by bodies of Christians " [p. 60]. And the Boston Platform says, " Councils are called (1) by a church desiring light or help ; (2) by a church and pastor (or other member or members) in case of differences, when it is styled a Mutual Council ; or (3) by either of these parties when the other unreasonably refuses to unite, when it is styled an *ex parte* Council " [Debates, Nat. Council, p. 132].

What we need is, that hereafter it shall be left in no manner of doubt that the terms " mutual " and " *ex parte* " apply strictly and only to Councils in cases of difficulty arising within local churches, called concurrently by all parties, or (under just safeguards) by one of them ; and that all other assemblings of the sort be known as a *tertium quid*, under the simple name of Council, or, perhaps better, under that name under which our English brethren have been lately debating them, — Councils of Advice.

To apply this reasoning to the case in hand: I submit, Mr. Moderator, that, inasmuch as an *ex parte* Council can never be justified — and so can never be rightly called — between different Congregational churches, because there exists no tribunal under heaven over them which can render final decision against any party in interest in such manner that an *ex parte* Council becomes the only expedient possible for relief: this, under no conceivable circumstances, could have been an *ex parte* Council. I submit, therefore, that while it would have been a much more grateful thing, and one pregnant with brighter hopes for best results, if the Plymouth Church had thought it well to have stood side by side with its sister churches in asking the Congregational churches of the land to come hither, to seek to show them the way of light and peace; still, as their consenting to do so would not have made it a Mutual Council, in the technical sense, so their declining to do so cannot make it an *ex parte* Council in any sense. I submit, further, that this view of the case precludes all necessity of inquiry as to any minor and subordinate steps and events; as to what specifically may have been asked, and what refused, by either church. Interesting in itself, and having its own importance as revealing the animus of the parties, such an inquiry could offer no result to impair the right of this body to assemble and to act. That right is found in the invitation of the Church of the Pilgrims, and of this on Clinton Avenue, and in the action of the churches invited by it, in response to the same. So that, as a quorum of the body has reported itself, this Council has, by Congregational principle and usage, a fixed, incontestable, and perfectly legitimate existence, and is ready at once to advance to the work before it, as set forth in the points of the Letter-Missive which has created and which must control it.

Hon. Mr. BARSTOW of Providence: I rise to move an amendment to this Resolution, — to strike out so much of the

Resolution as declares that the Council is neither a Mutual nor an *ex parte* Council ; so as to make the Resolution read : —

Resolved, That, in the judgment of this body, this is an Advising Council, regularly called, in accordance with the provisions of the Boston Council of 1865, and in the exact line of Congregational law and precedent, and, as such, is legally competent for, and is now ready to proceed with, the work which is presented to it.

I make the motion for these reasons : first, that the Resolution is unusual and unnecessary. The usual course, after the Council is organized, is, for the Moderator to declare that the Council is organized, and is ready to proceed to business. It is not usual to adopt a Resolution declaratory of this ; and we have no authority to pass this Resolution. It has been well intimated, if not expressed in words, that the Letter-Missive is our fundamental law. Indeed, it is our only law in this Council. These churches invited our churches to convene, and advise them upon certain points ; and our churches consented to meet these churches, and advise them upon those points. These delegates are authorized to give advice upon these points ; and are not authorized to give advice upon any other points, nor to make any declarations of principles outside of these. It has been said by Dr. Dexter, that we want to settle this question at once and forever. We have no authority to settle any question at once and forever. I do not know that we can settle any question forever. I am quite sure that we cannot settle any question outside of the Letter-Missive ; and my feeling is, that we have no right to introduce it here.

Another reason for my motion is, that it is inexpedient, and that we have no authority in the case. The questions presented in the Letter-Missive are delicate enough, certainly, and are numerous enough to keep us here quite as long as we shall want to stay ; are delicate enough in themselves, without increasing their number. Now, we come here to try to make peace between neighboring churches. We shall not be able to accomplish that unless we have peace and harmony among ourselves. A question like this cannot be introduced and attempted to be decided here, outside of the Letter-Missive and harmony be preserved among ourselves.

My next reason is, that the Resolution itself is **not true.**

That is my opinion about it. My opinion is, that this is an *ex parte* Council. I am sorry to differ with reverend gentlemen whom I so highly esteem as I do the pastors of the churches calling the Council, and the Moderator of the Council, for I have an esteem for these men amounting almost to veneration ; and yet I do differ with them, upon this point.

It is said that this is an Advisory Council. All Councils are advisory. Some go so far as to say that a Council can only advise. I cannot take that position. I suppose that a Council can do what it is invited to do by the Letter-Missive ; that questions may be submitted to the Council for decision ; and in that case, that the result which they reach is declaratory, and in a sense judicial. But when called for advice, all they can do is to give advice. As to this being a Mutual Council, it was supposed that a Council could be mutual between these parties if they invited a Mutual Council ; but, if there can be a Mutual Council called by churches, then there can be an *ex parte* Council called by a church. It seems to me that the one proposition proves the truth of the other.

It is said that an *ex parte* Council can only exist as growing out of grievances of individual members in a local church. What is a church but a congregation of individuals ? And if a church has a difference with a sister church, and one desires, and the other declines, a Mutual Council, why cannot that church, or those churches, call an *ex parte* Council, to advise them in this matter of difference ? It is said, because it can have no power or authority. Neither has any other Council any power or authority. It is merely called to give advice : the only power is to give advice, and just the advice asked.

For these reasons, I should prefer that the whole Resolution should fail ; but I desire very much that this part of it shall be dropped. If the mover is willing to drop out of it so much of it as declares that this is not an *ex parte* Council, I shall be content ; but, if not, I hope the Resolution itself will be lost, for I see no reason for our attempting to decide a great question not submitted to us. One fear I had on the assembling of the Council was, that some attempt might be made to create some canon of ecclesiastical law. I believe that all power resides in the local church ; that all the power in the church of Christ resides there ; that Councils are simply agents of the churches, and that they have no authority over the churches, — no authority to create law for the churches, for that is outside of our power, and we would better hesitate before we attempt it.

Rev. Dr. QUINT moved that the subject lie upon the table, in order to afford an opportunity to the committee appointed to communicate with Plymouth Church to make a report.

The motion was agreed to.

Prof. SMYTH : The committee report that this morning we went to Plymouth Church, and were received, in accordance, as I understand, with a vote of the church, by its pastor, and were conducted at once to the church assembled, and were invited upon the platform, and requested to present our communication, and to address the church. We presented the Resolution adopted here last night, and accompanied it with a few words expressive of the sentiment expressed, I believe, universally, here last evening, by all the members of the Council who took any part in this discussion, and by our votes. We were listened to with courtesy ; and, immediately upon the conclusion of our communication, a motion was introduced by the pastor of Plymouth Church, which was passed, and is now in the hands of the Scribe of this Council, who will communicate it.

Rev. Dr. QUINT : I hold in my hand a copy of the communication made on the part of Plymouth Church, which was accompanied with verbal assurances of kind feelings towards the Council. It is this : —

Resolution of Plymouth Church, in answer to the Committee of the Council, now convened in Clinton Avenue Congregational Church.

Resolved, That our thanks are expressed to the gentlemen who have so courteously presented us with the Resolution of the Council, and that this church will, without delay, instantly reply.

This Resolution was offered by the Chairman. When we left, the committee was already in session considering the draft of the reply, which will probably be here before long. They have promised to send it to us at a very early hour.

I now move that we take up from the table the matter under discussion.

Rev. Mr. BARTLETT, Pittsfield, Mass. : It is very important to determine the character of this Council. It is necessary that we understand its nature, in order that we may proceed intelligently. I have listened with very great interest to the learned Dr. Dexter ; and still, I think, he has not followed out these Councils to their end. I am willing to admit that there is a difference between an *ex parte* Council and an Advisory Council, though all Congregational Councils are advisory, and nothing more. An *ex parte* Council is advisory, an ecclesiastical Council is advisory, and has no authority except to advise. There is a difference between the occasion of this Council and that which usually calls an *ex parte* Council. But there were back of it two parties ; on the one side, Plymouth Church ; on the other, the two churches calling this Council. There were these two parties, and they failed to agree upon calling a Mutual Council. One of these parties then calls a Council. An *ex parte* Council is a Council called by one party. The judgment of Dr. Dexter, that it refers simply to the local church, and not to churches, in my judgment, and I submit it with all modesty, is simply arbitrary. It is a new addition to his own work. He states that a Mutual Council is one in the calling of which all parties to the difficulty or perplexity concerning which relief is sought, unite ; an *ex parte* Council is one called by one of those parties. These two churches are one of the parties. They call the Council ; and, if we may go further, in order to designate the difference between this Council and one which should have been called by these three churches, we might call it an *ex parte* Advisory Council, if you choose. There certainly is a distinction between this Council, called by one party, and the Council which might have been called by these three churches. If, then, we decide that there is this difference, existing because of there being two parties, and one party only calling us, we must get some term that will designate us. We are a different body than if we had been called by these three churches. We have been called by one party.

We are, therefore, an *ex parte* Advisory Council. I am not particular about the name : I am only particular about the fact. Now, it seems to me that we have had a little too much of the tradition of the church. Dr. Dexter, in his valuable work, tells us that Congregationalism grows out of the Bible and common sense. We are told the same in this Platform of 1865, — that the Holy Scriptures, and especially the Scriptures of the New Testament, are the only authoritative rule for the constitution and administration of church government. We are not dependent upon the former Councils and Manuals. We are to go back to the Bible and common sense. Common sense tells us that there are two parties, and only one party has called this Council. It is therefore an *ex parte* Council ; or, if you choose to distinguish it from that which would be called by a party in a church, it is an *ex parte* Advisory Council.

The MODERATOR: There is an ambiguity in the phrase *ex parte*. An *ex parte* Council is a technical phrase in the usage of the Congregational churches, and of the Manuals of Congregational church polity. Dr. Dexter has defined the meaning of the phrase, in that technical use. *Ex parte* is a phrase used in law : it is used continually. A man wants a deposition to be used in a suit ; and if he cannot get the other party to be present in person, or by attorney, when the deposition is taken, that becomes an *ex parte* proceeding on his part. The word is constantly thus used ; and, in that vague or loose sense of it, of course this is *ex parte*. All this proceeding is *ex parte*. But, in the technical sense in which the rules as laid down in the platforms apply to *ex parte* Councils, this is not an *ex parte* Council, I apprehend. I suggest that for the benefit of the brother, and the Council.

Rev. Mr. BARTLETT: I would like to ask what is the distinction made between a Council that is called mutually of three churches, or by the two parties, and one that is called, like this, by one party ? If the Moderator will enable us to distinguish between these two, I think I can move along with more light.

The MODERATOR : The brother has made it very distinct indeed ; and he may give to it what name he pleases : only do not let us, in calling this *ex parte*, undertake to apply to it the rules and precedents that belong to a different kind of Council.

Rev. Dr. RANKIN of Washington: It seems to me that the suggestions of the last brother are worthy of consideration, and have a good deal of weight. It was implied, in the proposition that there be a Mutual Council respecting these matters, that there was power to call that Mutual Council; and I think that involved the power to call an *ex parte* Council, if the proposition to call a Mutual Council failed. An Advisory Council, that is not *ex parte*, must be antecedent to the consideration of the questions of difference. For example, if these brethren, before calling upon Plymouth Church in any manner, had called this Council, it seems to me it would have properly been called an Advisory Council: but they have gone further with these matters of difference; and now our decision must be in some sense, and will be in some sense, accounted an *ex parte* decision. Our churches will so regard it, because the difference has begun: they have moved in the matter. Our decision has some relation to this other church. In coming here, it seems to me we cannot but regard ourselves as *ex parte*, unless this other church be represented here.

Rev. Dr. TAYLOR, Binghamton, N.Y,: It seems to me it takes a great while to baptize this child! Here it is a quarter past eleven o'clock, and we are asking what we are. Now, I know what I am. I know I am called here from Binghamton for a certain purpose,—to give the best answer I can to seven questions. That is just it. That is what I came for. Let us go to work, and take up the questions, and answer them, and not spend half the day on the question what we shall call ourselves.

Rev. Dr. PIKE, of Rowley, Mass.: Perhaps I may call the attention of the Council to the fact that you, Mr. Moderator, decided the question last evening, that this is not an *ex parte* Council. I supposed that that decision removed this subject from all further discussion, until an appeal was taken from your decision to the body here assembled; and I take it, if a motion had been offered here, expressly stating that this is an *ex parte* Council, you would have ruled it out, instantly. You have allowed this motion of Dr. Dexter, because it was a repetition of your own decision; and the importance that was attached to the motion was, because we could have, from the highest authority among us, the discussion of this subject ; and, furthermore, because there was included in the motion this idea, at the least, that we were to go about the proper business for which we were assembled here. Now, I sympathize very strongly with some of the measures last evening, for this reason, that I wish that we may appear to have acted with honor, and with the highest Christian principle, toward each of the parties in this controversy ; and I think we have shown that honor, and that accordance with Christian principle.

Now, it was delicately insinuated, though not directly expressed, last evening, by the chairman of one of the committees, that it seemed to be appropriate that a Council assembled for a special purpose should give their attention, first, to all of the facts, as they would be presented by the committees that had called them ; and therefore I sympathize with this proposition to go now immediately to the parties that have called us, and hear their statement of the facts. We do not know how long we are to be detained, before Plymouth Church shall send us its answer ; and, certainly, they could not expect us to wait here all the day before we received that answer. On the last evening we delayed ourselves on preparatory questions, and we are going through the same work all day to-day. Now the night is past, the day has come, and we should go to work upon the proper business for which we were called here ; and my impression is, that, if we cannot go about this work soon, we shall hear the rising voice around us, "What doest thou here, Elijah?" and be in the position of some legislative bodies, that spend so much of their time on preparatory steps, on the threshold of their work, that they never get about their work, until it is time for them to go home.

Rev. Dr. DEXTER : I ask permission of the Council to accept the amendment of Mr. Barstow. I think it might facilitate business. I am not in the slightest degree anxious to have the first part of the Resolution passed. It is within the knowledge of all of us, that this Council has been stigmatized as an *ex parte* Council, which had no business to be here. That is in the papers. I want the Council to declare itself so far as to stand somewhere. If it declares itself to be an Advisory Council, properly called, that is all I ask. I accept the amendment, with pleasure.

No objection being offered, the Resolution was accordingly amended.

On motion of Dr. CHAPIN, of Beloit, the discussion was suspended, for the purpose of hearing the minutes of the last evening read, the Scribe having returned.

The minutes were accordingly read, and approved.

Rev. Mr. BARTLETT moved to lay the Resolution of Dr. Dexter upon the table, and immediately proceed to hear the statements of the committee, and to the regular business.

The question being taken upon laying the Resolution upon the table, it was not agreed to.

Rev. T. M. POST, D.D., of St. Louis, Mo.: I am unwilling to take up the time of this body; but I believe we are standing at a point of very great consequence, of vast importance, both as regards the effect of this Council, and the history of our denomination in this country. There is danger, unless we treat this question before us with the utmost fairness, a fairness that approves itself to the public mind, — there is danger that you will fret this difference into a schism, and that it will go through all the States; certainly through the State from which I come. It is a very important question before us. I do not think we shall settle it by special pleading. I believe that it must be settled upon great, catholic, Christian principles. I believe, further, in order to settle difficulties ofttimes, the more delicate they are the more it is necessary to adhere to certain established usages. Now, it matters very little to my mind whether you call this an Advisory Council, or an *ex parte* Council. It matters very little what you term it. It is the effect and intention of it that we have to do with. And the same principles that would regulate in part the calling of an *ex parte* Council, if not in precedent, I think in Christian reason, apply to this; and also if we consider the effect and the weight which this Council is ultimately to have in its decision. As I understand it, a Mutual

Council must be asked before an *ex parte* Council can be called, in order that both parties may be represented in calling a Council, that they may be equally privileged in securing the judges, and in order that the decision of that Council may have weight and force with the public, and not represent a party. If one church calls a Council of its own, and the other church goes and selects its own judges, you have Council against Council, and you have a schism in the body. I therefore regard it as very desirable, — I regard it as quite as desirable as in any case that I can suppose, — that these churches should have united in calling a Council ; and that, until it was found that such effort was unavailing, it was in the interest of Christian unity, and of the permanent settlement of this question, that the effort should have been prosecuted ; for the reason that when a Council met it should be considered as representing all the interests of all the churches that were implicated.

Now, by the questions that have been proposed to us, we do virtually put on trial a church that is not a party to the Council. We advise, to be sure, our brethren how they shall treat that church. That, of course, involves a question of facts. We have to examine facts, and determine them, and then apply the rule of Christian reason to those facts, in the case of a church that says that it has had no opportunity, at least that it has had no voice, in selecting the Council, or the members of the Council, who are thus trying it. I do not wish to have that state of things go before the public. I think if we settle these things rightly, and I believe we shall — I have great trust in the Christian integrity and the Christian intelligence of this body of men ; I rely upon them, — but I do not wish to have it go before the Christian public, that here a church is put upon trial, and has not had any voice in selecting those that are to try it ; for we are trying that church in advising the other churches, — that is very obvious. It is on this question that I hesitate, somewhat, in adopting the Resolution which would command my respect from the learned character of the brother who has presented it, and my general confidence in the correctness of his judgment in ecclesiastical masters, as well as in the judgment that I see has been already pronounced in anticipation by other members of this body.

In coming here I left a church in the midst of a revival. I
have been traveling two days and two nights in order to be
here, because I wished to aid in restoring Christian peace and
harmony among the friends of my youth, from whom we are
so far removed that we have not been drawn into sympathy
with the questions which have agitated you here. But this
question strikes further. It will strike to the Pacific sea. It
is necessary not only that we do the right thing, but that we
be understood to do it in the right manner. Some of you
will say, What shall we do? Why have I come here at all?
I was in hopes that the Plymouth Church would have accepted
the offer to come here, and adopt us as a Council in common.
But, if not, there are still questions for us to act upon. We
are competent, as a law court, you may say, to settle great
questions of law; but to go into the trial of a special church,
to investigate certain facts with regard to that church, and
then pronounce upon it, it strikes me we are hardly competent
to that. I had it in mind rather to divide the questions before us. Upon some I hope we shall testify, and testify clearly.
Upon the other questions, where we have to find a decision of
facts with regard to another church, and where I see in the
letters written by that church in response to those addressed
to it by the other churches, it expressly denies the statement
of facts and allegations of principles contained in them, I think
our decision, if it goes forth in the face of these denials, without a trial on an issue with that church properly represented,
will not carry the weight that we wish it to carry with it.
The published documents on one side lead to a construction
which is directly contradicted by the other side; and so with
regard to the Resolutions presented, upon which we are invited
to act, in these letters. Different constructions will be put
upon them, by the different parties.

Now, Brethren, I am hardly ready to adopt this Resolution
in full. I think that this is, perhaps, the point that it is best
for us now to determine. I am satisfied you are doing something, now, that is going to reach much further than you are
aware of; and that it is important that in all these things we
be guided by those principles that will approve themselves to
those who are far removed from the immediate sympathies of

the interests, passions, or prejudices that are moving in this city, or in this part of the country.

Rev. Dr. QUINT : The remarks of Dr. Post have brought the matter to a point where I wish to propose an amendment which I had before written. The Resolution closes thus : " and as such (Council) is legally competent for, and is now ready to proceed with, the work which is presented to it in the provisions of the Letter-Missive." I move to add, " so far as they do not involve censure on any church which is not actually, or constructively, a party to this Council."

The MODERATOR : Is there any objection to the acceptance of the amendment ? If no objection be made, it will be added to the Resolution.

Rev. Dr. RANKIN : I object to the word "constructively."

Rev. Dr. QUINT : To avoid any doubt whatever, I will say that where a body ought to be a party to a Council, but will not consent to be, it is constructively a party to that Council.

Rev. Dr. BOARDMAN : I object to that amendment. It is something we do not come here to-day to do. We need the facts first. It is prejudging the whole case ; and I object to the amendment.

The MODERATOR : The amendment is objected to ; and therefore it is before the house as an amendment, and not as a part of the Resolution.

Rev. Dr. SAMUEL HARRIS, of New Haven : It seems to me, Mr. Moderator, that this is a question which it is necessary that this Council should settle ; but that, in its whole breadth, this is not the proper time to settle it. We are here as a Council ; and the pastors and delegates are sent here by the churches, and authorized by the churches, to take the matters submitted to them into consideration. On that point there can be no doubt. But the question whether the subject-matter submitted to us is all of it matter upon which, as a Council, called as we are, we can properly determine, is a question which we cannot properly decide until the whole case is before us ; and it seems to me that the decision of that part of the question should be postponed until we have heard the whole case, and retire by ourselves. Then the question will be, — how much of this matter is legitimately within the sphere of this Council, and how much is not ?

Rev. Dr. STEARNS, of Amherst : It seems to me, sir, that, whatever view we may take of the technical name of this Council, it comes at last to the same thing. We are called to give advice : there is no question on that point. The Letter-Missive calls us to give advice. We are called by that letter to advise two churches : that is what we are called for. The committee of those two churches stated, last evening, that that was the interpretation which they put upon the words of the Letter-Missive, — that this Council was called to advise them. Whatever name you call it, Mutual, *ex parte*, or what not, it is a Council to give advice to two churches ; that is the object for which we have come together. In doing it, if another church be in any way implicated, or in any way especially interested, whether we call ourselves *ex parte*, Mutual, or Advisory, we are bound to show them proper respect and courtesy. If I understand the action of this Council last evening, we presented to that church an invitation to appear in this body, and to represent their views on all the questions which may here be presented, just as fully, just as freely, and with no more limitation than is put upon the committees of the two churches which have called us here. What could we do more ? If the Council were *ex parte*, if we were called *ex parte*, all we could do in that case would be to send to the Plymouth Church, and invite them freely, in Christian love, to meet with us, and present their own views, in their own way. This we do out of love to that church ; not to put that church on trial at all : that is a question which does not come up now, if it ever shall come up ; but our position is, that we invite that church. We have invited that church to appear in this body, and to stand on an equality with the committees of the other churches, in presenting their own views, of their own case, and of the whole case. Well, under these circumstances, what can we do better than to proceed to hear the reasons why we are called to give advice ; and if the Plymouth Church appears,— and we have no reason to say that they will not appear, — we shall give them an opportunity, in Christian courtesy and in Christian love, to say all they care to say, — to make as full statement of facts as they please to make, and such representations, in every particular, as they please to make. Why not, therefore, acknowledge that we are an Advisory Council, whatever other name anybody may wish to put upon us? For we certainly are an Advisory Council; and we shall act in this Advisory Council very nearly as we should do if we were an *ex parte* Council. We are certainly, by the terms of our Letter-Missive, and by the interpretation of the committee, an Advisory Council; and as such we invite another church to be heard, so that we may give advice more properly. I am, therefore, in favor of saying at once, and settling the whole business, so far as this is concerned, that, whatever else we are, we are a Council called to give advice, — a Council for light, and for peace, in the way of advice.

Rev. Mr. BUTLER, of Fairport, N.Y.: I have but a word to say, Mr. Moderator, as to this question; and it is this: that if this amendment of Dr. Quint, with the construction that I give it, passes, it seems to me we might as well have stayed at home. Now, we have come to advise these two churches; and the point most essential in the whole advice is, whether or not a case of discipline, if it were carried out by either of these churches in the manner that it has been carried out by other churches, would be good, sound, Congregational discipline. If, therefore, we advise them on every thing else, and run around this, because it must some way seem to censure another church, then it impresses me that we might as well have stayed at home. I think the thing we want to settle, more than any thing else, is precisely the point that comes in here; and it seems to me that we need not necessarily censure any church, nor mention any church. It is this that they desire to have settled; it is this that we desire to settle for them: and if I had my preference in this matter, I would have this whole matter laid upon the table. We are debating this Resolution, not for any bearing it has on this gathering, but simply to satisfy the gabble of newspapers; and when we have debated it half a day, they will take more advantage of it than if we had not debated it at all. I think the quicker we get about our business, the sounder we shall be.

Rev. Dr. QUINT: As I introduced this, and gave no rea-

sons for it, I would like to say a few words. I do not agree
with the last brother on this matter. The object of the
amendment is not to satisfy the gabble of newspapers, as he
called it : it is to satisfy the instinctive sense of justice that
there is throughout the denomination, and throughout all
Christian churches. Unless we can strike the average com-
mon-sense idea of churches, we had better not have come.
Now we have come to a rather new phase in Congregationalism,
and the precedents are extremely difficult to find. That is,
there are precedents for what is called an Advisory Council ;
but I know of no precedent, for the last one hundred and
twenty-five years, of an Advisory Council called to censure
another church ; and there is our difficulty, that this is so far
beyond the memory of the most venerable of the Fathers here
present, that it does not seem to be a precedent. Now, the
Resolution says that this is an Advisory Council, and can go
on ; but it goes on to say that it is legally competent to consider the questions that have been brought before it, and to
proceed to advise. I say "legally competent," and "ready to
advise," provided you limit it to an Advisory Council distinctively so called ; provided it is not called to censure a church
which is not a party to this Council. There is the limitation.
If it is called simply to advise two churches, that is one thing ;
if it is called to advise two churches, and in advising two
churches to pass judgment and express an exact opinion upon
the exact case presented, whether another church did right or
wrong, that is trying that church ; and there is no dodging it
before the common sense of the community. Now, these Letters-Missive, for example, — I merely quote, not stating how
I shall vote on the whole question, — ask, " Was the action
of the Plymouth Church in the case of discipline issued by
it Oct. 31, 1873, as presented in the public documents, in
accordance with the order and usage of Congregational
churches ? or was it an apparent departure from these, tending, in the circumstances, to injure and offend other churches
in fellowship, and warranting apprehension and remonstrance
on our part ? " That is a square question, on which to try
Plymouth Church, and you cannot avoid the look of it.

The MODERATOR : " As presented in certain documents :" we

are not called upon to affirm the veracity of those documents. It is a hypothetical case that we are to act upon.

Rev. Dr. QUINT : I presume that this decision of our respected Moderator is not his official decision as Moderator, but merely the expression of his opinion ; and therefore I have great respect for it. If it were the opinion of the Moderator, as Moderator, I should object to this decision from the chair. If it be discussion, of course some other brother is in the chair ; and, if it be, I shall address my remarks to the Associate Moderator.

The point to which we have come, is this : Here are two churches, who find a difficulty on account of the alleged action of another church. That is a matter of record. The records, however, are supposed ; and we must ascertain whether they represent the facts. If those facts exist, — if certain acts were done, — the church, of course, which committed those acts may be able to explain them, be able to justify them. We will say then, We will give them an opportunity to be heard. Suppose they say, " We don't acknowledge the tribunal," what have we got to say ?   In an ordinary case you can have a certain kind of tribunal, — that is, a Mutual or *ex parte* Council ; because, if a party will not join in a Mutual Council, you can call an *ex parte* one ; but, if this principle prevails, without this limitation of powers, it is simply saying this : Whenever any one or two churches throughout the country, anywhere in the country, wish to object to the conduct of a third church, complain of something that has been done by it, they can go and call any Council they please, to pass judgment upon that third church, with or without its being present. In this case it is notified, but all of this is involved. Now, the question comes to-day, whether, with that construction, we are willing to say that any one or two churches can call a Council of their own motion, call it Advisory, and avoid the point of the Mutual Council which they first tried to get here, and avoid being called an *ex parte* Council, by saying, " We are willing you should be heard ; " but yet try the question by a Council of their own choosing ?   We had better have it understood, that when you try a third or second church, the first one must have given that church a fair opportunity to take part ; that it must have a sufficient notice, and then, that failing, call one in the nature of an *ex parte* Council ; because that will not only give an appearance of right, but will give it actually. If you adopt the first part of this resolution, and make it simply an Advisory Council to those that have asked advice, we are not warranted in going beyond the line which separates two churches, the one from the other, and in any way passing judgment that involves censure upon that third church. Whether they have an opportunity to be heard or not, makes no difference.

Rev. Mr. BUTLER : I want to ask this :— If, in a settlement of any difference, between churches or individuals, the decision of it on the one side does not somehow imply a fault or mistake on the other ?

Rev. Dr. QUINT : Any tribunal competent to pass, can pass such censure ; but a tribunal not competent to decide cannot.

Rev. Mr. BUTLER : Are we not just as likely to censure these two churches ? If we say the other is right, will we not do so ?

Rev. Dr. QUINT : Well, they have called us. I wish to say only one thing more : before we drop this matter, and go on and take up the questions, it seems to me we had better have some principle in the thing, so as to decide whether we shall act upon it or not, simply by this principle.

Judge WALKER, of Detroit : Mr. Moderator, it seems to me that the time is not misspent this morning ; that we should be in no haste to get at our action. The first question is, What have we before us ? The question of jurisdiction — of its own jurisdiction — must always be settled by every tribunal that is called upon to act. Has it jurisdiction of the subject-matter ? Has it jurisdiction of the parties ? That is a preliminary question, which, in the first instance, every tribunal, whether inferior or superior, must settle for itself. If there be an appellate power — and are the churches here an appellate power ? — that decision may be reversed. But, in the first instance, it must be settled by the tribunal that attempts to act. What is its power ? — what its extent ? — and what its limits ? Now, I think this question is one of exceeding importance ; and one that depends somewhat upon the nature of this Council, and its object and purpose. I have been very much instructed by the very learned discussion by Dr. Dexter, and have been profited by it ; and I am led to the conclusion, by what he says, and by what our Moderator, learned in these questions, says, that this is not technically an *ex parte* Council, and, clearly, it is not a Mutual Council. What, then, is it ? It may be well enough to call it an Advisory Council. But then comes the question, What is an Advisory Council, and what its powers ? what the limits of its power, and what may it do ? Now, I can easily conceive that there is a very large class of questions that may arise, where a church may call a Council for advice, and that advice may be given without restraint, because the nature of the question is such that there is no adverse party ; there it is right that they should go on and act. But when the questions presented for consideration involve the conduct of a third party, which may properly come before the tribunal, whatever you call the Council, should it not proceed in analogy to the principles that govern Mutual and *ex parte* Councils ? Must not those principles apply ? If there can be no *ex parte* Councils between churches, technically, after all, must not the principles that govern *ex parte* Councils govern the action when the proceeding is, in its nature, adversary ? Now, here, the proceeding is, in its nature, adversary. This is a question whether the Plymouth Church has conducted properly ; whether these churches that have called us have conducted properly in relation to that church. Now, can there be any question but that, in some sense, before this Council, and before the country, the Plymouth Church is on trial ? I submit not. Their conduct is up before us for examination, and that we may pass our judgment upon it. Then, it seems to me, that the only question remaining is : Will the Plymouth Church come here, as we have invited them to come ? If they do come, then we can proceed in analogy to a Mutual Council, or to an *ex parte* Council when the party complained of appears. Suppose they do not come. Then, is not the question this : In analogy to the rule applicable to *ex parte* Councils, has every thing, that ought fairly to be done, been done, to get them here ? Now, if there has been, even if this is not governed by the technical rules that govern *ex parte* Councils, I submit, in analogy to those rules, if these two churches have done all that they could fairly do to get the Plymouth Church here, and it refuses to come, — refuses to come now, in answer to the invitation of this Council, — that then we may proceed, in analogy to the rule applicable to *ex parte* Councils, and pass upon these questions. Then this becomes a question of fact. Has every thing been fairly done to get them to come before the Council, and submit these questions ? Or have they acted in such a spirit, — in such a way, — as so utterly to discourage any further advances toward them, that these churches were justified in calling this Council ? It seems to me that this is the question of fact which we have got to determine. Have these brethren, and these churches, acted with a reasonable Christian spirit, in seeking to submit their mutual differences to a Council ? and is not this Council now fairly justified in going forward and acting, if they do not choose to appear ?

Hon. CHARLES DEMOND, of Boston : It seems to me that we are ready for something now besides this. We all agree, I think, that we are a Council assembled for some purpose ; and I think there is force in the suggestion that we had better hear the parties, before we decide questions even as important as this. If the parties who have called us present their case, there may circumstances come out which will throw light upon our minds in regard to the very questions at issue here ; and, at the close of the hearing, retiring, we may come to decisions upon all these questions, — what kind of a Council we are, what are our duties and powers, and what result we should come to. Perhaps, we shall come to a decision that may be wiser than if we undertake to decide this question now. We all agree that we are a Council to hear these brethren ; and, therefore, I shall move, in a moment, to lay this question upon the table, for the purpose of moving that we proceed to hear the parties. I should vote for the Resolution, if I were called upon to vote now ; for I believe what the Resolution says : but my opinion may be altered when I hear all the facts ; and I prefer, if we are to come to a decision, that we come to it after hearing all we can about it. I therefore move that it be laid upon the table.

The motion to lay upon the table was seconded, and agreed to.

Hon. C. Demond : I move that we now proceed to hear the parties who have called us, and the other parties, of course, if they come in.

The motion was seconded.

Rev. Dr. Quint : I would simply ask whether it is courteous to proceed with that until we hear from Plymouth Church ?

Rev. Dr. Webb : I was about to suggest the same thing, — whether, having sent a message to this church, it is proper for us to proceed without having a reply ?   I have been highly edified and instructed by this discussion, and was greatly in hopes that it would have gone on until a reply was received. I do not think we could do better than to have kept the Resolution where it was yesterday, and discussed it until the other matter was settled.

Rev. Dr. Richard S. Storrs : I merely wish to say this, on behalf of the committees, and of the churches which they represent : that our main apprehension, so far as we have had any apprehension in regard to the action of this Council, and its deliberations, has been, that so much time might be occupied in preliminary discussions, on questions naturally arising, and then afterwards so much time occupied in the presentation of the facts and the views of principles which it is our desire to present, if the Council will hear us, which we have asked you to come from points two thousand miles apart that you might weigh, and concerning which we have desired, and do desire, your advice, — so much time might be thus occupied, that the final and private sessions of the Council, into which we shall not be admitted, but in which these subjects will be discussed by you personally, and where your result will be moulded and arrived at, would be, in the nature of the case, hasty ; the time would be so limited that the mind of the Council would not be fully and adequately expressed on the subject.   That has been our apprehension, and we have had no other ; for this is your business as much as ours. You are as much interested in Congregationalism as we are. If it goes to pieces, we are not to be the sufferers alone.   But we do very much desire, that so much time may be given for the Council to be by itself, when, after hearing whatever we have to say, it considers the questions, and considers whether to give us advice about the questions, — we desire that so much time may be spent in that, that your conclusions will be arrived at deliberately and wisely. Now, if you can stay indefinitely, all right : we will take care of you as long as you stay ; and we shall be glad to have the preliminary discussion protracted as long as you please. We do not wish, certainly, to make any suggestion that looks toward a termination of it, until you are perfectly satisfied to have that termination. But do remember this : that you will need many hours for private discussion. I have been in a Council where we terminated public discussion on Thursday at noon, and reached our result on Saturday morning at two o'clock. You will want all the time you can get ; and if it seems proper, if it is according to your mind, we shall be very glad to make our statements as early as we may, that you may have them distinctly before you. If it be desirable to wait for the Plymouth Church to appear, possibly it might not seem improper to the Council that some preliminary things, which may be said before approaching the discussion of the principal questions, may be permitted now to be said.

The MODERATOR announced that a committee from the Plymouth Church had just arrived, and was in waiting, with a communication from that church.

On motion, the Scribe was requested to invite the Committee of the Plymouth Church to appear before the Council.

The Scribe conducted the committee, consisting of Rev. Dr. EDWARD BEECHER, Mr. HENRY W. SAGE, and Prof. ROBERT R. RAYMOND, into the church ; and seats were assigned them to the left of the MODERATOR's desk.

The MODERATOR : I am very happy to present to you, Brethren, the brethren who are here as a committee from the Plymouth Church, among whom I recognize the Rev. Dr. EDWARD BEECHER. The other members of the committee are personally unknown to me ; but I beg leave to assure the members of that committee, that, with whatever message they are charged, this Council receives them in Christian affection and confidence ; that this Council is, as relates to the questions on which it has been convened, impartial, and uncommitted ; that, so far as any expressions of opinion have been uttered, in the Council itself, or in the intercourse which I have had with members of it, if there are any whose prejudices are in favor of the inviting churches, there are as many whose prejudices, pre-judgments, or sympathies, are in favor of the Plymouth Church; and that, as I estimate the average of the Council, it is as impartial in reference to the questions at issue as any Council could be. We shall be very happy to hear from the committee.

Rev. Dr. BEECHER then said, —

The authority under which we act will appear by reading the following vote: —

At a meeting of Plymouth Church, held March 25, 1874, it was unanimously resolved that Edward Beecher, Henry W. Sage, and Robert R. Raymond be appointed, as the messengers of this church, to convey the reply of Plymouth Church to the Council now assembled in the Clinton Avenue Congregational Church; and that, upon delivering said reply, they take no further action in behalf of this church.

ATTEST:
THOMAS G. SHEARMAN, *Clerk.*
PLYMOUTH CHURCH, BROOKLYN, March 25, 1874.

As Professor Robert R. Raymond is more familiar with the document, I will request that he read it to the Council.

Professor RAYMOND then read the reply of the Plymouth Church, as follows: —

REPLY.

TO THE COUNCIL OF CONGREGATIONAL CHURCHES, NOW SITTING IN THE CITY OF BROOKLYN, PLYMOUTH CHURCH SENDETH GREETING:

Reverend and Beloved Brethren and Fathers in God.

Having been notified by the Church of the Pilgrims, and the Clinton Avenue Congregational Church, of your assemblage, under their call, for purposes specified in their Letters-Missive, and having received from those churches an invitation to appear before you by our pastor and a committee, simply for the purposes of correcting any statements of fact which might seem to us erroneous, and furnishing any further and specific information which you might request ; and having declined this invitation on the ground that these churches thus called us before a Council in the convening of which we had been permitted to take no part, in which we had never been offered the rights of equal members, and in which it was not proposed now to give us the rights even of ordinary defendants, we nevertheless desire, out of our respect and love for you, beloved brethren and venerable fathers, to make a brief statement of our position, and to lay this our solemn Protest before you.

It is not against your convening or organizing as a Council that we desire to remonstrate. So far as the Letters-Missive under which you have assembled state matters which do not relate to any other church than the two churches issuing those letters, we make no complaint. We do not even object to the consideration in your body of the question whether those two churches have made a mistake in their manner of approaching us, and therefore owe us an apology, instead of our owing them an explanation. Although this is a question in which we, as a church, have some interest, yet an *ex parte* discussion of that point, for the sole enlightenment of those brethren, may be of great profit to them, and cannot seriously encroach upon the rights of Congregational churches at large.

Neither do we object to the consideration of the abstract questions submitted to your body. Bearing, as these questions doubtless do, upon the internal economy of the two churches which have called you, it is for you to decide whether there are difficulties arising, or likely to arise, within those churches, of sufficient importance to justify their asking for advice upon those points, in the light of which they may judge of their own past acts, and guide their future course. We are bound to presume that such is the case.

But when they call upon you to examine into *our* action for *their* edification, a far different issue is presented. You have been called to determine whether the action of *Plymouth Church*, in a specified case, was justifiable, whether *our* pastor's name was left without proper vindication, and whether *we* are to be retained in the fellowship of Congregational churches.

Brethren, we approach this part of your duties, if we know any thing of our own hearts, in a spirit free from all personal motives. We will not pretend, that, at all times past, we have felt unconcerned for ourselves as a church, or for that member of our church who, by reason of long and faithful service, and of his signal success in bringing home to our hearts a living and ever-present Saviour, has become to us the best beloved of men. But these things are of the past. The Lord hath given us peace and strength ; and we rest in him, with absolute confidence and absolute content.

But we still owe a duty to our weaker brethren. Not every church could pass through such a storm in safety. Not every church could withstand the decrees of a Council so worthy of respect as yours, even though the Council were known to have been called *ex parte*, and informed erroneously. Lest, therefore, our silence should leave the way open for the oppression of other churches, less powerful and less united than our own, we speak.

In the name of our Congregational polity, in the name of our feebler brethren, in the name of justice, even as administered by those who know not God, but, above all, in the name of that God whose throne is seated in justice and judgment, we protest against any action whatever by this Council, upon any issue relating to Plymouth Church.

And this we do for the reasons following, as well as for others, to set forth which, time would fail.

First. This is an *ex parte* Council, convened without any regular and sufficient steps to obtain a Mutual Council, — without any refusal upon our part to join in such a Council, — called to consider our affairs for the sole instruction of two other churches, and carefully fettered, so as to make it impossible by the terms of its call for the council to alter itself into a Mutual Council. Yet it is a well-known and fundamental rule of Congregational polity, that no *ex parte* Council can be called until a Mutual Council has been distinctly offered and clearly refused, and that every *ex parte* Council should be at liberty, and should offer, to make itself a Mutual one.

Second. If it is claimed that one or more churches, acting on the pretext that they are not in controversy with a sister church, and desire instruction only for themselves, may call a Council to instruct them as to their relations with that church, free from the rules governing the call of ordinary *ex parte* Councils, this claim appears to us subversive of the whole system of Mutual Councils. If this Council has been regularly called, and is competent to advise the churches calling it as to their duty toward us, then our

pastor can call a Council, without consulting us, to advise him publicly what is his duty toward his church. We have inquired in
vain for a precedent of this kind, and have every reason to believe
that none can be found. The present case is a most dangerous
innovation, which, if sanctioned by the churches, will do more to
disorganize Congregational polity than all the alleged errors of
Plymouth Church could do, if ten times repeated.

Third. This Council is summoned to advise, precisely as we were
originally summoned to take advice, under distinct menace and
moral coercion. Just as Plymouth Church was in one breath requested to explain the facts, and informed that it must be cut off
unless the facts had been misreported, so this Council is called
upon to advise whether the action of Plymouth Church has been
conformable to Congregational usage, and is at the same moment
informed, that, if such is indeed Congregational usage, the two
churches "cannot sustain such a position;" that it would be
" entirely unreasonable to expect it from " them ; that, "even if they
could continue to hold it in view of the past, they should feel it
indispensable to be extricated from it in forecast of what may
occur in the future ; " that "such a position is simply insupportable;" and that, "if this is to be Congregational practice, many
churches [clearly meaning their own] will certainly prefer to identify themselves with some other communion."

While we do not for a moment assume that such threats will
intimidate you, any more than the threats which for nearly a year
past have been uttered from the same quarter intimidated us, yet
we conceive it possible in the future that a combination of large
and powerful churches might select a Council of weak and dependent ones for the purpose of crushing one still weaker ; and, in such
a case, menaces like these would have a controlling and disastrous
effect. We resist them *now*, when they seem to us idle and vain,
lest they should be left by our silence to be drawn into a precedent
fatal to the liberty of other churches.

Fourth. Officers of the great institutions to which Congregationalists have been accustomed to contribute most liberally, — the
Home Missionary Society, the Congregational Union, the Board
of Commissioners for Foreign Missions, and others, — having been
invited to attend this Council, in which their wisdom, experience,
and devotion to the great work of the church make them distinguished and valuable members, are singled out for special and
almost personal dictation, and are warned in most pointed language that the callers of this Council do not intend to contribute

any more funds to the support of these Christian enterprises, if their theories of Congregational fellowship and discipline are not indorsed by this Council.

This attempt to pervert great missionary organizations into engines of ecclesiastical power, to stop the fountains of Christian benevolence, and to overawe members of Councils by appeals to their fears for the special branch of the Lord's work in their charge, tends to destroy the moral force of all Councils, and constitutes an assault on the independence of both the churches and the societies, entirely without parallel in the history of Congregationalism.

Fifth. In so far as this Council is called to consider the points of conflict between Plymouth Church and neighboring churches, the whole frame of the Council, in its widespread constituency and national character (so appropriate and admirable, if called only to deal with large and general questions) is directly in opposition to the genius of Congregational polity, — one great aim of which is to confine local troubles to their own locality, and to settle them in the neighborhood, by the aid of neighboring churches, without spreading the tale of local dissensions over the whole land.

Sixth. The charges brought against this church are partly based upon the reported speeches of its pastor, although it is well known that Plymouth Church, with the hearty concurrence of its pastor, has from the beginning of its history delared that no man, however beloved and revered, may usurp the rights of the brotherhood, and has always insisted, and does now insist, that by its own acts and declarations, and by these only, it will be judged. And the maintenance of this rule with respect to all churches, we hold to be an essential part of Congregational polity.

Seventh. It is proposed virtually to arraign this church for alleged violations of Congregational usage. But Congregational usage itself derives its sole authority from the Word of God ; and no Council may call to account a Congregational church for the alleged violation of principles not declared by the Word of God.

Nor can we assent to any action by which the tradition of the elders shall be placed upon even equal grounds with the commandment of God, nor agree to receive for doctrines the commandments of men. And we therefore protest against any attempt to formulate the usage of churches into a code of ecclesiastical law, to be placed on an equality with the Word of God, as binding upon the conscience of the churches.

In the presentation of the case to you, it happens naturally enough, from the fundamental error of the whole proceeding, that our views and practice in cases of discipline are not correctly stated. We shall not correct these errors of detail. Nevertheless, for the purpose of informing you frankly, as brethren beloved in the Lord, what are our views and practice concerning church discipline, although not recognizing your power to act upon this subject, we append to this paper our past and present rules of discipline, and a declaration of our practice under them, adopted unanimously by this church, and representing not merely the course we have marked out for the future, but that which has been followed in the past.

Our doctrine of church fellowship is in like manner gravely misinterpreted. We have never claimed (as asserted) that "fellowship binds to silence the churches which have pledged it." We have never denied the right of churches to offer to each other advice in a Christian spirit, nor the duty of churches to receive such an offer in the spirit of brotherhood. We *have* asserted the right of every church, acting in the like spirit of fraternal love, while receiving the offer, to decline the advice, and to judge for itself, when, according to the laws of Christ, an occasion has arisen for exercising this right. And, having received an offer of advice which seemed to us to be tendered in a spirit not according to the mind of Christ, we did decisively exercise our right, by declining to listen to advice conceived in such a spirit. Nor can we ever assent to any doctrine of church fellowship which shall be destructive of the liberty of the local church, or which shall convert that which the Lord ordained as a safeguard and an instrument of sympathy, into an irritating espionage, and an instrument of oppression.

But we rejoice to live in affectionate fellowship with all churches of the Lord Jesus, and especially with those who are in all things like-minded with us, holding to the same faith and order, not only in things fundamental, but in things less essential, yet dear to us by conviction or association. In asserting that this church was not responsible for the doctrine, order, or discipline of other churches, we never for a moment intended to cut ourselves off from relationship to them. There is a certain vague and general sense in which all Christians are responsible for one another. But this is not the sense in which the word is generally used. The responsibility of members of the same church for one another is the mildest form in which the word is commonly understood. And it was just that degree of responsibility between churches which we meant, and still mean to deny. Members of a church can put each other on trial before the church : we deny the right of any church to put another church upon trial, before any ecclesiastical body whatever.

Yet we cheerfully admit, that whenever any church shall openly and avowedly change the essential conditions upon which it was publicly received into the fellowship of neighboring churches, or shall by flagrant neglect exert a pernicious and immoral influence upon the community or upon sister churches, it is their right, either by individual action or by council, to withdraw their fellowship.

We hold that, preceding disfellowship, in all such cases, there should be such affectionate and reasonable inquiry as shall show that the evil is real, that the causes of it are within the control of the church, that the evil is not a transient evil, such as may befall any church, but is permanent, and tending to increase rather than to diminish.

It was with this meaning, and reasoning from this point of view, that we used the word "responsibility." We do maintain that we are responsible for no other church, and to no other church. But we use these words in their ordinary and popular sense, and not with reference to all those shadowy grades of meaning which may possibly be attached to them. In short, we used this language for the purpose of repelling dictation, and relieving the conscience of other churches from a sense of any such responsibility as necessarily implied the right to dictate. The responsibility of *affection* we gladly accept : the responsibility of *authority*, even in its lightest touch, we utterly repudiate.

We pray for the divine blessing upon you and your deliberations. We commit you and ourselves to the care of the great Master, in whose service we are all united here, and who will, out of perplexities, conflicts, and doubts, bring us all into an eternal unity of love, and through love to peace.

––––––––––

Thus much, brethren and fathers, it was in our mind to say to you, before receiving any other invitation than that of the two churches. But having now received your invitation to appear before you by our pastor and a committee, we are constrained to decline it, lest by our acceptance we should seem to renounce our conscientious convictions, and to withdraw our solemn testimony against the violations of Christian liberty, courtesy, and equity which have characterized the calling of this Council, and the steps which led to it, and lest we should establish a precedent full of danger to smaller churches, as encouraging irregular and unwarrantable proceedings on the part of strong churches, which the weaker party might afterward, by the force of our example, be compelled to condone. We are not responsible for the errors which have been committed in the treatment of this church, and in the calling of this Council; and we are not willing to cover them with our consent.

By order of

PLYMOUTH CHURCH,

THOMAS G. SHEARMAN, *Clerk.*

F. M. EDGERTON, *Moderator.*
BROOKLYN, March 25, 1874.

Resolved, That Edward Beecher, H. W. Sage, and Robert R. Raymond be appointed as the messengers of this church to convey the reply of Plymouth Church to the Council now assembled in the Clinton Avenue Congregational Church, and that upon delivering the said reply they take no further action in behalf of this church.

DECLARATION OF PRINCIPLES.

PLYMOUTH CHURCH, believing that care in the admission of members is of more value, in maintaining the purity of the church, than severity in dealing with them after admission, attaches great importance to the evidence given by candidates for membership of vital faith in Christ and of spiritual life begun. The Examining Committee must be satisfied upon these points before recommending the candidate to the church; and letters from other churches are not accepted as substitutes for personal examination. All persons who enter Plymouth Church are, in effect, admitted upon profession of their faith.

The active membership, numbering about 2,300 souls, is so organized that a systematic watch and care is extended over all, in the form of visitation, inquiry, fraternal advice, encouragement, and assistance, and, in the case of non-resident members, by regular correspondence. We recognize it also as our privilege and duty to reprove and admonish one another with all fidelity, provided it be in love; and all these duties, while not neglected by the members of the church as individuals, are moreover laid upon special officers of the church, and so distributed and discharged that no single member is omitted from this fraternal vigilance.

By the assiduous use of personal, social, and spiritual influences, by preventing or healing disputes and reclaiming wanderers, we seek to avoid the necessity of judicial discipline; and this we hold to be not only wise policy, but Christian obligation. Nevertheless, when these means fail, the discipline of this church is express and energetic. If any member of our body brings dishonor upon the Christian profession, we hold it our duty to reclaim him if possible, with all long-suffering and patience, but, if unsuccessful in this, to make it known that we are no longer responsible for the dishonor which he has brought or may bring upon the name of Christ.

If any one desires no longer to be known as a member of this church, or as a professed follower of Christ, we hold that, while we cannot release him from the special obligations to Christ which he has assumed by the public profession of his faith, we may, and should, after having endeavored to change his purpose, release ourselves from our responsibility to and for him, in whatever method the circumstances of the case may require, regard being had to the best good of the individual, the well-being of the church, and the honor of the Master.

While we are ready at all times to receive suitable inquiry, and to give to sister churches every reasonable explanation, concerning our action in cases of public interest, we hold that it is our right, and may be our duty, to avoid the evils incident to a public explanation or a public trial; and that such an exercise of our discretion furnishes no good ground for the interference of other churches provided we neither retain within our fellowship, nor dismiss by letter as in regular standing, persons who bring open dishonor upon the Christian name.

RULES OF DISCIPLINE.

I.

AS ADOPTED APRIL, 1848.

RULE 5. No member can be deprived of church privileges, except by regular process. The presentation of complaints may be first made to the Examining Committee, who shall, upon sufficient cause, prefer charges to the whole church, or the complainant may present his complaint in person to the church. When a member is accused, he shall be seasonably furnished with a copy of the complaint, and shall have a full hearing.

RULE 6. — The censures which may be inflicted on offending members are, according to the aggravation of the offense, either (1) private reproof, (2) public admonition, (3) suspension, or (4) excommunication. In cases of excommunication, notice thereof must be given from the pulpit on the sabbath.

II.

AS AMENDED IN 1865.

RULE 4. *Discipline.* — Members cannot be censured by the church, except by the process herein stated. A complaint may be made either to the Examining Committee or to the whole church. In the former case the clerk of the committee, and in the latter case the clerk of the church, must reduce the complaint to writing, if it is entertained, and must use due diligence to forward a copy to the accused, and to give him personal notice of the time and place of hearing. The accused must have a full opportunity to be heard in his own defense. An accusation presented to the church must always be heard, either by the church or by the Examining Committee, unless the application for a hearing is rejected at a meeting of the church by a three-fourths vote.

RULE 5. — [Same as Rule 6 above.]

RULE 7. [Adopted, 1859; amended, 1871.] — Members may be dropped from the roll of the church, with or without notice to them, as may be deemed just, by a two-thirds vote of the church, upon the recommendation of the Examining Committee, either upon their own application, or, in case they have abandoned their connection with the church by prolonged absence or otherwise, upon the application of any other person.

III.

AS AMENDED IN 1874.

RULE 4. *Discipline.* — Members cannot be censured except by the process, herein stated.

1. Complaints must be made in writing, either to the Examining Committee or the whole Church.

2. If the complaint is made to the Examining Committee, the facts must first be investigated by it, so far as to determine whether there is reasonable probability that the charges can be sustained by proof.

3. If the complaint is made to the church, it may order a similar investigation by the Examining Committee, or by a special committee, before deciding to proceed.

4. If the Examining Committee or the church decides to proceed with the case, the clerk of the church must use due diligence to forward a copy of the complaint to the accused, and, if practicable, to give him personal notice of the time and place of hearing.

5. The accused must in all cases, when a trial is had, have a full opportunity to be heard in his own defense.

6. The church may refer any case of discipline to a committee, to hear the evidence, and report its opinion on the whole case, or any part thereof.

7. When a complaint is made to the Examining Committee, the accused, at his first appearance, may require the committee to submit to the church the question, whether the complaint shall be taken out of the committee for trial; and the committee cannot proceed meantime.

8. Proceedings before the Examining Committee shall be kept private until otherwise ordered by the church; and the committee, unless the complaint is sustained, or unless it desires instructions, or unless a report is ordered by vote of the church, shall make no report upon the case.

9. No member of a committee can vote upon its final report in case of discipline, unless he has heard or read the evidence and arguments in the case, except by consent of both the complainant and the accused.

10. If the evidence has been taken by a committee, the church is not bound to hear evidence on either side.

11. Final censure can be inflicted only by the church, and by the concurrence of two-thirds of all present and voting.

Rules 5 and 7 unchanged.

Rev. Dr. BEECHER : On retiring from this Council, I desire to reciprocate the kind feelings expressed by the Moderator, and to say, that with the utmost cordiality, and with the utmost Christian affection, we reciprocate all of these kind feelings expressed toward us, and toward the church with which we are connected.

The committee then retired.

The MODERATOR : The communication is now before the Council.

Mr. E. F. Brown, of Harlem, N. Y.: I suppose it is proper to receive this communication. I move that it be received, and placed upon the files of the Council.

Hon. A. C. Barstow : I will move, as an amendment, that it be placed on the records of the Council.

Mr. Brown : I will accept the amendment.

Hon. C. G. Hammond : I would rather that the motion should be divided.

Mr. Brown, with the consent of Mr. Barstow, then withdrew his motion.

Hon. C. Demond : I now move that we proceed to hear the committees of the churches.

Rev. Dr. Dexter : I move, as an amendment, that the hearing of the committees of the inviting churches be the order of the day on the re-assembling of the Council after recess, at three o'clock.

The amendment was accepted by Mr. Demond, and the motion, as amended, agreed to.

The Council then took a recess, until three o'clock, p.m.

COUNCIL convened at 3:30 p.m.

The MODERATOR : The Council will now hear the statements to be presented by the Committees of the churches which have called it together. The members of the Council will please give their attention to Dr. R. S. Storrs.

Rev. G. B. WILLCOX of Jersey City, N.J. : Mr. Moderator, before Dr. Storrs begins, I would like to say that, as it will probably be desirable to have an evening session, it may be well for the Council to fix now upon an hour for our adjournment this afternoon. I move, therefore, that the Council adjourn at half-past five, to meet again in the evening.

Rev. Dr. STORRS : Mr. Moderator, I hope Mr. Willcox will not press his motion. I do not know how much time I shall occupy in what I have to say. It may be that I shall be wholly through with my remarks by the time he has mentioned. But if I should not be, I should much prefer to finish what I have to say before the adjournment, instead of leaving a part of it to go over to the evening. I will get through by six o'clock, and as much earlier as I can.

Rev. Dr. QUINT : There is one item of business, which will only occupy a moment, before Dr. Storrs begins. The Committee on Credentials wish to report, with the consent of the Council, that, the church in Orange Valley, New Jersey, having sent two delegates to the Council, the Committee recommend that the delegates should decide between themselves which one shall act in representing the church, the other retiring.

The Committee report, also, that, in four cases, acting-pastors have been sent to the Council by churches invited, and recommend that these be received as members.

The Report was accepted, and adopted.

The MODERATOR : The brethren of the Council will now give attention to Dr. Storrs.

Rev. Dr. STORRS addressed the Council, as follows : —

FATHERS, AND BRETHREN : — I am quite aware of the seriousness of this occasion, and of the seriousness which attaches

to the remarks which I am to make ; not merely in view of
the fact that they are to be addressed to so large and influential an assembly, but also of the fact that they are to go forth,
through the fingers of the reporters and the types of the
press, everywhere, to-morrow. I desire to speak very simply,
and very seriously ; and I pray the Spirit of God to help me,
and to guide me, — not that I may be detained from saying
any thing untruly, beyond the truth or against the truth ; or
any thing maliciously ; or any thing with a secret sting beneath it : for I am certain that my own heart would revolt
from either of these, instantly, vehemently : but that I may
be kept from saying any thing hastily, inadvertently, as one
may in the freedom of remark ; any thing the import and the
relations of which may be other and wider than I, in speaking,
may be aware of. I pray the Divine Spirit to keep my mind
under His influence, that I may be preserved from that peril,
which cannot be altogether guarded against. And I am encouraged in the hope that this prayer will be answered, by the
letters which have come to me within a day or two, from distant points, and from men whose faces I have never seen,
telling me that prayer was there being offered for a Divine
blessing upon the deliberations and the results of this Council.

We, of the committees, greatly regret that we are prevented
in the providence of God from having the aid, on which we
had largely reckoned, of one of our most eminent and able
laymen, a member of the committee from the Church of the
Pilgrims, the Hon. Joshua M. Van Cott ; known in this city,
in the State, and in the country, as an eminent lawyer and
jurist ; fully informed concerning the principles at issue here,
and the discussions through which we have come to the present point ; intensely interested in them ; and upon whose
ability to present the matter, upon whose experience in delib-
erative assemblies — far surpassing that which either of us
possesses — we had based large expectations. To his regret
as to ours, but to ours more than it can be to his, he, by a
painful accident, has been confined to his house, and pinned
to his bed, for six weeks past, and is unable to be here. We
have to do what we can without him.

The committees have requested me to present for them, after some preliminary remarks, the views which are common to our churches on our first five Questions. You will see, therefore, that, in order to do this with any completeness, I shall have to trespass largely upon your patience. But I pray you to hear me with all the measure of patience which you can bring to it, remembering that this burden which you now take up, for a little, we have been carrying for months ; and that my remarks, so far as they shall help to illustrate the state of mind prevalent in our churches, concerning this subject which has brought you together, may be helpful to you.

I need not say that we are glad at last to have an assembly, before which we can freely speak our minds. We have been subject to measureless misrepresentations, during the months that are closed ; misrepresentations not altogether willful or intentional, perhaps not in the larger part so ; arising often from entire misconception of the facts themselves, and of the principles involved in the facts : misrepresentations, however, which have constituted, in the aggregate, a formidable power against us, the energy of which, and the ubiquity of which, we have never had hidden from our eyes. To such misrepresentations we, of these committees of our churches, have answered never a word. I am not aware that any single member of either committee has ever written a line in answer. If any one has done so, he has done it as his private privilege, and on his private responsibility, without any communication with the committees on the subject. For we have felt, Brethren and Fathers, that some time or other our opportunity would come, when we could state the facts under the influence of which we had been acting, and the principles which seemed to us involved in them. And, if it never came, personally to us it did not matter ; for we thought we were right, and we knew we were honest ; and God knew it ; and under our responsibility to Him we have done what we have done, and have waited for this occasion. But we are glad it has come.

A word as to the constitution of this Council. It has been said to be a " picked " Council. And it *is* picked ; as the generals of an army are picked, for their courage, and soldierly

qualities, and strategic skill ; picked, as the members of the ju-
diciary are picked, for their acquaintance with the law, and for
the spirit of equity which rules within them ; picked, as reporters and editors are picked, — men of intelligence and skill,
quickness of insight and discernment, and of power to represent fact and thought to the public mind.

We intended to have the most wise, and weighty, and impartial Council that we could obtain.   We took churches from
the West, and churches from the East, — ancient churches
with eminent pastors, ancient churches with recent pastors,
recent churches with younger pastors, that it might not be
felt by any one that we were overlooking the modern spirit,
and the temper of the time.   We took men from the head of
great institutions of learning, and of great societies for missionary and beneficent purposes ; because we wanted the
judgment of the ablest men whom we could assemble, on the
questions which we have presented, as looked at in the light
of the facts and arguments which we have to exhibit.   And
we should have taken more, but that we could not depopulate
the country of its most eminent ministers and laymen in
order to settle a matter even so grave and important as this.
And having started with the intention of having forty
churches, and finally reached eighty, as we supposed,— through
a mistake in the count it turned out to be seventy-nine, at last,
— we there stopped.   It is a picked Council, in the sense that
we intended it to be : — the best, and most absolutely impartial, and, so far as advice can go, the most authoritative Council
that we could convene.

It has been said, however, to be a "packed" Council.   You
know how that is : you have shown how that is.   You have
heard this morning, before we who called you together had
opened our lips on the subject, the views presented at length,
presented ably, presented in a paper prepared beforehand, of
Plymouth Church, which is not a party before this Council, as
it insists, and which, after presenting those views, contrary to
your invitation given explicitly last evening, retreated from all
the questions which, being answered, would have shed much
light upon the paper.   We do not complain of this in the
least.   We called you together because we confided in your

wisdom. We accept this as an illustration of your wisdom ; but we are sure that this shows, at least, that this is not a packed Council.

We may well insist upon it, that in allowing your minds to be colored and moulded, before we had said a word, by the formal and elaborate presentation of the views and alleged facts on the part of another party, not appearing here to give evidence before you concerning matters on which further inquiry would to us have been important, you have shown at any rate that you are not a "packed" Council. And for our vindication I wish to say, further, that the statements which have been made, that we corresponded with individuals to know their opinions beforehand, as a condition precedent to inviting them, are simply and absolutely without foundation.

Here are seventy-five churches represented. If we corresponded with a single pastor, to know what his opinion was beforehand, he can rise and state it, and put us to an open shame. If we engineered the election of a single delegate, in a single church, that we might obtain one friendly to our views, in distinction from one whose sympathies were on the other side, he can rise and state that, and bring us to confusion. We did absolutely neither, and nothing of the kind. Our own brethren in the city, living near to us, we did not speak with ; holding ourselves aloof from them on this subject with a reserve which we felt and showed on no other possible question ; until we ourselves felt that they might think we were uncommunicative and repellent,— because we did not wish to prejudice their minds beforehand. And the only information we ever received concerning these brethren in the city, in regard to their opinions on this subject, we received through the report of a newspaper in this city, which has been furiously and foolishly hostile to us from the beginning. It sent out one of its interviewers, those indefatigable Paul Prys of the modern civilization, to find out what these brethren thought ; and it reported what purported to be the substance of their replies, — whether correctly or not we never inquired.

Some of them were favorable to us, and some were not. The names of some of them were on our list ; the names of others were not. The list had not been sent out, but was completely in our hands. Not a name was added; and not a name was dropped. Now, if any man hereafter asserts that this is a "packed" Council, in the face of this declaration of mine, on behalf of these committees, I say that either he or we have a deliberate lie to give account for.

It has been said, furthermore, that we called it by trickery; as one paper, with characteristic courtesy, expressed it, by "a barefaced ecclesiastical trick." Well, I shall not use harsh language. I will simply say, therefore, that this is an utter and irredeemable untruth. We are not as wise as our critics, undoubtedly; but we are not absolute fools: and we should not have called eighty churches together, with eminent divines from all parts of the country, to detect us in a trick. Here we are, Brethren, in your hands. We have said that we accept and solicit your admonition, if you find that we have acted wrongly; and, if you find that we have acted in any spirit of trickery, toward you or anybody else, you may put the lash on as hard as you like, and as long as you like. We will not complain, and we will not flinch.

What trickery can there be? A and B have a difference in business, and A desires B to unite with him in submitting it to a referee for adjudication; but B declines, or does not accept; till at last A, weary of waiting, goes himself to some disinterested person, wholly impartial, wise, experienced in business, friendly to both parties: he does not ask him to investigate B's accounts, or to call B up to answer to any charge; but he asks his advice as to the propriety of the course which he, A, has followed heretofore, and what he had better do in time to come. Certainly, if that is a trick, it is a great pity there are not more tricks in this world. They would tend to amity and to honesty among men.

Let me clear away one or two other misconceptions, which may possibly be present in the minds of some of the Council. It has been said, not unfrequently, that we have been animated by a secret hostility to Mr. Beecher. The assertion has not a particle of fact, as large as a grain of dust, to rest upon. These two pastors who are before you, at the head of these committees, had been the true and tried friends of Mr.

Beecher for many years ; one of them from the time he set his foot in this city. We were the two men whom he selected, from the entire range of his ministerial acquaintance, to be with him in the crowning festival of his life, — his Silver Wedding with his church. What has occurred, since then, within us, suddenly to change the sweetness of that affection into an acid hatred ? What has occurred, within us, to change the admiration and the pride we felt into jealousy and envy ? Brethren, it is with the profoundest sadness we have known, that we feel that we could not stand in the same relations, on the same platform, with him, now, which we occupied then. But the change has not been in us, through any deterioration of character, through any such sudden revulsion from friendly feeling toward a friend.

It has been said, not unfrequently, that we are actuated by some secret jealousy of Plymouth Church. I am almost tired of repeating words of denial ; but certainly that has not the smallest possible basis to rest upon, except the meanness of the mind that utters it. Why should we be jealous of Plymouth Church ? It in no way interferes with us. We have been proud of it, for a quarter of a century ; and no voices have been more ready and eager than ours in rendering it the heartiest meed of praise, in all the past. Are we jealous of other churches ? — jealous of the Tabernacle congregation, in New York, with its immense assembly, filling its superb building, under the fruitful and magnificent ministry of our friend, Dr. Taylor ? Are we jealous of the Central Church, with its beautiful audience room, and the great multitude which crowds that room, to hear the vivid and powerful appeals of our Brother Scudder ? We should as soon think of being jealous of Yale College, as of being jealous of Plymouth Church. When it works as a Congregational church ought to, it works for the benefit and blessing of every church and of every citizen ; and we most heartily rejoice in it.

It has been said — and this is one of the most intolerable things — that we have desired to investigate a scandal which has passed away. I will not suffer myself to speak of that imputation as it deserves. But if we remember that it has been impossible, in the nature of things, to investigate that, ecclesiastically, since the 31st of October of last year, — the church which had primary cognizance of it, and sole cognizance, having ended and excluded the case, and made it impossible to bring it up again ; and if it be remembered, further, that we had no desire, or wish, or willingness whatever, under any circumstances, to touch a pitch which it did not belong to us to handle, — I think ultimately that story will stop. Plymouth Church itself could not now investigate it, if it wished to. It cannot call back into itself the member charged with having circulated scandals, whom it has put beyond its jurisdiction. It might as well undertake to investigate, and this Council might far better undertake to investigate, any scandals concerning any former occupant of the mayor's chair in New York, or concerning the late James Fisk. It is a business with which we have never had any opportunity to meddle ; and, most certainly, we have never desired any.

There is another misconception, which perhaps it is more worth while to answer. It is the feeling which some have that we have been magnifying, tremendously, a single case ; that we have lost perspective. We have "got a bee in the bonnet," as the Scotch say. We have failed to distinguish the larger from the less ; and we are making a prodigious ado, and calling together a great Council from all parts of the country, on a question which is really simple, concerning a single case, and upon the whole insignificant. Well, of course, it does not seem so to us.

Here are two churches, large in numbers, and, to a degree certainly, intelligent and cultivated, in general information and in the Christian graces, which have been for five months steadily at work trying to bring light upon the questions which have now come before you. Stormed at by the incessant rain of opposition, thundered at and lightened at, laughed at and scoffed at, and treated with all derision and contempt, they have marched, as soldiers march through the rainstorm, not breaking ranks because of the rain. Of course they have felt the case, and the principles involved in it, to be important. Here are Committees. Who are they? Hot-headed youngsters, that take fire at a spark, and go out as quickly? To a large extent they are the wisest, the most experienced, able, sober-minded men we have. Some of them are younger, most of them are the older members of our churches. And it would be just as possible to ignite yonder pavement by drawing on it the end of an extinguished match as it would be to stir these committees, the committee of my church or of the other, to any undue excitement, by the mere appeal of passion. You might as well set the granite walls of my church-edifice to dancing hornpipes.

Look at the case itself. Is it insignificant? Is it not one of the most startling, bewildering cases which have occurred in ecclesiastical history, anywhere? Here is a man of brilliant and popular powers, widely known, and widely welcome, in the lecture-room, and on the political platform; wielding large influence in the country; formerly editor of one of the leading religious newspapers of the country; for seventeen years a member of the church; converted under the ministry of the pastor of that church; active, and prominent, and enthusiastic in it; I believe, but I won't affirm, once superintendent of its Sunday School. Suddenly he ceases attending. Living in the city, passing it every day, he never crosses its threshold. Rumors arise attributing to him scandalous allegations concerning the pastor of the church. He is charged with the offense. He is called up before the church, — before the Committee through which that church exercises its power of inquiring into the action and character of its accused members. He makes no answer, either way, to the specific charge. But he himself appears at last, in the church-assembly, in what looks like any thing but a mood of repentance or confession, in what seems to be a mood of defiance; and he is as tenderly sent forth from thence, so far as appears to us, as if he had been the Israelite indeed, in whom there was no guile. Is it not a startling case, — most impressive in itself, in its history, in its incidents? well adapted to attract attention? a volcanic case among common cases? If Bald Mountain in North Carolina, after its long rumbling and thundering, were to fling off its crest of pine, — if it has one, — and burst into an American Ætna, I do not believe the surrounding population would be more startled and amazed than we were.

But then, while the case itself was remarkable, and not to be minimized into a trifling affair, — any more than the tumbling torrents of Niagara can be interpreted into an ordinary cascade, or the gleam of the meteor bursting in the air can be made to be nothing but the flash of a firebug's wing, — the principles involved in it are more remarkable still. For it is the peculiarity of such cases that they involve principles ; and you cannot escape the principles, no matter how simple the case may be. Hampden's ship-money was twenty shillings. It involved the right of the king to lay taxes without the assent of Parliament ; and, for less than a guinea, England went to war, and the stately head of Charles the First fell in front of Whitehall, while England became a Commonwealth. Our fathers refused their three-pence a pound duty on tea. Lord North always said that it was nonsense, because they absolutely made nine-pence on every pound, since there was a drawback, in England, of a shilling a pound duty on tea exported to the colonies. No matter. More or less, they felt that that involved the right of taxation without representation ; and the war that followed was no three-penny affair, but a new empire emerged into the world in consequence of it.

Principles therefore, as connected with cases, make the cases noble in significance and relations, while they dwarf them in their incidents. When the negro Somerset was brought before Lord Mansfield, the only question at issue was : Can an English master compel a slave to leave England without his own consent ? Lord Mansfield decided that slavery was an institution so odious that it could only be suffered to be supported by positive law, and that the law of England did not accept or allow that case. And slavery was swept from the British Empire by the principles emerging from that single case. Therefore, even if this case had not been so startling in itself, it would have compelled our serious and continuing attention by the principles involved in it. For principles are powerful.

I learned from you, Sir, [turning to the presiding Moderator, Rev. Dr. Bacon], many years ago, when we were both younger than now, that " tendencies are stronger than men." It rang in my ear, has been a watchword in my life, from that time to this. And tendencies come with principles. Principles are powerful. If they are evil, they work mischief beyond the generation by which they are accepted, and by which they are applied ; and, if they are good, they have an immortal life upon the earth, denied to men. They are powerful ; and they admit of no compromise, as our fathers have taught us. You may not shape them, and trim them, to meet an exigency ; but, if they are borne in upon you as connected with an action, evil in its nature or good in its nature, you may not shrink from the acceptance of such principles, or from their service.

And principles are all that Congregationalism has. It has no ritual, venerable with the memories of the past, and beautiful in the rhythm and cadence of its majestic sentences. It has no hierarchy, transmitting a succession from the apostles onward. It has no elaborate and extended system of minute rules. It has a few great and vital principles, of church-membership and of church-fellowship ; and these are all. The life of the system is in its principles, as the life of the animal is in the blood ; and, if you stab and shatter those principles, there is an invisible and silent hemorrhage that destroys the life itself.

So we felt. So we feel. And, in our deliberate conviction, if the principles applied by the Plymouth Church are to be accepted as the principles of Congregationalism in this country, the system has already gone to pieces. That which our fathers knew, and loved, and honored, no more exists. Therefore we took up this discussion, when it came to us, in the providence of God. Therefore we have gone on with it as God seemed to require that we should. Therefore we have stood in our lot, and have learned what it is to bear burdens and carry crosses, and to fight what seemed to us the good fight of the faith and of the fathers. The fact that Congregationalism is spreading so widely in the country seemed to us to make the duty more commanding ; and the fact that it was a duty which we disliked to perform, from which our hearts instinctively drew back, only made it more imperative upon us, when God had sent it.

So, then, I have aimed to set aside, at the beginning, some

of the misconceptions which may have been silently present
in the minds of members of the Council, and which certainly
have been present widely in the newspaper press, and in the
public mind so far as that press affects it.   I wish it might
be understood, as it ought to be understood, that as to my
dear brother and myself, as to the members of these committees, each in his especial relations, this has been one of the
most painful passages in our personal experience ; — in our
ministerial life the *most* painful which has hitherto met us.   I
wish it might be understood that we are too old to be fickle ;
and, while I say it modestly, concerning ourselves, I will say
it frankly and energetically, remembering our churches, we
are too strong to be jealous.   We have no personal end to
answer ; no personal grudge to gratify ; no spark of malice
or bitterness in our hearts toward the pastor of Plymouth
Church.   And upon the occasion, at last, of addressing this
Council, we hope to say nothing that any one will regret ; we
mean to say nothing that we shall regret, here or hereafter.

Now, Brethren, for the Letter-missive, and the Questions.

First : Is it in accordance with the order and usage of Congregationalism that a member may terminate his membership in a
church by absenting himself from its services and communion ?
Or is a corporate and consenting action on the part of the church
necessary to such termination of membership?

We hope the Council will give an answer to this, not only
prompt, but very emphatic.   Let us state our conception of
the matter, as this is and has been, that we may interchange
our minds with yours on the subject ; since that is the object
of this conference with you.

By universal consent, and universal custom, the man who
enters a Congregational church, enters it by the consent of the
body, expressed by a vote, conditioned upon his acceptance of
certain Articles of Faith, and a Covenant.   That has been the
custom and rule of Congregational churches since there were
churches of that sort in the land.   It is the distinctive
peculiarity of Congregationalism.   Into the Anglican Church,
out of which our fathers came, a man is born, a birth-right
member.   He comes to church-membership, as he comes to

citizenship, through the accidents of birth and physical growth. The Congregational churches were founded upon the idea of gathering out from the community around them those who had personal faith in the Son of God, and a personal conse- cration to him, and uniting them together, in the vital and enduring bond of a covenant ; a personal covenant, accepted by each man for himself. Then he becomes a member of the church, and not before. He enters into reciprocal obligations with the church, — obligations which are more or less fully recognized and manifested in this covenant which he accepts.

The question before us, then, is a very simple one : Can the man who has entered into these reciprocal obligations with the church terminate those reciprocal obligations by his own action ? Not by his own positive action, even ; by his own negative action, with no notification made to any officer, with no public and declarative act, by a mere absence from the service, by an unexpressed change in his own state of mind, — can he thus terminate his reciprocal obligations to the church ? It seems to us that to ask the question is to answer it.

There is some definite point of time where his membership ceases. It is not like water gradually leaking out from a pail, — more to-day, and less to-morrow. A man is not a complete member of this Clinton Avenue Church to-day, and next week nine-tenths of a member, and the next week four-fifths, the next two-thirds, and, by and by, a half, then a quarter, then a fifth, until finally a vanishing point has been reached, and his membership has gone into the air. There is some definite point of time where his membership terminates ; and, having continued entire up to that point, it ceases entirely beyond that point.

Where is that point of time ? We say it is where the member, having expressed his desire to be released from the church, is released from it, by the church's action. It is said, upon the other hand, that that point is found where the mem- ber himself, by his own volition, without declarative action, even, without express notification, chooses to terminate his membership. It seems to us that this is a dangerous, and most eminently an absurd proposition

It wholly makes void the Covenant of the church. You see that in a moment. The covenant of the church reads how? Merely for illustration, I will read the covenant of the Plymouth Church. [Rev. Dr. BURTON, of Hartford, Conn: Is it the last edition?] It is the last that has been published, given to me by the Clerk of the church, and so, I presume, authentic : —

Do you solemnly covenant and agree to study the peace, purity, and liberty of this church? to love and watch over its members as your brethren? to receive from them all needful care and admonition? Will you labor together with us in the maintenance of its public worship and ordinances, submit to necessary discipline, and avoid all causes of scandal and offense, so long as in the providence of God you shall continue among us?

Now, there is a sense, no doubt, in which that expression, — "the providence of God," — as representing the divine superintendence over the creation, includes Satan himself ; includes the worst choices of the worst men ; but, as the expression is ordinarily used, it represents the chances and changes of our life, external to our own choices, as the things by which our life is shaped and governed. And, if it is not used in that sense here, it would apparently have been more appropriate to say : "so long as in the providence of your own mind, you do not elect to absent yourself from our services." A man who has entered into the covenant, on this hypothesis, may terminate his membership in that church, five minutes after he has publicly assented to this agreement. He may terminate it at the end of his first communion. He may have entered the church, and been solemnly received, and go out from it, with no more relation to it for all time to come ; and nobody would be the wiser about it until four years had passed away.

What is a Covenant? Not a legal contract, of course, where it concerns moral and spiritual interests, and is based upon no pecuniary consideration ; but it is a mutual agreement, for moral and spiritual ends. It is, at any rate, a solemn promise, on the part of the man who enters into it ; and a promise is a declaration of something which he will do, or will forbear, on conditions : of which promise or declaration the other party has a right to claim the fulfillment. Now, if you say that any

man may terminate these reciprocal obligations, expressed in
the covenant, at any moment after that expression, by his own
unuttered volition, certainly you make the covenant of no effect
or value afterward ; and no church, in our judgment, that was
self-respectful, would long continue to maintain it.   It could
not stand up in its great assembly, and welcome a man into
solemn reciprocal obligations with itself, who was at liberty to
wholly terminate those obligations, by his own inward choice,
the moment he walked from out its doorway.

Such a theory makes all Discipline impossible ; the very
suggestion of Discipline becomes absurd.   If a man's volition
is every thing that keeps him in the church of Christ, how are
you ever to reach him for any offense?   You may take the
most extreme offense you please.   We have all heard of Sher-
idan, how, when he was found drunk in the gutter, and a
watchman shook him and said, "What is your name?" he
said, in reply, in his drunken wit, "William Wilberforce."
Now, I suppose the case of a deacon in the church, who, after
a communion at which he has officiated, goes to his home, and
is found there in the evening drunk, — not dead drunk, raving
drunk, beating his wife and children, threatening them with
lethal weapons, uttering profane, foul, and licentious language, with the very spirit of the Devil flagrant in him, and
no more of the spirit of Christ.   He is found in this very state
and act by the Pastor, and the entire Examining Committee ;
and he looks up at them and says, "Gentlemen, I am not a member of your church.   I left it at the end of the communion
this afternoon."   And there is not a thing to be done to him ;
and there is not a word to be said to him ; and the church cannot even put on record an expression of censure against that
man ; — for, if he is out of its jurisdiction, it has no more right
to pass censure on him, than it has on the Shah of Persia.

Discipline is farcical, the very idea of it is preposterous, if
you accept this principle.   A picnic party might just as well
undertake to erect itself into a tribunal for the trial of offenses
against the State, as a church of Christ, no matter how large,
how intelligent, or how powerful, to make itself a tribunal, on
a basis of this sort, for the trial of an offender against the
most sacred and solemn laws of God and man.

The principle dissolves the Church, as an organized body, and reduces it, at once, to a mere casual and incoherent assembly, in attendance upon a particular ministry. For the same principle applies everywhere, if it is admitted as proper anywhere. If it is merely a man's volition that holds him to the church, and the covenant has no binding force upon him after he has refused to be bound by it, in his own unexpressed state of mind, what is there left to organize that church ? The church cannot retreat from its obligation to the individual without a vote ; but he can retreat from his obligation to the church without a word. Inclosing such a church from the world would be just as easy and wise a thing as undertaking to inclose a field by building a fence along one side of it, and leaving all the rest an open common. That is precisely what the Church of Christ is, on such a theory of church-membership.

The same principle applies, instantly, to every officer. They have applied it, in one of the churches of this city, in the case of a Deacon who resigned after years of as faithful service as I believe has often occurred in that church ; and it was ruled, and voted by the assembly, that his resignation made the vacancy, and there was no occasion whatever for accepting the resignation on the part of the church, the vacancy occurring, and being complete, at the instant the resignation was resolved upon. They might have gone still further, and affirmed that the moment he absented himself from his duties in the diaconate, without any notice, those duties had no longer any claim on his attention : the office was vacant, and the vacancy was complete. And precisely the same principle applies to the Pastor of the church ; so that no man can tell, unless he can enter into the interior state of mind of the eminent Pastor of the Plymouth Church, when he goes out of the door at night, after the Sunday service, whether that church has a Pastor or not, or whether he continues a member of it.

If that principle is to be recognized and allowed, — that the membership ceases when a man's state of mind in regard to it changes, — it would dissolve human society itself, if the principle should be carried out. For human society stands upon covenants, upon contracts, and upon the power to enforce them. That is the office of government. That is the office of the courts. And while, as I have said, the covenant which a man enters into with a Congregational church, when he becomes a member of it, is not for secular purposes, or upon pecuniary conditions, and therefore is not a contract of which the law can take cognizance, and to the fulfillment of which it can hold him, it is as binding as any, in the forum of conscience. If, then, a man can relieve himself from the obligations of that covenant, so solemn, so public, so formal, with a large assembly, by a mere change in his inner purpose, why should he not be at liberty to release himself, in the same way, and with equal facility, from every covenant ? As a citizen he cannot be thus released. Society says he shall not be. But as a being responsible to God, if I can terminate my relation with the Church of the Pilgrims, this instant, by determining not to go inside its doors any more, I can terminate my relations in human life to any party with whom I am in reciprocal obligations. You carry out that principle, and you inevitably disintegrate human society.

There was a prodigious noise made in this city a year ago, or somewhere thereabouts, — I don't remember the exact time, — when it was said that a member of one of the churches of the city had violated his covenant not to repeat certain statements, which were included in a certain important private paper. Why on earth had he not a right to violate it, if he had chosen to ? If a man may terminate obligations by his own change of mind, at any time, with the church of Christ, who is to quarrel with one who does that, outside of the church, which he is permitted and authorized to do within it ?

Brethren, I speak within bounds on this subject when I say that if you admit this principle, then a bridge of air is a solid structure in comparison with a Congregational church. It seems like arguing that the earth is solid, and not a gas, — like arguing that the sunshine casts light and not shadow, — to argue the principle. But we have to argue it, because the opposite has been affirmed.

And now a word about a matter incidental.

It has been said that we were offered a Mutual Council on this question, on condition that we would make it read: "Does the Word of God, and the usage of the Congregational churches," and so on. The statement is not precisely correct, although, undoubtedly, in intention it was so. We were not offered a Mutual Council; but the pastor of the Plymouth Church offered to use his influence with that church, to induce it to unite with our churches in calling such a Council, on that one point, provided that change should be made. He did not agree, however, to do the same thing in regard to two other subjects, which were to us of grave and essential importance; so that this became a minor matter. But we were not able to assent to even this modification; and possibly we may have been criticised for it. We were honest in our judgment about it, and I will state the reason of that judgment.

Congregationalism, as we understand it, is a definite, actual, historical system, which has its rules, and usages, and laws; which is supposed, believed, by those who live in it and love it, to be based upon and in accordance with the Word of God. It is the function of a Council to come together and testify what Congregationalism is; not to testify what Congregationalism ought to be. That is a question never presented, within my knowledge, to a Congregational Council. It may testify what the customs and rules are; but it cannot interpret the Word of God, to show that those customs and rules ought to be changed. That is a function which belongs to Councils in the Roman Catholic Church, if anywhere, and not among us. That is a prerogative which threatens the right of private judgment, of individual churches and persons, if Councils shall ever assume it. And when they undertake to enter on the performance of it, the field opened will be found illimitable.

Suppose, for example, that the Plymouth Church, in this city, were to vote hereafter to hold its services on the seventh day, instead of the first, and to baptize everybody by immersion, as it now baptizes a number, — in other words, were to connect itself with the Seventh-day Baptists. It would be legitimate to call a Council to ask whether that is in accordance with the order and usage of Congregational churches. But would any Council come together to consider and decide the question whether the views of the Seventh-day Baptists are scriptural and Divine?

Suppose an eminent Congregational divine should come to the conclusion, through much study, that when the Lord spoke of everlasting punishment in the Gospel of Matthew he did not mean a punishment "everlasting," in the ordinary sense of that word, but a punishment which, whether it be longer or less, belongs to the life to come; and that, after preaching in Universalist pulpits for some time, he at last should receive a call from a Universalist society. It would be legitimate to call a Council to consider whether it is in accordance with the order of Congregational churches to install such a minister over such a society; but would a Council come together to determine the question whether that interpretation of the Lord's word is in harmony with the teachings of Scripture, and with the teachings of the Fathers? and whether that is sound or unsound which has been written on the subject in modern times? If it did, it had better bid farewell to its homes and churches; for it would take its punishment in this life, and that punishment would be as nearly eternal as any thing in this world ever will be.

We affirm, then, that the Question, as presented by us, is the proper question here to be considered; and that it must be decided by the Council, absolutely, that a member does *not* terminate his membership by simply absenting himself from the services of the church, into which he was received by a formal covenant, and with which he entered into reciprocal obligations. Unless our whole conception of the matter is untrue, — radically, thoroughly, completely untrue, — that must be decided thus.

So we come, then, to the second Question : —

Second: During the voluntary absence of a member from the ordinances, if specific charges, of grossly unchristian conduct, are presented against him by a brother in the church, to which charges he declines to answer, is it in accordance with the order and usage of Congregationalism that the church shall withhold inquiry as to the alleged wickedness, and, in face of such public assertion of his offenses, shall treat him as if still unaccused, dropping his name from its roll "without reflection upon him"?

You observe, Brethren, that the question is very specific. "During the voluntary absence of a member:" not when he is out of the country, and cannot appear; not when he is deadly sick, and cannot appear; while he is a voluntary absentee. "If specific charges:" not general intimations. "Of grossly unchristian conduct:" not of venial offenses, peccadillos, improprieties of manner, occasional lapses; "grossly unchristian conduct:" — acts that show the absence of the spirit of Christ, and the presence of the opposite; acts which may be criminal even in the eye of human law. "Are presented against him by a brother in the church:" not by public rumor; not by one outside of the church, and so not responsible to it; but by a brother in the church. "To which charges he declines to answer:" neither affirming nor denying. "Is it in accordance with the order and usage of Congregationalism," *then*, that the church shall treat him as if not accused, and shall drop his name from its roll without censure?

It seems to us a strange thing that this question should need to be asked, and need to be answered, at this day, after so long a development of Congregationalism, in its purity, in the land. But it does require such an answer; and we trust that you will give this also with emphasis,— will give it, as they say in the French Assembly, "with effusion."

Of course, neither of our authorized Platforms knows any thing of such a practice. The Cambridge Platform knows nothing of absentees, even: they did not, I suppose, exist in that time. The Boston Platform speaks of the matter in these words:

"A church-member, removing his residence to another place, does not thereby throw off his responsibility to the church with which he is in covenant. If his removal is permanent, he ought to seek, and unless he is liable to some just censure, — in which case he must be dealt with as an offender, — he has a right to receive, a letter of dismission."

In one of our letters we copied from a former Manual of Plymouth Church, of 1854. I do not quote it now to show what is the present practice of Plymouth Church. I quote it to show what its views then were, as expressed in its careful and large Manual, seven years after it was organized as a church.

It says that in all large churches, especially in all city churches, where the membership is perpetually changing, it comes to pass, in the course of years, that there are numerous absentees enrolled upon the list of members, whose names are entirely unknown to the active members of the church.

" It is proper, therefore, that the church from time to time appoint Committees of Inquiry upon the cases of absentees, or of members who, though residing in our vicinity, are supposed to be living in the neglect of Covenant obligations. . . . If, in the course of their investigations, they find matters worthy of discipline, they should act precisely as it is proper for church-members to act in any case where facts requiring the discipline of the church are brought to their knowledge."

We suppose that to be the early, the ancient, the general, and the proper conduct of the matter.

Observe carefully the distinction between this question and any other, and do not let it become confused with any other, in your minds. We do not ask : What shall be done with a man who has been a member of the Congregational Church, who has become converted to the Roman Catholic opinion, and has connected himself with the Roman Catholic Church, but in whom we still discern the spirit of Christ? We do not ask : What shall be done with one who has become a Unitarian, and joined a society with which we are not in intercommunion and public fellowship, but in whom we recognize yet the spirit and temper of the Master? We do not ask, even : What shall be done with a man who has become honestly convinced that he entered the church under a mistake, and has never been a regenerated person? We have no quarrel, we raise no issue, with the provision, for example, in the manual of the Plymouth Church of Chicago, — a church which we invited and desired to be present to-day ; whose brilliant pastor, and some delegate from whose very earnest membership, we wanted to welcome, representing views sympathetic with those which we oppose, so far as we understand them. We wanted every church ; but most of all we wanted, if there was any distinction, those which were probably opposed to us. We do not, I say, make any issue with this provision : —

" If any member be convinced that he is not truly regenerated, but that he professed religion under self-deception, and shall request a dissolution of his connection with this church, if there be no scandal in his life requiring discipline, his request shall be granted, he having first been duly labored with, by a simple vote declarative of the facts ; which vote shall be publicly announced at the next succeeding Communion season."

I suppose that that principle may be, to some of you, unfamiliar, at any rate ; but here, in our question, we raise no issue concerning a case of that kind. We limit it to the case where there *is* scandal in his life, requiring investigation, and, if it be found that the charge is justified, requiring discipline : can he then be treated as if unaccused ?

We never saw the Manual that allowed it. The only instrument that has ever been referred to as giving any sanction whatever to such a thing is what is called the "Heads of Agreement," familiar to you, I suppose, which was quoted, with a ludicrous incorrectness, in one of the principal meetings of the Plymouth Church in this city : —

"It may sometimes come to pass that a church-member, not otherwise scandalous, may sinfully withdraw and divide himself from the communion of the church to which he belongeth ; in which case, when all due means for the reducing him prove ineffecttual, he having thereby cut himself off from that church's communion, the church may justly esteem and declare itself discharged of any further inspection over him."

He must be "not otherwise scandalous." His withdrawing is sinful. "All due means" must have been used to reclaim him. Only when these have proved "ineffectual," can the church declare itself discharged of further inspection over him. And this is included under the head of "Censures." And this is contained in an instrument which never had any general authority among Congregational churches ! To justify such a practice by such a rule — misquoting it, after all — is like founding a title to real estate upon an incorrect copy of an insufficient conveyance ; and you can tell us, Mr. Moderator [turning to the Associate Moderator] of how much value such an instrument would be.

It is a dangerous thing, as well as unknown to Congregationalism ; — dangerous, because the man is either innocent or guilty. If he be innocent, being still within the jurisdiction of the church, it is the business of the church to investigate the facts, and, finding him innocent, to give him its verdict and vindication, and send him out with no spot upon his name, with his banner high uplifted, and unspotted in the air. And if, on the other hand, he be guilty, it is the business of the church to find that out, and to use all possible means for reclaiming him. For it seems to be strangely forgotten, sometimes, that the office of discipline is remedial; the end of it is reformation, the re-establishment of the offender in his relations, not with the church merely, but with God, whose Spirit speaks and works in the church. And the church is false to its duty to the man, derelict to the obligations it solemnly took upon itself, unless it find out whether he be guilty, and, if it find him thus, make strenuous and continued effort to reclaim and restore him.

Whether he is a brilliant and powerful man, or whether he is the humblest man, that is no matter. The soul is that which Christ loved and sought, and suffered for, and the soul is that which the church ought to work for; and, if it find that its member is guilty, and cannot be reclaimed, after all fit means are earnestly used, then it is to send him out with a verdict of censure on him, — which he has deserved, which he has properly incurred, which he has brought upon himself by his violation of the obligations he was under to the church, and the obligations he was under to God.

This is for the education of the church. A man is not so much educated by what he hears, as by what he does. It is character revealed in action that trains a man. A church is not educated by hearing splendid sermons. It is educated by working those sermons into practice, and by incorporating them in its life; by setting itself to hard work, to difficult duties, and not shirking things because they are disagreeable.

It is necessary for the vindication of the church before the world. This Platform says properly, that though vice be tolerated and even honored in the public community, it may not be tolerated in the Church of Christ. A church has its power by manifestation of its zeal for righteousness; by showing that the distinction between truth and falsehood, between purity and unchastity, between fraud and honesty, is something which it recognizes as important and Divine. So, if it has a guilty member within it, it must try to reclaim him; finally, failing in that, it must exclude him, with censure, as unrepentant; for its own training, for its own vindication of its name before the public, and for the honor of Christ,— who taught Timothy to keep himself pure, and not to be partaker of other men's sin ; who said, by James, that the wisdom which cometh from above is first pure, then peaceable ; and who, by Paul, commanded the Corinthians to cast out from among them the wicked person.

We hold that when a man, no matter though he be voluntarily absent, not having yet sundered his connection with the church, the church not having consented to any such termination of his membership, is accused of specific and gross offenses, by a brother in the church, himself responsible to it if he fails to prove his charges, the church has no right to drop that man "without reflection upon him." It must investigate, to be true to its trust, true to its obligations, to the man, and to the Master.

And I wish to say one word more ; because there have been rumors stealthily and widely circulated in regard to our churches,— the church of which I am the pastor, and of which I have had the honor and happiness to be the pastor for almost twenty-eight years,— that this has been a common practice with us ; certainly that cases similar to this have occurred among us. I therefore say, here and now, on my responsibility as a Christian man and minister, knowing whereof I affirm, and appealing to every member of the church to verify or correct the statement, that no such case has ever occurred among us ; and that no such case, with the rules under which we have lived all these years, ever could occur.

I suppose it is the experience of every pastor that now and then there come to him intimations concerning and against the Christian character of some of his church-members ; intimations which, in our commercial communities, are very often connected with a man's business affairs. He is unsuccessful, has been caught in the grip of some sudden panic, and his property has been wrested from him. Other people feel that he has deceived them, as to his means, resources, credit; that he has obtained from them more than they would have given had they known the exact facts. Therefore, they are moved to feel that he has been intentionally dishonest ; and they say so. Or, sometimes, such intimations come through family disagreements, or social entanglements, of one sort or another. I have invariably said one thing, in substance : Vague intimations I cannot receive. They pass me as the wind does. I may hear of such some time about you, and I shall not suffer myself to be prejudiced by them against you. If you have any knowledge of facts, which you will put in a specific form, giving dates and names, with facts and witnesses, and present them to me as charges which you are willing to be responsible for to the church, they shall come before the Committee, without a day's delay. They shall be prosecuted to their issue, without fear or favor of any man.

That has not once failed to be done ; until it came either to excommunication, on the one hand, or to acquittal and vindication, on the other. We have no power to drop a man "without reflection upon him." He goes out excommunicated ; or he goes out with honorable and affectionate letters of commendation ; or he goes out by withdrawal of watch and discipline, which is a censure of the church, only less than excommunication, but the infliction of which implies no moral blame, no scandalous offense, on the part of him against whom it is issued. A man has sometimes gone to a religious society with which we were not in fellowship, — as has happened in two cases, — for whose character we had respect, in whose character we had a degree of confidence, but who did not go, through change of opinion, into any church with which we were in communion. In one case, where a man went to another church, joining it without giving us notice, without applying for any letter, in a spirit of sudden anger and half-insane hostility against some of the church-members, we did the same thing. Where they have been honest and upright, and no accusation has been preferred against them, we have simply withdrawn from them watch and discipline ; there being no charge whatever against their moral character.

I make this statement emphatic. I cover with it the entire

history of the church. I have no doubt Dr. Budington
would make as emphatic a statement in regard to this
church. But, after all, this is comparatively unimportant.
Even if we had done this thing, which we certainly have not,
with our earnest convictions we should ask you to condemn
us. And we ask you for an answer to this second Question,
which shall be explicit and decisive.

We come, then, to the third Question : —

Third : When such a member is charged with having "circulated
and promoted scandals derogatory to the Christian integrity of the
Pastor, and injurious to the reputation of the church," if he be publicly released, by the church which he confronts, without examination of the facts and without censure, from all further responsibility
to it, has the rule of Christ in the xviiith chapter of Matthew, concerning the treatment of a trespassing brother, as commonly
administered in Congregational churches, been maintained ? or is
it distinctly disregarded, in a case which called for its careful observance ? "

In this question you observe a specific offense is pointed
out, that we may know from you your judgment as to whether
that particular offense is one that ought to come under the
cognizance, and, if it be proved, under the condemnation, of
the Church of Christ.

It has been sometimes said that, while it would be admitted
that a member of the church who should assail another with
personal slanders ought to be brought before the tribunal for
investigation, and for the adjudication of the case, when a
member of the church makes statements concerning the
pastor of the church itself, it is the business of the pastor
alone to make any complaint, and no member of the church
has a right to interpose if the pastor does not take up the
case ; that it is not a personal offense, in any proper sense,
in any such sense as brings it within the ordinary administration of church discipline. And that is the question which
you are asked to consider.

We hold that it is ; that it is not merely an offense, that it
is one of the gravest of offenses, to utter statements scandalous in their nature, and having no justification, against the
character of a minister in Christ, who is established in the

pastorate of a numerous congregation. It is to strike at the life of the Gospel there. It is to put a hand upon its influence, to limit it. It is to put a hand upon infidelity there, to invigorate it. It is to lay its hand upon Christ himself, so far as He is represented in his ministers, and to hold Him back from his kingly march along the earth.

We hold it to be one of the gravest of all possible offenses, — an offense which shows, if it be committed, one of the worst of tempers ; an offense which works more widely for mischief than almost any other that can be committed by any member of any church. We hold that, as concerning the humblest pastor of the humblest congregation, where men meet together to worship God ; for the usefulness of that pastor depends upon his character, and upon their confidence in his character. If that confidence be diminished, or destroyed, his influence for good is thereby checked or killed. The ermine is said to die if its fur be soiled, with a stain which sticks to it. The minister's usefulness dies, if his name be clouded with a suspicion, started by the scandal which some one has circulated, and which is not afterward and utterly thrown off. And the most transcendent abilities, the most eminent genius, cannot accomplish the work of usefulness and of divine service which is due from them, and glorious to them, if there be any ultimate suspicion left upon the name.

And if those statements be made concerning one so eminent in the pulpit that his words go everywhere, on the wings of the press ; are read everywhere with admiring love and with responsive enthusiasm, — by the invalid in the sick-chamber, by the merchant in his counting-room, by the operatives in the factory, by the legislators in the halls of Congress, by the gatherings of men upon the remote frontier, — then we count that offense, the circulating of scandals unjustified against such a name, an offense against every invalid, and every merchant, and every frontiersman, to whom the unblemished name and fame of that minister are dear, and to whose welcoming hearts his words bring their ministry of consolation and of strength.

If his name be known wherever the English tongue is spoken, it is an offense against Christendom. It is the crime *de Lèse-majesté;* an offense against sovereign abilities and renown. It is an offense that strikes more directly at the life of the Gospel in the world than any other which it comes within man's reach to commit. It is a public offense; and the humblest member of the church in which it has been committed has right not only, but is under the highest possible obligation, to complain, to formulate charges, to urge charges, to prosecute charges, and to demand that the church which has the jurisdiction of the case shall not let the offender go beyond its reach until he has shown himself innocent, or has repented in dust and ashes.

Brethren, it is more than setting the torch to the Ephesian dome. It is striking at the essential soul-life of multitudes of men and women throughout Christendom. And if that is not an offense of which church-members may complain, — if that is not an offense of which the church should take cognizance, — then the member who deliberately shoots his minister dead at the communion-table may as well be sent out " without reflection upon him ! "

The fourth Question is : —

Fourth: Was the action of the Plymouth Church, in the case of discipline issued by it Oct. 31, 1873, as presented in the published documents, in accordance with the order and usage of Congregational churches? Or was it an apparent departure from these, tending, in the circumstances, to injure and offend other churches in fellowship, and warranting apprehension and remonstrance on our part?

What was that action? The published documents which are referred to will be found in the pamphlet, from pages 22 to 26.* You observe that we do not ask you for a final judicial judgment concerning the Plymouth Church. We ask whether there was so much appearance of a departure from the ordinary custom and rule of Congregational churches as, under the circumstances, justified us in remonstrating ; and that is all that we ask. What was the action, then, as it appears in these documents ?

The first of these was published, you will notice, by the member himself, accused of the offenses, in the paper which

---

* Pp. 23 to 26, of this volume.

he edits and owns. The second of them was published by the pastor, in the paper which he edits and controls. The third is the card of the Clerk of Plymouth Church, published in the New York Sun. We have evidence, if it be needful, that these are the authentic and exact documents. The action, then, will be found in the final Resolution adopted by the church, on the 25th page : "*Resolved*, That this Committee recommend to the church that the name of —— be dropped from the roll of membership of the church, as provided by Rule No. 7 of the Manual." Rule No. 7 is quoted in the next document, and is quoted correctly : —

"Members may be dropped from the roll of the church, with or without notice to them, as may be deemed just, by a two-thirds vote of the church, upon the recommendation of the Examining Committee, either upon their own application, or, in case they have abandoned their connection with the church by prolonged absence or otherwise, upon the application of any other person."

It does not appear from the report of the Examining Committee that any application had been made by the member referred to, to be dropped, or that any application had been made on his behalf, by any other person, to the same effect. But this may have been. It would, at any rate, be only a formal departure from the rule. It does appear, from the Report which precedes this Resolution, and upon which the Resolution is founded, that charges had been made against this gentleman, by a brother in the church, — the charge itself showing, in the expression "a member of this church," that he who presented it, as well as he against whom it was brought, was within the membership. It appears that these charges had been sent to the member accused, on the 6th of October ; that he had replied that he did not consider himself a member of the church, and had not been for nearly four years an attendant of it, that the pastor did not consider him a member, and that he did not hold himself amenable to its jurisdiction ; that the Examining Committee did not receive that reply as a bar to further proceedings, and a sufficient answer, but again sent to him the charges, in writing, with a notification of the time at which they desired that he should make answer to the same ; that he did make such answer, repeating what he had said before, — that it was nearly or about four years since he had terminated his connection with the church, and, therefore, the document addressed to him as a church-member he could not receive.

Then it appears that, without further investigation of these charges, and without any subsequent communication with him, so far as is here shown, the Committee recommended, and the church adopted that recommendation by a two-thirds vote, that he be dropped from the roll.

It further appears, from the charge itself, which is upon the 23d page,* that it alleged his "having circulated and promoted scandals, derogatory to the Christian integrity of the pastor, and injurious to the reputation of the church." They were statements not as to the pastor's manner, not as to his modes of speech, not as to any thing concerning the externals of his life, but as to his "Christian integrity," and, therefore, "injurious to the reputation of the church." It appears that these alleged statements were such that the member controlling the paper in which the charge was printed, did not feel at liberty to give, from motives of proper delicacy, any currency to the specifications.

These things appear in the published documents; and we are not dependent upon other evidence, or upon newspaper report, for any of these facts. Then it appears, from the card of the Clerk, — an official card, written the next day, and published two days afterward, — that the name of the member so specifically and so seriously accused, was, "in accordance with the facts, with the rule, and without reflection upon him, taken from the roll."

These are the facts, which plainly, and in their successive order, appear, from these widely published documents : that a member of the church, absent from its services, but not as yet released from his connection with it by the church, was accused by another member of having committed this grave offense ; that he neither affirmed nor denied in regard to it ; that, when called upon finally to answer to the charges, he still neither denied nor affirmed ; and that at last his name was

---

* P. 23, of this volume.

dropped from the roll, under the rule as it is said, by a two-thirds vote, and "without reflection upon him."

We were startled and surprised by these extraordinary facts. It seemed to us that the case came properly under the legitimate and necessary operation of those principles which I have already been discussing, and our conception concerning which I have aimed freely, frankly, simply, fully, to set before you. It seemed to us, that, if the member accused was innocent, it should be made to appear, and his name be freed from all complication or suspicion of the offense. If he was guilty, it should be equally made to appear ; and if he could be reclaimed, and brought to repentance, he should be thus restored to fellowship with the church, and with the Master ; and, if he could not be, he should be shown not to be worthy of a place in the Church of Christ, against which he had been sinning, if what was alleged was true, so seriously, so certainly, and so long. This was the way it seemed to us ; and that the very last and worst thing to be done was to drop his name without any reflection upon him, in the face of these charges, not withdrawn, not explained, and not even denied.

If the Committee had said, "The charges are frivolous," that would have been right. If the Committee had said, "The charges are not proven," that would have been right ; provided the facts were so, the action based on them would have been right. If they had said, "We cannot get evidence ;" if they had said, "The man is insane ;" that would have been right. But they received the charges, sent them to him, heard his answer, sent them back, requiring a further answer ; received his repetition of his former reply ; and then terminated the case by their Report adopted by the church : — leaving the accused without vindication ; leaving, as we thought, the honor of the church in danger of being deeply stained.

In the circumstances, this seemed to us to warrant apprehension and remonstrance on our part. What were the circumstances ? I shall not refer at all to any matters of private scandal and personal gossip which went on in the streets, and on the ferry-boats, and over the country, as I suppose and

have been told, and which makes our passage through a good
many months, preceding that 31st of October, to be remembered as one might remember a journey through a valley full
of grinning skulls and horrid stenches. I shall not refer to
that. I banish it from recollection; and have only to speak
of circumstances which are as patent as the highway, as indis-
putable as the earth.

The first of them is, that a long, circumstantial, defamatory
statement, concerning the pastor of the Plymouth Church,
was published in a certain newspaper in New York, in November of 1872; the authority for the statements therein contained being attributed to this member of Plymouth Church.
I accept the statements as absolutely false. What I affirm
before you is the fact of their publication; and nothing else.

The second circumstance is, that no denial of his authority
having been given for these statements was made by the member to whom reference had been made. Such a denial would
have ended the matter, instantaneously.

The third circumstance is, that two months after, there came
from him a letter, published in the newspapers, in which he
spoke of the necessity of telling the true story, if he should
deny the false, and adding that when the truth was a sword,
God's mercy commanded it to be sheathed; with other
remarks to the same effect, which I will not quote.

The fourth circumstance is, that out of this preceding train
of events there arose wide concern and alarm among the
multitudes of fervent, enthusiastic admirers of him whose
genius had so long made the pulpit of that church famous,
and whose influence had been so great a power for the furtherance of the truth and of liberty, in this land and in others;
an alarm which was represented by articles in leading papers;
particularly, perhaps, by articles in the leading religious paper
of the West, of our denomination, published in Chicago, to
which I will not further refer.

The question arose in many minds: What can all this
mean? It was perhaps still further urged upon many by the
appearance of an article in the newspaper owned and edited
by this member of Plymouth Church, in the month of April
of last year, in which it was said of Mr. Beecher: —

"He is an instance of a man who, seeking to save his life, is losing it. Long acknowleged as the most brilliant popular preacher in the country, a compliment which nobody not in any sect begrudges him, but cheerfully pays, he is, nevertheless, year by year, declining in moral weight, not only with the church, but in the community at large. To think one thing and say another, to hold one philosophy in public and another in private, to offer one morality to the multitude and keep another for one's self, is a degradation to no man so much as to a minister, and a blot upon nothing so much as upon religion."

I do not know whose pen traced the lines. I know that they appeared, as I have stated ; and I know that the impression made by them was sharp and painful.

What did it all mean ? That it did not mean that Mr. Beecher was guilty of the offenses charged against him, in the original scandalous statement, was made plainly to appear by a card from him, published in a Brooklyn newspaper, widely circulated, on the 30th of June of last year, in which he pronounced the stories that had been circulating concerning him grossly untrue, and stamped them as utterly false, and without foundation. I may not have given the words exactly ; but that is not important. That was the substance of his statement ; which carried relief, unquestionably, to multitudes of minds, and which brought him into direct antagonism with all these stories which had been circulating concerning him ; which affirmed the circulation of these stories, now stamped by him whom they concerned as utterly and absolutely false, a crime against the truth, of the grossest kind, as well as a crime against the purity of manners and of speech.

After that card, these charges were presented to the church ; by a member of the church, who professed to be moved by so strong an impulse that he felt it was from the Spirit of God. He must vindicate his pastor ; he must vindicate his church. He asked no advice ; he would take no advice to the contrary, from anybody. A respectable member of the church, formerly one of its officers, of unblemished character himself, he was moved to this office by that strong inward impulse, without suggestion from any one else.

This train of circumstances, then, had preceded ; and now we advance to the action of the Committee, sending the charges ; then to the fact that the member who was accused of this offense had been recognized up to that time as a member of the church — I will speak of that more at length in a moment ; then to the fact that he was present himself in the final church-meeting, and offered to answer to any charge, not of having circulated scandalous statements, but of having slandered the pastor.

All these circumstances together, coming one after another, seemed to us to make that action not only contrary to the usual custom and rule of Congregational churches, but such an action as would be fruitful of mischief, as we felt, to the church itself, to the pastor, who had declared his innocence, and to all the churches neighboring and in fellowship.

But here the question arises : Was the member dropped ? or was it a mere clerical correction of the roll, recognizing the termination of a membership which had absolutely terminated four years before ? Of course much light will be shed upon this question by the answer which you shall give to the first of those which we have presented in our Letter-Missive.

In our particular answer to it, all that we need say, or nearly all, is derived from the Manual of the church itself. Its Covenant seems to contemplate a more permanent relationship of the member than would be one terminable by his own volition, expressed by nothing but his absence. Its rule in regard to the Dismission of members is this : " It is expected that members, on removing from the city, or to other churches in the city " — will what ? — will notify the clerk that their membership with us has ceased ? — " will ask for letters of dismission and recommendation ;" as members, of course. " A request for such a letter may be announced at the weekly prayer meeting. If no objection is made to the clerk, he must issue a letter accordingly, and strike the name of the member dismissed from the roll of the church." Dismissed when the letter is issued ; but not before. " If objection is made, the matter must be submitted to the Examining Committee." Why ? If the member, in consequence of his removal from the city, perhaps months before, is out of their jurisdiction, what have they to do with him ? Clearly, in the contemplation of this Rule, in spite of his removal, he is within the jurisdiction still.

Observe, also, Rule 7 : " Members may be dropped." Members may be dropped ! Not, " members terminating their membership, by absence, may have their names erased from the roll." " Members may be dropped, with or without notice, by a two-thirds vote of the church." Suppose it is only a majority vote ? — they continue Members, not dropped.

It seemed palpable, to us inevitable, that in the contemplation of this Manual, in the contemplation of the Examining Committee, who had once and again sent these charges, in the contemplation of all the precedents and principles of Congregationalism, this member, accused of having circulated these statements, which the pastor, over his own signature, had denounced as utterly, grossly untrue, and stamped as false, was still a member of that church.

And there was a witness concerning it which appeared entirely unimpeachable. It was the witness of the pastor himself, who, writing in April, 1872, concerning two gentlemen, members of that church, of whom this was one, said : " If I have said any thing injurious to the reputation of either, or have detracted from their standing and fame as Christian gentlemen, and *members of my church*, I revoke it all." That was written in April, 1872. If this membership had terminated at all, until the church terminated it, it had terminated four years before, at the end of 1869 ; and the testimony of the Pastor should certainly be received as showing, at least, his personal conviction at that subsequent point of time.

It was represented to us as well, — we will present, if it is wished, evidence for the truth of the representation, to the Council, — that two years after this member had withdrawn from Plymouth Church, and ceased to cross its threshold, the Examining Committee had sent a sub-committee to him, to confer with him about the continuance of his relations ; that three years after, they had sent another. They treated him as a member to the very last ; and we felt that he was a member, accused of as grave an offense as could well be alleged against any man, brought, properly, as a member, before the jurisdiction of that church, and then left to depart from it, without investigation, and without censure. And it seemed to us, that, by such extraordinary action as that, all the ends of discipline were sacrificed.

There was one thing shown, and that was all. And that was noble, that was superb. It was the magnificent loyalty of that church to its pastor, — a loyalty which he had deserved by twenty-five years of faithful service, splendid and eminent, in it, and in the land ; a loyalty that was most honorable to it, for the affectionate and chivalrous qualities from which it sprang, and which it revealed. That was shown. I honored the church before. I honored it for its great and noble Christian work, in many departments and many directions of Christian effort. I honored it for the sweet and saintly souls that are within it. I honored and I loved it, for the friends of my own, friends of almost thirty years, who are members of it, who now look on me, no doubt, with disfavor, perhaps with a hostility which I in no degree reciprocate ; from whom I will not be divided, by any change within myself, while life continues. But I never honored the church so much as for that splendid outburst of loyalty to its pastor. But that was *all* that was shown.

It has been said that the minister had vindicated his own name fully, perfectly, already. Let it be admitted that that had been done, for all fair and sympathetic minds. It would have done no harm, after that, to have had the further and final vindication of a judicial verdict from the church, against the member who was alleged, and provided he was proved, to have uttered the calumnies. It would have saved the pastor from assaults and stings which come against him now, whenever a paper in the interest of the liquor-seller, in the interest of a political party opposed to him, feels itself moved to strike him with its stab. It would have done that, though it were not needful for fair minds, certainly for sympathetic minds. It would have done no harm ; and would have gone into history forever, with honor to the church

But every thing else was sacrificed. The ascertainment of innocence or guilt, the apportionment of blame, the reclamation of the sinful, the punishment of the guilty, the assertion by the church of the governing authority of righteousness and truth, the vindication of the honor of the Master,—all were sacrificed. We felt that a stigma had come upon the name of Congregationalism itself. We felt that our churches would be considered as in the habit of adopting the same principles, and applying them in like manner, in their own practice. We felt that the great interests of purity and truth in the world were not maintained and advanced, but were lowered and hindered, by that action. And, therefore, we remonstrated. Our question with you is, whether we were not justified in remonstrating?

We wrote earnestly, because we felt strongly. We wrote earnestly, because we thought our constant Christian friendship, of so many years, gave us a right to write with earnestness. Were we not justified in remonstrating against action like this, involving principles like these? If you decide that we were not, tell us so frankly, and we will do the best we can to take back our fault. If you decide that we were not, we shall know, at any rate, what privileges Congregational churches do not possess. And if you say, that in front of that case, signal as it was, prominent, startling, involving all these principles, throwing this shadow on ourselves, threatening the fame of every similar church in the city, we had no right to make remonstrance and protest, because we were in fellowship with that church,— then I know this: that never again, so long as life continues, shall I give the Right Hand of Fellowship to any church, or be in a Council which gives the Right Hand of Fellowship to any church, till I have been permitted to share the omniscience of God Himself as to what that church will do, to the end of my life on earth, and as long as the church which I represent continues to exist!

We come now to the fifth and last Question on which I am to speak.

Fifth: In view of the aforesaid action of Plymouth Church, and of the fact that this is maintained as in accordance with its customary policy, what is the duty, concerning that church, of the churches calling this Council? Especially, what is their duty in regard to continuing in their fellowship with it?

It is so maintained, as you will observe, as in accordance

with their customary policy. It is said to have occurred in the orderly, proper, customary operation and administration of Rule No. 7, of the Church. That is distinctly affirmed in the card of the Clerk, which follows the report of the Committee, and the action of the church. The case has never been referred to in any document which I have seen, representing the mind of the members of Plymouth Church, as in any degree an exceptional case. If such representation has been made, I am not aware of it. The arguments which were presented in the church-meetings, at which the action was adopted and was afterward defended, all contemplated it as natural, normal, a customary incident of the administration of the usual rule and law of the church.

The same principle has been subsequently applied, as I have said, in the case of the resignation of one of the Deacons, an honored and useful officer of the church. Plymouth Church, I believe, takes the ground that this is the right and proper thing for it to do, in accordance with its own sense of Christian propriety and duty; in accordance with its own rule; and that there was nothing whatever unusual or exceptional in this case which has been brought before us. It simply exhibits the preferred and permanent policy of the church.

Now the question is as to continuing, what is our duty as to continuing, in *our* fellowship with it? — not the fellowship which we have with Baptists and Methodists, excellent Christian brethren, whom we respect, and with whom we are in kindly relations, of common work and common hope, but who are in no sense responsible for us, and for whom we are in no sense responsible. Our peculiar fellowship with Plymouth Church is one, as we understand it, of denominational alliance; of mutual responsibility; of common responsibility before the public. It is that more intimate fellowship which is referred to in the Platform, as the more intimate communion exercised in asking and giving counsel, in giving and receiving admonition, and in other related offices. What is our duty in regard to continuing in this peculiar, denominational, intimate, responsible fellowship with Plymouth Church?

We feel, Brethren, that, unless we have the right to remonstrate against what seems to us wrong in that church, we must in some way be extricated from our relations of mutual responsibility to it, and with it, before the public. We have not the least desire to cloud its reputation, or hinder its usefulness, or diminish its numbers. Let it go on and build larger structures, and gather in more numerous audiences,— more admiring and attentive it cannot gather. Let it break forth and spread on every side. But when it does an act like this, adopts a policy destructive as this, we feel that we, dwelling near it, in this public fellowship and intimate communion, must be released from all the responsibility. Our churches have been steadily, for five months, working toward that result. We shall wish this church God-speed; we shall heartily rejoice in their prosperity. But we cannot be, as we feel now, in public and permanent fellowship with them, and be liable at the same time to have every remonstrance urged by us, on behalf of principles which to us are vital and organific, resented as an intermeddling and an offense.

Therefore we have asked you, from different and distant parts of the land, to meet us here, and hear our case, and then to advise us what to do. We are sorry that that advice should imply, in the mind of anybody, censure upon Plymouth Church. We can't help that. We do not ask you for that censure. We ask you for advice to *us;* and we ask for that advice upon a presentation of the facts which we are able to make but very imperfectly, which we could have made far more perfectly if we had had the opportunity to ask some questions of the representatives of that church, on the floor of this Council. In some way or other, it seems to us we must be extricated, — extricated speedily, easily, and without any further vehement and protracted contest. We have not time enough to carry on such a contest. The Master summons us to work while the day lasts; and as the day now drawing to its end is darkening on the earth, the other day, we know, is darkening over some of us. We have not other months and years to give to such a discussion as this, strenuous, prolonged, painful, tearing our very hearts asunder, sometimes. We must be able to to be out of this more easily.

If not, Congregationalism is condemned. If not, men will say this Congregational fellowship is the strangest force on earth! It does not hinder a man from preaching what he likes, whether it be the Calvinism of his fathers, or its exact opposite. It does not hinder a man from inviting to his communion Universalists, Unitarians, Quakers, and Catholics. But when any church desires to be extricated from it, any church which had never shown any thing but friendship up to that point, the reflections thrown upon that church are like the pelting of ice-pellets in a winter hail-storm. A member accused of gravest offenses against the pastor, against the church, goes out of that church, whose reputation he is alleged to have injured, whose tenderest feelings to have outraged, "without reflection upon him." We, who had never uttered an insinuation against that pastor, whose lips would have been blistered if it had passed them, standing afterward to maintain principles which to us are vital, have "reflections" raining upon us thick as snow-flakes, and stinging as Indian arrows. Luckily our armor is steel-plated, and they have neither stung nor hurt. But we must be out of this. Why, it is like Victor Hugo's devil-fish, — cold, but clinging ; and it sucks a man down, and holds him fast, and pulls him in, whether he will or no.

Brethren, we were said, here this morning, by the accomplished reader of the document from Plymouth Church, to have threatened you. Exactly as much as we threatened ourselves! We said we were afraid that missionary societies would suffer ; they are our societies, as much as yours. We were afraid that churches would leave our communion. We were afraid for our own sakes ; and we did not threaten you, or anybody. We were afraid for the Congregationalism which our fathers brought hither.

We have heard much of the power of the Plymouth Church. It is a great, energetic, wealthy, powerful, resolute society, with immense force in the city and in the land ; which has used its force for the most part nobly, for the country and for the Lord. We have heard much of the great services of Mr. Beecher, to the cause of the land, and the dearer and grander cause of Christ. We feel it all, Brethren. I think of that church as I have loved it, and my heart bleeds as I ask you to show me what my church shall now and henceforth do concerning it. I think of him whom I loved so long, who buried my child, whose children I have helped to bury, — of all the fond love and admiration of the vanished years, — and I vow within myself, with a vow that shall not be broken, that if my hand shall ever add, intentionally and of malice, any sorrow to that whitening head as it journeys toward the grave, that hand may wither at my side!

But there comes before me another form, grander and mightier than that of Plymouth Church, clothed upon with more consecrated memories than its minister. It is the august and venerated form of that Congregationalism which our fathers brought hither ; which our ancestors preached, and loved, and served, two centuries and a half ago ; which my personal ancestors in this country have preached and served for two hundred and forty years upon these shores, since Richard Mather left the English Church to become the pastor of the Congregational church in Dorchester. It has spread across the land. Its hands have everywhere been clad with might, and brimmed with blessing. It has made the wildernesses blossom into Christian commonwealths. I carried to the grave, last summer, the form of one who for sixty years had loved it, preached it, and maintained it, and who had taught it unto me, — from whom my life had come. Its power to him was in its purity ; its glory to him was in its discipline within the church, and in its fellowship of the churches. Let us maintain the glory, and vindicate the purity, of that venerated form of Congregational polity, if it be, as I believe it, living still. If, like him from whom I learned it, it has fallen feeble, and finally lifeless, let us carry it to its grave, and carry it here, — we never shall have a grander funeral assembly ! — and bury it, with tearful eyes and aching hearts. But if it be living and strong as ever, ancient as the Gospel, living as the Master, mighty as the Truth, let us here declare and re-affirm it, and give it new impulse for its mighty advance, across the land, around the world !

Council adjourned until 8 p.m.

Council convened at 8 p.m., and was opened by singing.

Rev. Dr. Stearns of Amherst College, Mass., offered prayer.

Rev. Dr. Budington addressed the Council, as follows :—

Fathers and Brethren : — I do not know that I ever rose to address my fellow Christians and my fellow ministers, under circumstances that at all compare with these, as to the power they have to awaken my sense of responsibility. I commend myself in Christian faith to the guidance of Him, who we trust is in the midst of us to-night. I remember the somewhat similar circumstances in which I was placed some months ago, when it was given me to follow the brother who has preceded me, to-day, in addressing you. On that occasion, he gave utterance to the feelings of his heart, and the gathered memories of many years, in the admiration, and love he bore to his friend of a quarter of a century, the son of the friend of his own revered father ; and when that magnificent tribute of Christian and ministerial friendship was ended, I remember how impossible it was to proceed : and now I cannot but think how impossible it would have been for me to obey your mandate, had the Resolution passed, summoning me to address you at the close of that speech. I thank you for sparing me the trial which would then have befallen me.

And now that I rise to speak, I beg you to bear in mind, what has been repeated more than once, the delicacy of the subjects upon which we are called to speak ; and I ask you, brethren, to relieve me from anxiety with regard to the words I shall employ. Once for all, I commit myself to your charitable construction, assuring you that I have nothing to keep back, and nothing whatever to communicate having any personal bearing. I have nothing to do with the guilt or innocence of any person whose name has come before you in connection with church discipline. I am only concerned for those principles which are involved in that history ; and I stand here to-night in behalf of them, identifying myself with them if I may do so, and asking you to receive what I say, as bearing singly and alone upon the exposition of the princi-

ples underlying the practices of which we are to speak.
Indeed, Brethren, if we, of these churches, have not been identifying ourselves with Congregationalism, then the advice
that we ask from you must be a censure; for we have
felt from the beginning that we had no mission whatsoever
in this matter, unless we were sent for the conservation
of principles underlying the constitution of the Christian
Church, and inseparable from its triumph in ages to come. I
will not deny, that, when we began this history, we were fore-
warned that we must expect opposition and misrepresentation;
we were even told that we must expect schism and alienation
in the midst of our own churches; and we have found it so.
Had I known at the outset all that I know now, I will not say
that my fortitude, as I confronted the difficulties of my position, would have been adequate; but to-night I give thanks
to God that I did not know the future, that I ventured into
it under the guidance alone of loyalty to Christ, and adherence
to the principles I have received from Christ through the
fathers that have gone before me.

I shall endeavor, in presenting what remains of the case, to
be as brief as I possibly can be; and I will therefore proceed
at once to ask your attention to the next Question, — the sixth
in order, upon which we ask your advice. This Question
reads as follows: —

Sixth: In view of the Resolution adopted by the Plymouth
Church, Dec. 5, 1873, in which its rules are interpreted publicly, and
with authority, "as relieving all other churches from responsibility
for the Doctrine, Order, and Discipline of this church, and this
church, from all responsibility for those of other churches," what
is the duty, concerning that church, of the churches calling this
Council? Especially, what action, if any, should they take to
release themselves from the mutually responsible connection with
it, in which they have stood before the Christian public?

You know where to find these Resolutions. They were
referred to this afternoon, and they are two in number. The
first of them reiterates the principles contained in Rules 1
and 2 of the Manual, and affirms the fundamental principles
of the Congregational polity, which are these two, — so fundamental that they may be called the two poles upon which the

system revolves, — the independence of the local church and the fellowship of the churches with one another. These principles are common to all our churches ; and the language in which they are expressed is, in this instance, almost identical with the language you will find currently used in all our Manuals. The independence does not exclude the fellowship ; nor, again, the fellowship the independence. Independence denies authority, outside of the local church, to govern and call to account ; it does not share constitutional self-government with any body of men outside of those who constitute the local church ; and in this respect the Congregational churches differ from those under the Presbyterian and Episcopal government. The fellowship of the churches, on the other hand, is as real and absolute in its sphere, which is distinct from, and in perfect accordance with, the independence of the local church, being absolutely voluntary, prescribing simply the way in which the churches use their liberty, and in no sense an abridgment, much less a transference of liberty. There is, therefore, no objection to the language of these Resolutions referred to in this sixth question, so far as the reiteration of Rules 1 and 2 of the Plymouth Manual is concerned.

But when we come to the second part of these Resolutions, — that which affirms an interpretation of them, — we at once reach another language, and we find that interpretation putting a sense upon these rules which utterly destroys the fellowship of our churches, and changes Congregationalism into an Independency that disowns and repels fellowship. You will remember that this Resolution was passed in connection with the reception of our letter of admonition. It was passed specifically, to use the language of the Preamble, "that the relations of Plymouth Church with other churches should be clearly understood." It is, therefore, a public and authoritative interpretation of the principles of Plymouth Church in regard to their relations to other churches in respect of independency ; and the language used is definite and exclusive. It relieves all other churches from responsibility for the Doctrine, Order, and Discipline of the Plymouth Church ; or, in the language of the pastor at the preceding meeting, which found its formulation in this Resolution : "Our ecclesiastical basis," he says, "puts us on precisely the same relations with Baptist, Methodist, and Presbyterian churches, that it does with Congregational churches." But those denominations,—the Baptist, Methodist, and Presbyterian,—as you know, never assumed, and never were understood to assume, responsibility for the Doctrine, Order, and Discipline of the Plymouth Church. The Congregational churches, on the other hand, did assume such responsibility. They were present, as in the case of the formation of all the other Congregational churches of Brooklyn ; and they publicly received the Plymouth Church into the fellowship of our fraternity of churches, giving them our name, and assuming a spiritual responsibility with regard to their Doctrine, Order, and Discipline. Now, however, these churches which have thus entered into public and responsible fellowship with that church, are, by this interpretation of their rules, relieved from all responsibility. Their doctrine may be changed to any extent. It may become Unitarian, Universalist. It may go to any extent in derogation of the faith received from our fathers. They may surrender discipline ; they may revolutionize their order ; and we, who have given our common name to them,—and given it publicly, — have no recourse, in the way of withdrawing it, but are to be held to the fellowship pledged to them at the outset, when they submitted their principles to a fellowshiping Council. Those principles were found, at that time, to be in accord with the well-known ancestral principles of our churches. To make it still stronger, the new interpretation asserts the right, on their part, to judge, in every case, what fellowship or advice may be offered or received. Instead of being a reciprocal right, it is, by this interpretation, their exclusive right ; and however great their aberration may have been, or may hereafter be, the only right to judge with regard to fellowship resides in that church. What can be more positive and definitive than this,—the declaration of an absolute surrender of their relation to the Congregational churches, in the way of fellowship, and the institution of an Independency which absorbs and annihilates the fellowship hitherto recognized among us ?

Now, we maintain that this interpretation destroys, in a

vital and essential point, the fellowship of our fathers, and substitutes another thing in the place of it. That new thing, we hold, should bear a new name, that it may not be mistaken, and that other principles may not be confounded with ours. Independency, we have from the very beginning, for two hundred and fifty years, pointedly, systematically, and uniformly disowned.

I need not multiply instances of this. The *Cambridge Platform*, and the *Platform of the Boston Council*, in 1865, maintained the same language in regard to it ; and that language is unmistakable. Indeed, the Plymouth Church Manual, which was quoted this afternoon, issued seven years after the institution of that church, is in itself a sufficient testimony to the fact that this Independency, instead of being consistent with Congregationalism, is antagonistic. A common name imports common principles. Congregationalism is as well known where Congregational churches prevail, as Methodist, Episcopal, Presbyterian, and Baptist churches are ; and the principles that belong to our name are as uniformly recognized, where that name is spoken, as the principles of any other denomination of Christians. These common principles, inhering in the name *Congregational*, are three : First, the orthodox interpretation of Christianity. Our fathers, when they came here, came together, as they expressly said, for the purpose of giving their consent and adherence to the principles of the orthodox faith affirmed by their brethren on the other side of the water ; and they affirmed in almost the same words the faith which had been set forth by the *Westminster Confession* and by the *Savoy Confession ;* and when, in the earlier part of this century, a portion of our Congregational churches departed from the orthodox platform, they adopted, righteously adopted, necessarily adopted, another name, and left us ours, so that the *Unitarian* denomination, coming out from the midst of us, was not and could not be popularly confounded with the Congregational.

A second principle, inhering in this common name of ours, is the great and fundamental one, which characterizes our history more than any thing else, namely, the covenanting of believers together in mutual watchfulness, and the maintenance of an orderly discipline. Perhaps, historically speaking, this more than any thing else characterized the Congregational churches of our country, as they started upon their history under the forming hand of our fathers in the faith. There is no conception of the Christian church, grander, more Divine, and more sacred, than that which the Puritans had. The Bible was only a silent testimony to the truth of God ; but they believed that the Church of God was a living witness to the truth of God ; that a renewed man was the doctrine of regeneration set up in a human life ; that the doctrine of sanctification was a history drawn out into a human life ; and that the Church of God, in their love for one another, and in their common loyalty to their Moral Governor, was a state within a state, a kingdom within a kingdom, which had the sublimest mission on earth, the work of redeeming the world to Christ. Now, to ignore this Puritan idea of the Covenant of the Christian Church is to dishonor Puritan history, and to make all their sacrifices, to which we owe our country and our churches, a mistake and a crime.

The third and last element, belonging to this common name, is the carrying out of this idea of covenanting between Christians in the local church, so that neighboring churches shall be bound together in the bonds of a similar covenant, to watch over one another, in the Lord. I need not call your attention to the evidence of this. It is beautifully expressed in the Platform of 1865. You will find it on the forty-first page of that Platform. It is a covenanting between churches ; not at all in the way of rule and domination, but a voluntary and spiritual fellowship ; an agreeing together to exercise their acknowledged liberties within these voluntary bounds ; a consenting together in the owning of the same faith, and a walking together in conformity with the rules of the same Christian discipline. It is voluntary, and voluntary on both sides. Each local church is voluntary in entering into the fellowship, and the churches around are voluntary in the extension of fellowship.

Now, we say that a change in any of these fundamental principles should be expressed by some change of name. It is a mere matter of honesty, — honesty on the part of those who have changed, and honest dealing on the part of those who have not changed. And this is not only honest, but necessary to the proper life and action of our churches ; for, Brethren, common principles are the only enduring basis upon which common Christian work can be done. The work of Christ, which he has given us to do, — to publish his Gospel over the earth, and gather believers into churches, — can be accomplished only upon the basis of common principles, and the assurance that these common principles will be perpetuated.

It is upon this basis that our home missions are prosecuted ; it is upon this that foreign missions rest. For the Gospel is a definite system of faith ; the church is the Gospel in the form of an institution ; and this fellowship of the churches, by which they promise to watch over one another in the Lord, is the only method of determining whether the faith once delivered to the saints is really maintained, and whether the life which Christ requires is really lived. Why, Brethren, it does not matter what the doctrine is, whether orthodox or heterodox : it must be formulated and adhered to, or missions, the evangelization of the world in any sense, is at an end. Our Unitarian friends, who left us a generation ago, in leaving behind them the orthodox faith, left also behind them this responsible fellowship and communion of the churches ; and what to-day is the testimony from that class of Unitarian ministers and churches who bear the name, and fitly bear it, of *Evangelical Unitarians,* — what but just this ? that the Independency into which they launched themselves when they departed from the faith of our and their fathers, has made the future of Unitarianism discouraging from weakness of organization. Fellowship has been lost through extreme Independency ; and, losing this, they have lost unity, life, growth. They have no means of keeping *in* their pulpits the gospel they own, and of keeping *out* the infidelity they disown. So, too, our English brethren are less called Congregationalists, than Independents ; not that they disown in theory the fellowship of Congregationalism ; but that this part of our polity has, in England, been paralyzed, until, as we hear, they are now driven to the study of our American Congregationalism, in order to save themselves and secure their development. That body of Christians, as you well know, is highly intelligent and devout. It is a missionary body. We love them and honor them ; and when their distinguished ministers came over here, a few months ago, to the Evangelical Alliance, we were heartily glad to see them ; and I believe they were glad to see us, and especially the fellowship we maintain by our system of Councils. They have been engaged, of late, in gathering funds for the support of superannuated ministers, and widows and children of deceased pastors. They have found no difficulty in gathering moneys for this sacred end ; but they have found their work embarrassed, and, I believe, seriously interrupted, by such an Independency of their churches, as prevents them from defining what a Congregational minister is. Without the protection afforded by a Council of neighboring churches, unfit ministers, not only unsound in doctrine, but stained in life, may work their way into churches. So, Brethren, our churches in the West, under the fostering care of our Home Missionary Societies, and the churches now spreading over the Turkish Empire and other fields of the American Board, if this theory is to prevail, will be thrown into confusion among themselves, and be disowned by those under whose patronage they have sprung into existence.

Now, this Independency has been claimed, not as a new departure, but as genuine Congregationalism. As a new departure, we are free to say, we should have no quarrel with it. It was competent for our friends of the Plymouth Church to declare themselves Independent. Their reserved rights included this right, and we at first supposed this was their real intention. In that case, we intended only to recognize and record it in some orderly way. A Council might not have been needed. If a Council was needed, instead of being a National Council like this, a local and small Council would have been adequate for the purpose. To the import of this action of theirs we called special attention, in the Letter, as you will bear witness. At first the Pastor seemed disposed to take this view of it, and accept the position. " It would be an infinite relief," he said, "if I could stand on a platform where no man on earth was responsible but myself for the

12

things I said. I do not think it fair," he said, "to put such a responsibility on my brethren." These were generous words, and generously spoken; and all we wished was to ascertain whether the Plymouth Church meant what the Pastor did, and then to deal with them as fairly as we could. But, in their last letter, the Plymouth Church claimed their interpretation to be the true Congregationalism. In their last letter, you find them saying that, "Congregationalism is the conduct of the affairs of the church by the whole brotherhood, not embarrassed by the unasked interference of other churches." Mark it. "It is the conduct of their business by the whole brotherhood, *not embarrassed by the unasked interference of other churches.*" Again, "the position of Plymouth Church, deliberately taken at the beginning, and *never changed,* is Congregationalism as we understand it, hold it, and are determined to maintain it." "We have no desire to interfere with the churches you represent, in any course they may feel constrained to take. If they choose to withdraw from a truly Congregational fellowship, it is their right: we have not withdrawn, and we will not withdraw."

Now, Brethren, we ask you, in the advice you give us, to determine this question: Is this Congregationalism? To hold us in unwilling fellowship, not to say with such actual departures, but with the possibilities wrapped up in this interpretation, is, I solemnly believe, injustice and tyranny. It makes us contradict our convictions. Not to be able to leave and withdraw ourselves from a fellowship we freely gave, after the conditions of that fellowship are changed, is to do injustice to the deepest convictions of our consciences; and we ask how this can be made to harmonize with the doctrine which gives to each individual member of the local church the right to withdraw on his silent volition from that church, while we, as churches, are to be held to fellowship whether we will or no? We are forced by the continuance of such fellowship to give currency to principles our consciences oppose. And it is a tyranny as well; for, my brethren, in withdrawing from a church, we exercise no authority over that church. Not in the least degree do we put a restraint upon their liberties, when we ask to be released, from a fellowship which now does not represent our convictions and our feelings. As fellowship, when exercised, does not invade the liberty of a local church, so, when withdrawn, it does not impair that liberty. But when, under such circumstances, we are held to fellowship, *our* dearest, most sacred, and inalienable rights are taken from us. Under our polity, it seems to me absolutely preposterous to talk of tyrannizing by withholding a fellowship which has ceased to correspond to the truth of underlying facts. The only possible tyranny in the communion of churches, is to make that communion survive its terms, and outlive its voluntariness.

So, Brethren, we come to the practical inquiry, what action shall we take to release ourselves from the mutually responsible fellowship with the Plymouth Church, in which we have stood before the public ? There are two ways. As individual churches, we may withdraw, by the acts of our local churches, from fellowship. But this would be a violation of the principles of our denomination. Our platform lays down a specific course for us to pursue ; and, as law-abiding Congregationalists, we are bound to take the course prescribed. It would also be assuming, in us, to act without counsel, on so important a subject. We did not wish to act hastily. Nay, we did not wish to act at all, unless it was necessary, and the safety of our communion was imperiled. It would also be ineffectual, to take separate church action. The controversy would only be continued ; nay, more, become interminable, spread from church to church, and enfeeble every church that was involved in the discussion. It would be schism ; it would be anarchy ; it would waste us away ; it would give up our name, or, at least, share our name with any body choosing to adopt it, and to claim fellowship, however unlike, and however antagonistic their principles.

There must, then, be some public and orderly determination of the question. This is by a Council capable of affirming what Congregationalism is, and, as representing the mind of the churches upon the subject, authorized to declare their principles ; so that, in obedience to such declaration, we may keep along in the path of the fathers, and have an opportunity to affirm the distinctive principles of our polity, while we withdraw, in an orderly way, from churches that have departed from such principles.

There are, as was said this afternoon, two sorts of fellowship; one is of a non-responsible nature, which connects different denominations together, in mutual respect, and in the interchange of certain offices of Christian confidence. The Platform of the Boston Council recognizes this relation. We hold communion with all parts of the church universal. We recognize believers who come together in the affirmation of the common faith, 'and give evidence of fidelity to the common Head; we hold occasional communion with them; we have more or less intimate relations with them, according as their differences are more or less fundamental. But the relations we sustain to Congregational churches are more intimate. We give and receive fellowship in the way of organizing churches, recognizing pastors, and ordaining ministers. We give and receive admonition; and we bind ourselves to sympathy, and acts of helpfulness, toward those needing sympathy and help. When we are released from this mutually responsible relation of churches, bearing a common name; when the tie of common principles no longer exists, — and is no longer understood to exist, — the more generic and non-responsible communion is exercised, and this without embarrassment, and to the advantage of all parties.

Now, Brethren, we ask you to advise us in this matter, both as to the relation of Congregationalism to Independency, and as to the methods in which we shall release ourselves from a church which has substituted Independency for Congregationalism. Give us, we pray you, a deliverance on the subject of Congregationalism, which shall release us from a fellowship which has become misrepresenting to us, and therefore painful. Give us a deliverance which shall save the younger and weaker churches — whether at home or abroad — from misconception. Give us our natural and inalienable Congregational liberty. We have a right to march shoulder to shoulder with those who believe with us, and who act with us. We are not under the necessity of marching with those who do not believe with us, and who do not act with us. So much, Brethren, for this Sixth Question; and now I ask your attention to the Seventh, and last.

Seventh: Have the churches calling this Council acted, in its judgment, in substantial accordance with the principles of Congregationalism, as set forth in our authorized Platforms of Polity, in the remonstrances and requests addressed by them to the Plymouth Church? Or in what respect, if any, have they erred toward that church, and departed from these principles, in the representations they have made?

I beg you to notice the exact import of this Question. Observe that the Question respects the *remonstrances* and *requests* we have addressed to Plymouth Church. We do not ask you to give us advice on the methods of church action. In making such remonstrances, different methods are within the liberty of local churches. They are matters of internal administration. We do not ask you to advise us as to the way in which the churches took action, — whether by a meeting publicly called, with the business stated from the pulpit; or whether it were better to perform that duty at the regular meetings for worship, at the same hour, and beneath the same sacred influence under which we offered our prayers and held communion with the great Head of the Church. We do not ask you to tell us whether the business would better be done by Committees, or by the whole brotherhood assembled together. We say these are matters of local usage and right. But the question is specific. It asks if our remonstrances and requests have been in accordance with Congregational principles. You will find these remonstrances and requests in the first letter. Was that letter, as a whole, in accordance with our polity? That letter contains two prominent features, inasmuch as it has two parts, distinct in matter and unlike in language: that part which respects the question whether the Plymouth Church is charged justly or not with the practice and principles set forth in the letter; and then the part which deals with the character and tendency of the practice and principles in themselves considered.

In regard to the first part of the letter, we strove, earnestly and prayerfully, to make our address to the church as cautious, as *hypothetical,* if you please, as we could make it. We expressed, in the first place, the hope that the action complained of was not what had been reported; and we asked to be informed as to the reasons for it, in the hope that when we knew them, we should look differently upon what they had done. Again, we hoped that they would see reason to modify their views, when we gave them our views. It was on these grounds that we asked a conference. We assured them that any new light would be most welcome to us. We disavowed the slightest authority. The right we exercised we claimed simply in a fraternal sense, as involved in fraternal obligation. If we had duties to perform toward them, we held, as a matter of course, that we had rights ; and, as we had the duty of Christian watchfulness to exercise, we had the right to make this request for a conference with them. We did it, in the language of that letter, "in absolute kindness of spirit, but under the deepest convictions of duty." We founded our admonition upon a public report uncontradicted ; and so far from expressing, as we were charged with doing, a settled conviction that they were in the wrong, we suggested the possibility of misapprehension, and hoped for the removal of it.

Now, I ask, is it a Christian offense, in dealing with a Christian church, to express watchfulness and solicitude, as regards a report uncontradicted ? If so, times have greatly changed since the apostle Paul exercised this duty toward the Corinthian church. "It is commonly reported," said the apostle in his first letter to the Corinthians, that there exists among you a crime which "is not so much as named among the Gentiles ;" and this common report was the basis not only of a mention in that letter, but the basis as well for the judgment he pronounced : "For I verily, as absent from the body, but present in the spirit, have judged already as though I were present, concerning him that hath done this deed."

But, my brethren, coming to the second part of that letter, I ask if the vigor, the *severity* if you will, of that part which describes the novel, unscriptural, and injurious nature of the practice in question, was excessive and unchristian ? — was that practice unjustly characterized in its bearing upon the purity of the Church of God, and upon the reputation and usefulness of ministers ? Consider, my brethren, that when we were expressing our feelings on this subject, we felt that we were

speaking not for ourselves, but for Christ, — we were expressing
our zeal for the honor of our common Lord. And suppose
the language were too severe : I ask, is nothing due to Christian
jealousy for the truth and the honor of Christ? Were we
bound to act as in a court, not of equity, but of written law,
where verbal objections are to be taken, technical difficulties
availed of, and mistakes noted, however unintentional ?

Well, Brethren, in a subsequent letter, this charge wholly
falls to the ground. It is confessedly given up : we studied to
express ourselves in the least objectionable form possible ; we
avoided words which could give offense ; we expressed regret
that we had inadvertently used them ; said we should not
have used them if we had supposed them capable of such an
interpretation. But sending this second and unobjectionable
letter, did we make progress ? At that meeting you will bear
in mind, the non-fellowshiping Resolutions were passed. So
much, then, for our letter as a whole.

Look next at the details. Consider the remonstrances we
made. Were we warranted, in remonstrating against the
dropping from the roll of a member's name on the 31st of October, under the circumstances as described ?

I am not under the necessity of discussing this subject. It
has been done already. The answer to the question, evidently
depends upon this other question, whether that person was a
member of the church. This point has been, it seems to me,
satisfactorily settled. Besides, it was made, by the rules of
the Plymouth Church, incumbent upon the complainant that
he bring his complaint before the Examining Committee. This
was done in obedience to that imperative rule ; by it, that
complainant acquired rights ; he was entitled to have the accusation heard, either by the Examining Committee or by the
church, unless the application was rejected at a meeting of
the church by a three-fourths vote. Were those rules regarded ? Was he allowed so much as to mention the subject ?
And is it not in accordance with Congregational usage that we
should have remonstrated as we did ? Were we warranted,
again, in remonstrating against the refusal of the church to
examine charges against this member, because possibly they
might ultimate in charges against the Pastor? Remember

the circumstances in which we were placed. For a whole year, our city, and the churches throughout the land, were agitated by the question ; and we were appealed to not only, as you know, Mr. Moderator, from within the bounds of our own body, but by other Christian bodies, to know whether the Congregational polity did not prescribe some method of determining the truth or falsehood of such grave charges ? We were told, that we who were next to him, longest associated with him, were held by our brethren accountable to them, that our common name should not suffer through indifference or neglect on our part. Our reply was : " No one who understands the Congregational polity can hold us responsible for non-action, under present circumstances. Plymouth Church is a large, intelligent body, with multitudes of excellent people in it. It is only common Christian courtesy to believe that they will discharge their duty ; that they will take up the case when it comes regularly before them, and that they will give it an orderly issuing." Were we right in waiting a whole year in this deference to the rights of that church ? Ought we to have brought any complaint in the Ministerial Association ? But an Association is a voluntary body, and no minister is under obligation to belong to it. Was our delay in the first instance, and then the promptitude with which we acted after our hopes were disappointed, and the issue was had on the 31st of October, — was our delay in the first instance, and our promptitude in the second, warranted ?

Then, Brethren, was our remonstrance just, that absenteeism, instead of being regarded as a distinct offense, should be made an excuse for not investigating charges, regularly brought ? But, in this instance, absenteeism was simply a form of emphatic accusation. Were we warranted in remonstrating, also, against the injury done to our common name? But we found that we could not retain our own members in our churches, if we were silent on the subject. Nor could we release ourselves, in the forum of our own consciences, from the duty that devolved upon us as next neighbors to the church. So much for the remonstrances.

Our requests were two : first, for a conference, in hopes of finding the facts otherwise than what they had been reported, or that they might be changed.

Should a single church have begun this investigation? The Cambridge Platform of 1648 said that a single church ought to begin it ; but the Platform of 1865 modifies the rule, and apparently for good reasons. The maxim holds that the law endures, as long as the reason for it does. The reason for the law given in the xviiith of Matthew is, "that every word may be established ;" that is, that legal testimony may be furnished ; but this is not needed in a case like this.

Should we have approached the officers of the church, in the first instance? But it was church action that we complained of, and those officers would naturally, and ought in justice to, have referred us to the church ; and from the history that has transpired, it is now most evident that our decision was right, since it would have been more offensive than we supposed, at the outset, had we gone to them, instead of going directly to the church.

Again, should we have asked for a conference in few and simple words? But we felt that we had a *prima-facie* case to make out ; that it would be unjust to our convictions, and misguiding to them, to go before them with any thing less than a full, explicit, and earnest statement of all we felt and believed on the subject.

Well, Brethren, when we came to the request for a Council, was that a threat? Did we do wrong in suggesting an appeal to a Council? But what was the Council that we asked them to unite with us in calling? A *Mutual* Council. Is there any thing *threatening*, in asking brethren to meet us on common grounds, before a common tribunal, elected by them as by us? The idea of a threat never occurred to us ; and when it was imputed to us, it seemed the most inapt and preposterous objection conceivable.

Again, was our request for a Mutual Council so treated that we were released from the obligation to press it any further? I beg your special attention to this point. Consider, then, that a conference was a necessary step to a Council, and that the declinature of a conference carried with it the declinature of a Council. Were we not authorized to conclude, that, when they refused to meet us for fraternal conference, they refused *a fortiori*, to meet us in a Council? Such a conference being necessary as a preliminary to a Council, we could not have a Council without it; and had we gone to them to ask for a Council, it was asking for a conference over again, and in a form sure to be refused. Nevertheless, we did distinctly ask the question in our letter of Dec. 5; and they replied on Dec. 6, "We are not aware, on our part, of any question requiring the advice of a Council." They asked us, indeed, to state the points we proposed to submit, and they promised a prompt reply in answer. We stated the points; and then, on the ground of an inference drawn from another part of our letter, they declined to tell us how they regarded the points they had solicited, and upon which they had promised us a prompt reply. At the same time they voted themselves an independent church, with no obligation of fellowship; and this we understood to be a denial, not of one Council, but of all Councils growing out of a fellowship they disowned.

Their definition of Congregationalism, also, as "the conduct of the affairs of the church by the whole brotherhood not embarrassed by the unasked interference of other churches," seemed to us to forbid approach, and we were shut out from interposing until asked to do so. Then, you remember, they expounded the differences between them and New-England Congregationalism, showing that at the outset they had refused to allow a Council to organize them, and that from the very beginning they had dissented from the Congregationalism of the fathers. Then, again, they made it impossible for us to ask them for a Council, when they said: "documents are to be accompanied by proof of the authority of the whole brotherhood of your churches, regularly and deliberately conferred." They declined also to receive in any case, either from the whole brotherhood, or from us, the Committees of the whole brotherhood, letters, containing covert insinuations against the character of any of the members of Plymouth Church. Covert insinuations! What was this but a refusal to refer any matters of disagreement, upon which we could found admonition, to a Council? For, if there be ground of admonition, may not that ground assume the aspect of covert accusation against somebody? Then, Brethren, it seemed to

be a disingenuous and baffling reply, that, notwithstanding all
these forms of refusal, we found inserted in the midst of their
letter this sentence: "we do not decline to join in calling a
Mutual Council. It is you who seem to us to have first offered
an invitation under dubious authority, and then withdrawn it."
Were we not authorized in the conclusion to which we came,
that we were wasting time in renewing such offers? Was it
not obvious that no Mutual Council would ever have been
accepted? And that, too, for the reason that no action would
ever be permitted to take place growing out of the scandals,
or by any possibility associated with them, because it was
unalterably fixed that those scandals should never be investigated, or even mentioned.

Brethren, I will now relieve your attention. We ask your
judgment upon the questions submitted to you this afternoon
and evening. I will say again, what I said at the outset of
these remarks, that if we know any thing about ourselves, we
are standing here not more for ourselves, than for you; and
if the principles of our Congregational polity have not warranted the interposition we have made, then are we wholly
indefensible in the course we have taken. We have striven
to divest ourselves of any personal feeling. Personal considerations were all against the course we have taken: they were
so at the beginning, when with united prayer and mutual consultation, the sixteen representatives of the two churches met
together. God has given us one conviction: we have felt
that we were standing for you, standing for our fathers before
us, as their representatives, conserving the interests of our
children that are to come after us. In these days of moral
declension, when corruption has seated itself on the judge's
bench, in halls of legislation, and in municipal bodies, when
our hearts within us have been trembling for our country's
institutions, we have said to ourselves, "Except we can have
purity in the pulpit, and purity in the church, then indeed, is
our American civilization to pass away." We have stood for
God, and for the Church of God, in the feeling that we were
likewise standing for our country, and we could not do otherwise than as we have done.

Relatively, I have added very little to the wisdom of the

body with which I have had the honor to be connected ; but I am very thankful that I have entered into the fellowship of their sufferings. As it is the highest glory of the Christian to enter into the fellowship of the sufferings of Christ, so I esteem it a distinguished honor to enter into the fellowship of a true, faithful minister of Christ. As I have stood by my brother Storrs, and seen how his heart has ached, how like parting with his heart's blood it has been to part with the precious memories of by-gone and happy years, I have thanked God that it was my privilege to stand by his side, and in the humblest offices help him in the work to which he has been called. God grant that it be not too great a work for that frame, in years past overtaxed, and now again put to the strain, through the past winter, as he has carried upon his mind and heart, alike your interests and ours.

The MODERATOR : What order will the Council take upon the case that has been presented by the Committees of the churches that have called us here ? I will suggest, at this time, that, to whatever hour we adjourn to-morrow, the first half-hour of the session be spent in prayer-meeting ; and, if there is no objection, I will request Rev. Dr. WEBB of Boston, Mass., to conduct that service. I will take that to be the sense of the Council, unless objection is made.

Rev. Dr. R. S. STORRS : Mr. Moderator, it has occurred to me, that, as a great many facts have been stated in the course of our representation of things to day, it may be de-sired by members of the Council that they should have an opportunity to ask questions of us — representing the Com-mittees — to-morrow, as to the evidence of the things which we have stated, or as to the meaning of things which we have stated. I would simply say, — of course I have no right to make any motion, but I make it as a suggestion merely, — that if it be agreeable and desirable, and so appears to the minds of the Council, we shall be very glad to be here, to-morrow morning, and to spend as much time as may be de-sired, in answering any questions which may be addressed to us.

The MODERATOR : Of course it is desirable, and expected, that the representatives of the inviting churches and these

Committees, will be present with the Council, until the Council shall decide to withdraw for its own private consultation ; and, unless you, this evening, determine to be by yourselves in your session to-morrow morning, these brethren will be present, as a matter of course.

Rev. Dr. LORD, of Montpelier, Vt. : I would like to ask if the Committee desire to present any more statements of facts to the Council ?

The MODERATOR : The Committee have announced that they have presented the case, and have nothing more to offer unless questions are asked.

Rev. Dr. STORRS : I should be very glad, without having had opportunity to confer with Dr. BUDINGTON, that it might be understood that, provided new matters should occur to us after reflecting a little upon what has been said to-day, if we should desire to present some other things to-morrow, we may have the opportunity.

The MODERATOR : There is no objection to that understanding. That opportunity will be given, of course.

Rev. Dr. FISKE, of Bath, Me. : Is it, then, to be understood that the Council is to go into private session to-morrow, the Committees of the churches being in a convenient position to be called in to answer questions ; and the gentlemen of the Committees being permitted to add any thing which occurs to them, though not requested to do it ? With that understanding, if it be in order, I would move that our sessions to-morrow be private sessions.

The question was stated, to be upon the motion that the sessions, to-morrow, be private sessions, with the understanding, that, before going into private session, the Committees should have an opportunity to add any thing they may have omitted.

Rev. Dr. PALMER, of New York : It occurs to me that it would be better that the motion should be put in the shape in which Dr. Fiske offered it ; because we should be more likely, after we have begun our discussion, to think of matters upon which we desire information ; and, on the other hand, they will have an opportunity to confer together, and can make communications to us. I think if we begin in the morning, in an open session, we shall fritter away a portion of the time which is very valuable to us. I think we should vote now to have private sessions in the morning, with the distinct understanding that our brethren are to be at hand, that we may call upon them, or they may send to us, should occasion require.

Rev. Dr. QUINT: It seems to me it would be better not to vote, to-night, to have the session private to-morrow, entirely, or to begin so. We have heard the statements made by the Committees. We have asked no questions,— not a single question. We have heard no other statement, if anybody wishes to make one ; and the chances are that to-morrow morning these gentlemen will recollect something that has been omitted ; and it is far better that any further statement, or development, that is to be made, should be made here, where the public may come and hear it. The less we do in private, the better. The less statements come to us, in private, the better. The more public the better. We cannot make the whole thing more public than it is already. Inasmuch, as upon reflection, many of us will think of points upon which we desire more light, it will be far better to begin with an open session, and then everybody will know what statements are made to us ; especially as these things must, to a very great extent, affect another church not here represented.

The MODERATOR: I wish, as Moderator, to say that there ought to be nothing brought into the private session, before the Council, for consideration, that has not been presented before this whole assembly ; that we are not to go into private session for the sake of receiving further information on which we are to act ; and let me say that members of the Council are not to come in, each one with his own little budget of what he has heard elsewhere, as sometimes happens.

Hon. A. C. BARSTOW, of Providence, R. I.: I think it would be difficult to detain many members in session longer than the close of a long day, to-morrow ; and I hope we shall be able to complete our consultation upon the whole case, by using as many hours as need be, before midnight to-morrow night.

Rev. Dr. WEBB, of Boston, moved that the Council adjourn

to meet at 9 a.m., March 26, the first half-hour to be spent in a prayer-meeting.

The motion was agreed to.

Council thereupon adjourned.

The members of Council assembled at 9, a.m., agreeably to the vote at the close of the last Evening Session, for the purpose of prayer for the Divine guidance. The services were conducted by the Rev. E. B. WEBB, D.D., of Boston, who, after the singing of a hymn, offered prayer, and read a portion of the vth chapter of the Gospel of Matthew. Prayer was also offered by President CHAPIN, by Rev. H. M. STORRS, D.D., Rev. GEORGE E. ADAMS, D.D., Rev. H. M. PARSONS, Rev. JOHN O. FISKE, D.D., and Rev. WILLIAM M. TAYLOR, D.D.

The Council was called to order by the Moderator at a quarter to ten o'clock.

The SCRIBE read the minutes of yesterday's sessions ; and on motion, they were approved.

In the case of the Orange Valley Church, in New Jersey, it was reported by the Committee that Deacon John Wiley would sit as delegate from that church, the other delegate sent by the church having withdrawn.

The MODERATOR : It was expected that the Committees of the inviting churches would be present this morning, and would have the opportunity to make any additional communication which might seem to them important, and to answer any questions which the Council might desire to address to them. I believe that is the business immediately before us.

Rev. Dr. PALMER of New York : As I understand the Scribe, there is a motion before the Council which was pending at the time of adjournment. I would like to inquire if that is so.

Rev. Dr. QUINT : The motion was made that the sessions of to-day should be private. It did not come to a vote, and I suppose it has lapsed.

Rev. Dr. BROWN of Newark, N.J. : Would it be in order to present a motion or resolution now ?

Rev. Dr. QUINT : The Committee wish to make further statements, and will be present soon.

Rev. Dr. BROWN : If I were to make the motion, I should like to make a few remarks upon it.

The MODERATOR : The brother might proceed, if his motion is in order, while we are waiting for the Committees.

Rev. Dr. BROWN : I have a motion in my hand that I should like to make, because I am perfectly clear in my own mind as to what course the Council should take in the great matter which lies before it ; and, in my own thoughts, I have been clear in regard to it for the last ten days. I do not suppose that my views will agree with those of all the members of this Council, by any manner of means ; nor do I suppose that the Resolution which I am about to present will be adopted, in the form in which I present it ; and yet I do most sincerely hope that, if it shall be discussed for a few moments, it will have some sort of influence in making up the Result of this Council. I ought, Mr. President, to premise yet another sentence or two. When these papers came into my hands, — the papers calling the Council, — some ten days ago, I devoted one or two days to careful study, and I reached my own conclusion ; and that has only been confirmed by every step of progress and discussion thus far. I premise further, that, when I listened to that magnificent speech of Dr. Storrs, yesterday afternoon, I agreed with him on almost every point ; and, if this were a Mutual Council, I should vote in accordance with his views, on every point, so far as they were presented yesterday.

Rev. Dr. H. M. STORRS : May I interrupt the brother one moment, to put an inquiry to the Moderator ? Are we to understand that we are now to discuss the merits of the case before us ?

The MODERATOR : No, sir.

Rev. Dr. H. M. STORRS : If this bears upon the merits of the case, is it in order ?

The MODERATOR : It would not be in order ; for we are supposed not yet to have had the case entirely presented.

Rev. Dr. BROWN : That is the reason I raised the question at the commencement, whether it was in order to present a Resolution which touches the merits of the case. I will read the Resolution : —

Resolved, That inasmuch as this Council is, in point of fact, though not so styled, an *ex parte* Council, and as such was irregularly called, therefore, for it to give any advice that can rightly be construed as adverse to the Plymouth Church would be to violate the very principles of Congregationalism which we are here convened to vindicate.

It is on that Resolution, Sir, that I desire to speak.

Rev. Dr. QUINT: I object, as the special agreement was that the Committees should have the floor, first.

Rev. Dr. BROWN: I have no objection to its being deferred; but I shall re-present it at the proper time. I move this Resolution; and that it come up for discussion after the Committees shall have completed their statements.

Rev. Dr. QUINT: As the special assignment and understanding was that the Committees should have precedence, I object to its consideration at all, at this time.

The MODERATOR: It is not now in order. It will be moved, according to Dr. Brown's statement, the first time it comes in order. We are now ready to hear any further statement from the Committees of the inviting churches.

The Rev. Dr. BUDINGTON said: It escaped my mind yesterday to add a word with regard to the charges which have been made against our two churches, — that in the administration of discipline in these churches we have over and over again acted upon the same principles that we complain of in our correspondence with Plymouth Church. You have listened to the answer made by the Church of the Pilgrims, so far as the administration of discipline in that church is concerned. I will not occupy your time with any thing in detail. I will simply say, that, during the nineteen years of my ministry, there has never been any thing approximating to the principles of the case issued October 31, in Plymouth Church. Nothing of the kind.

I would like also to say a word with regard to the protest which was presented, in answer to the invitation given by the Council, to Plymouth Church, to be present here, to make statements of facts, and to present their views, putting them before you on precisely the foundation that we occupy in our addresses to you. That protest, I am sure, will enable you, in some measure, to understand the feelings we have had when, time and time again, we have approached them, as the published documents in your hands will show, with earnest entreaty

I may say, that they would meet us, and meet us frankly and squarely, with regard to the subject-matters that were lying on our consciences. The protest that you have received indicates the disposition which we have met again and again. You have asked them earnestly, respectfully, to give you facts. We have done the same, and have received as little in reply as you did.

It has occurred to me this morning, however, that perhaps the language of that protest, re-interpreting again their action — in which they define their sense of what Congregationalism is, in respect to Independency, and as ignoring Fellowship, — may possibly be regarded by some minds, in the Council, as withdrawing the subject-matter of our complaint. With reference to this thought, I wish to say this : we made up a case for you, presenting to you the action of that church, the view we took of it, and the reasons we had to take the view of it we did. We have presented to you the action of that church ; and we have asked from you a deliverance on the vital question, — whether that action was or was not in accordance with the fundamental principles of our polity. That case remains the same : it is upon that action, under the circumstances, that we ask you to give us your deliverance. The necessity for a deliverance and testimony on the part of the Council is as perfect with regard to the action taken by that church, up to the time of our issuing our Letter-Missive, as it could be under any circumstances whatever ; and the intermingling of fresh action, taken yesterday, does not alter the matter, or the manner, or the spirit of the action we have been complaining of.

Give us, then, your sense of the propriety, and the accordance with Congregationalism, of the action which has led to the calling of this Council. Give it to us explicitly. Enable us to understand it. Brethren, all we want to know, in the name of our common Master, in the name of God over us all, in the name of the children that are to come after us, is just this : are the principles upon which we have acted, the principles you accept ? Are they the principles that represent the inheritance we have received from our fathers ? Are you disposed to stand with us upon that platform ? Or have circumstances so changed, that in the time to come, there is a change needed in the exposition of the principles of our polity? Do we need a new departure? Is Fellowship less important? Was that movement of our churches which led to the National Council an unwise movement? Was the eagerness with which the weaker and newer churches of the West sprang forward to embrace that movement an insignificant indication? Do our churches cling to the principles of Fellowship which we have received from our fathers, as vital to our existence, and to our influence in time to come; or can we part with them? Can we become Independents?

Well, Brethren, it will be said that this protest re-interprets the interpretation of independence given on the 5th of December. Very well, Brethren, what I have to say about that is just this, and only this: If, after they gave us an interpretation which under the circumstances made it inevitable that we should understand just what we did understand, and which I endeavored to express to you last night; if, after that, they come forward with a new interpretation, and tell us that this second edition of their interpretation was the original one intended, — then I ask you what reflection it casts upon the spirit and principles of that church? In our dealings with it, as God is my witness, I say for myself and for the brethren with whom I am associated, we have endeavored to act as Christian men; to explain ourselves as fully as the English language would enable us to express ourselves; and successively, time after time, we have been baffled. Contradiction has come upon contradiction; and this protest, when joined to the other documents, reads the same lesson. You can draw the inference from it which I draw; you are as able to understand what light it casts upon the troubles we have been going through with, as I am. You can judge of this as well as I.

Does it indicate that the policy of that church has been presided over, and actuated, by principles of administration hitherto unknown in the management of churches? I will not answer that. It is a question I wish you to answer. But, with regard to that protest, I say two things. In the first place, whatever that protest now presents to your minds, for consideration, is not part and parcel of the action which convened you, and upon which we asked the deliverance of your testimony ; and, furthermore, if that protest is to be accepted as part of the action which you are to give a deliverance upon, as in certain respects no doubt it ought to be, — if it is to intermingle itself with the principles of the 5th of December, — you have an illustration of that flickering policy, that bandying of words for temporary purposes, which met our plain, uniform, unbroken, and unvarying request, and which will enable you to understand with what spirit we have been contending ; and how utterly impossible it has been, in our judgment, frankly to meet a spirit which has used such methods, and by them has confounded us again and again. I beg of you, Brethren, whatever action you choose to take with regard to that protest, give us a deliverance with regard to the action which was completed when the Letter-Missive was issued ; and tell us if that action is consistent with the fellowship of Congregational churches.

I have only one thing more to say, Brethren. I beseech of you, deal with us as frankly as we have endeavored to deal with you. We have rolled off from our shoulders a burden that we had taken upon ourselves, and which had been rolled upon us by the great Head of the Church. We put it now upon your shoulders ; and, under your responsibility to the Master, give us an answer which shall not be misunderstood. I ask it in behalf of the membership of these two churches. Give us an advice which is clear-toned, unambiguous, and self-consistent. Give us a result which Plymouth Church shall understand, without any mistake ; and do not leave the public round about us, and do not leave the greater public that is to follow in these churches of ours, to any ambiguity with regard to the sentiment of this Council, on the principles on which we ask your testimony.

I have just come in ; and deeply interested as I was by the proceedings of yesterday in common with yourselves, all day long, lifted up as I was by that tender flood of feeling which carried you all up at the close of the afternoon session, and then coming in the evening, as well as I could, to make deliverance to you of my thought on this subject, — I have been unable to give any thought to the questions which I have now attempted to answer, other than has occurred since I entered yonder door. Brethren, I have done. I have no doubt that my Brother Storrs has other thoughts in mind. Perhaps he has had more moments at his command than I have, — at least, I trust he has ; and I will give way to him to express any thing that may have occurred to him since the adjournment last night.

Rev. Dr. R. S. Storrs : One or two of the members of the Council have intimated to me that they wish to ask me some questions, in regard to some things which I said yesterday. I should a little prefer that the questions should be asked before I make any remarks ; because my remarks might afterward bear on them more directly.

The Moderator : Any member who desires any information or further suggestion from Dr. Storrs, can propose his questions now.

Rev. Dr. Rankin of Washington, D.C. : I have some questions that I desire to put, on the general subject, if they are in order now. I made a minute of some few questions, since the deliberations of yesterday morning, that I desire to ask. My questions are these : —

Are these Committees satisfied that, in their approaches to Mr. Beecher and the Plymouth Church, they pursued the method recommended by our Saviour in the xviiith chapter of Matthew? — I mean, in spirit.

Did any personal interviews with Mr. Beecher on the subject-matter of these two letters ever take place ?

Was any effort made to secure such interviews? and, if so, what?

What defined duty and authority have the Standing Committees in the churches calling this Council ?

Do these duties relate to the fellowship of the churches?

Could these Committees authorize a Letter-Missive to the churches ?

Could they initiate any measures where questions of church fellowship were involved?

Were the letters written to Mr. Beecher by these Committees first submitted to the two churches calling this Council ?

Was the expediency of this method of approach ever a matter of church discussion before sending them ?

What evidence have the Committees calling this Council that

the case of discipline in the Plymouth Church was not regarded and treated as an extreme and exceptional one?

Were these Committees acquainted with other instances of the kind?

The MODERATOR: Does anybody object to the putting of any of these questions?

Rev. Dr. CHAPIN of Beloit, Wis.: It seems to me that a portion of these questions should, no doubt, be put; but I have my doubts as to some of them.

Rev. Dr. R. S. STORRS: As some of the questions seem to me to overlap one another, I would rather make a comprehensive statement, in regard to the whole subject referred to in them. I shall, perhaps, answer them in that way more rapidly and satisfactorily than by taking them up *scriatim.*

Rev. Dr. RANKIN: The series of questions is topical. The first few relate to the same topic.

Rev. Dr. WEBB: Suppose we take the suggestion of Dr. Storrs, and hear his general statement; then, if we wish to repeat any of the questions, let them be repeated, and answered further.

Rev. Dr. RANKIN: I have no objection to any method the Council sees fit to adopt.

Rev. Dr. R. S. STORRS: As these questions are wholly fresh to me, — not having been aware of the nature of those which Dr. Rankin or other members of the Council intended asking, but only that they had some to propose, — and as others to follow may be equally unforeseen, may I suggest that all the questions to be put to me be put now? I may, perhaps, then cover them all in one general reply, and so save the time of the Council.

Rev. Professor SMYTH: I had prepared very much the same questions as brother Rankin, and therefore I will not repeat those. But there is one question, which he did not touch upon, that I would like to have Dr. Storrs answer, if it seems expedient to him. In his remarks, yesterday, he spoke of the advantage, in this community, of a vindication by Plymouth Church of the good name of its pastor. He said the vindication of Mr. Beecher's card was amply sufficient for fair or sympathetic minds; but that, since then, as I understood him,

Mr. Beecher had been made a target, and that it would have been for his repute, and for the interests of religion in this community, that the church also, by its action, should have vindicated his name. I should like to have him, if he deem it wise, explain a little further what was, in his judgment, the occasion and necessity for such action on the part of Plymouth Church.

Rev. G. B. WILLCOX : I would like to inquire whether every question that is offered here, unless protest is entered, is to be urged ? If so, I would like to object, decidedly, to the question of Professor Smyth. He has touched one of the most delicate and sensitive points in the whole controversy. It is a point which I know will awaken more feeling in Plymouth Church than any other that could be raised. I hope, therefore, that if it be possible to avoid that point, it may be allowed to pass in silence. I take it that we are not called to investigate the character of Mr. Beecher, or his reputation, or the danger of his reputation suffering, at our hands, or at the hands of his church.

Rev. Professor SMYTH: I have not raised the question of Mr. Beecher's character. We are not called upon to investigate that. But statements have been made publicly, and are in print, on an important point which will come before the Council for its action. It is a part of the *res gestæ ;* it is also a part of the documents which are submitted to us for consideration ; and I should be glad if Dr. Storrs would shed any further light that he may have upon it.

Rev. Mr. BARTLETT : I suggest that this question is excluded by the Letter-Missive. I hope your decision, Mr. Moderator, may be given on this point. My point is, that this question is excluded by the Letter-Missive.

Rev. Dr. PALMER of New York : I have heard some statements in regard to what Dr. Storrs said yesterday, on a certain point, and I would therefore like to have an answer to this question : did Dr. Storrs say that, in case the deliverance of this Council should not satisfy the churches calling it, he would never hereafter hold fellowship with any Congregational church ? or did he say that he never would give the right hand of fellowship to another new Congregational church, just organized ?

Rev. Dr. R. S. Storrs : Let me answer that, right off, for it is wholly unconnected with the preceding questions, stands by itself, and need not wait to be answered with them. What I said, as I believe, what I designed to say, was precisely this : that if our doctrine of fellowship in the Congregational churches connects us with other Congregational churches which have a right to do precisely what they like, — in respect to doctrine, giving it up ; in respect to order, becoming Methodists ; in respect to discipline, making the church, as was said in the letter from Plymouth Church yesterday, a covert for immorality, — and we are held to be bound to silence by the obligations of fellowship, and to have no right to remonstrate without its being deemed an intrusion and an offense, — then I will never give the right hand of fellowship to another such church, till God tells me what that church will do during its continuance.

Rev. Dr. Palmer : You did not mean that you would withdraw the right hand of fellowship which you had already given?

Rev. Dr. R. S. Storrs : I did not touch that subject at all.

Rev. Dr. Chapin : I have one or two questions to put, merely in regard to a fact. I do not wish, but quite the contrary, to open the delicate matter referred to in another question. But to some of us, who have studied this matter only at a distance, the correspondence between the churches calling the Council and the Plymouth Church seems to start with a set judgment and feeling, and seems to be met with a set judgment and feeling, which may have come in consequence of things that had preceded it. I would, therefore, like to ask, simply as a matter of fact : first, whether in the movement in the Plymouth Church, of bringing charges against the member referred to in the Letter-Missive, there is any reason to believe that there had been any consultation by the member bringing those charges with any of this Committee, or with members outside ; in other words, whether there had been a pressure from these neighboring churches at all affecting the urging of those charges ? I have my own judgment. I think we should say No. But I should like an explicit answer to that question.

And, secondly, whether, as preliminary or antecedent to any of these proceedings, there had been any private conference, or correspondence, between the pastors of these two churches and the pastor of Plymouth Church, with reference to the matters which seemed to implicate the character of the pastor of Plymouth Church? I ask only for the fact, whether any thing passing in that way, previous to the formal correspondence, will account for what seems to some of us the strong, perhaps the over-strong and over-vigorous putting of the case, with which the correspondence, as it comes before us, begins.

Rev. Dr. BYINGTON, of Brunswick, Me. : In the last letter of Plymouth Church, which is in this published pamphlet, they say that they understand the offer of a Council to have been withdrawn by the churches which had first invited them ; and I would like to inquire of the Committees whether that was their understanding, and whether, in their last letter, they intended to withdraw that offer?

Rev. Mr. BLAKE, of Concord, N, H. : On the 33d page* there is a sentence in a Resolution of Plymouth Church, beginning " In accordance with these her immemorial declarations," and ending with " admonition and censure : " I should like to know how the Committee understands that? and whether it is true that before any correspondence between the three churches, any of the Committee who are represented as calling this Council threatened any of the clerks of the church with the excommunication of Plymouth Church, as something inevitable in the future.

Rev. Dr. STORRS: Not to my knowledge. I never heard of any such remark, by anybody, or from anybody ; and I have no reason whatever to suppose that any such remark was ever made. If this brother will bring up before his mind sixteen gentlemen, some of them living in his own town of Concord, and some of them outside of it, and then will contemplate the proposal to him to be answerable for all their remarks in the course of six months, he will perhaps understand the difficulty which I should experience in making an absolutely negative reply to a question of that comprehensive sort. But, from what I know of the gentlemen of the Committee, I am perfectly sure that no such remark was ever made, by any one of

* P. 33, of this Volume.

them; as I absolutely know that no such remark was ever made by me.

Now, I am afraid I shall forget some of these questions, after all. President Chapin's strike me as important, and I wish he would repeat them.

Rev. Dr. CHAPIN : First, as to the fact whether the movement in the Plymouth Church, bringing these charges, was made under any outside pressure ? Second, whether there had been private conference, or correspondence, between the pastors of these two churches and the pastor of the Plymouth Church, respecting the reflections upon character that were involved in the matter ? I ask merely for the matter of fact, not at all to bring up that question.

Rev. Mr. BARTLETT: I am requested to ask, in addition, whether all of the pamphlet furnished to the members is official ; and particularly whether the card of the Clerk of the church, on the 25th page,* was an official declaration, or simply a personal one, upon the responsibility of Mr. Halliday?

Rev. Dr. R. S. STORRS : In reply to that, I have to say that the card, as printed here, is copied exactly, with typographical accuracy, from the paper in which it appeared ; and that in that paper, and at the foot of the card as there published, the Rev. Mr. Halliday signed himself as Clerk of Plymouth Church. That was not inserted by anybody else. It was inserted by himself ; and it has the same official stamp which the letter from Plymouth Church, addressed to us on Nov. 28th, on the 33d page has — "S. B. Halliday, Clerk of Plymouth Church." If we do not know that the first was official, we do not know that the last was official ; and we could have no proof of either communication, as having been official, unless we have it in each case equally.

I will now reply to Dr. Chapin. I am glad he asked the question which he did. I thought I had touched upon it yesterday afternoon.

The gentleman who made these charges, — I am not aware whether he is present now, as he was yesterday ; but if he were present, he would testify to this: that I had never exchanged a word with him ; that I did not know his name ;

* P. 25, of this volume.

that I did not know that he was living in the city, or was a member of the Plymouth Church, until he came to me to ask me a question as to how he should present a certain matter, which was heavily on his mind. And when he told me what it was, I found that it was this matter.

He told me that he desired no advice from me concerning it ; that he had had it borne in upon him, as a Divine impression, that it was the duty of some member, and, if of any member, his duty, to bring this matter before the Committee of the church ; that his soul was pierced and weighed down with the impression resting on him that the church was suffering ; that the name of the pastor was suffering ; that the minds of the congregation hearing the pastor were suffering, through the absence of an investigation ; that he asked no counsel concerning it ; that he had conferred with the pastor of the Plymouth Church, and felt that he approved of it ; and the only question which he asked was, whether a particular form was technically correct, so that it could not be objected to as technically irregular, and he be prevented from getting any hearing on the merits of the case.

I told him it was a delicate matter. On the one hand, I did not feel at liberty to refuse counsel, in regard to a minor matter, to a man who seemed to me to be standing in somewhat difficult circumstances, under a serious sense of responsibility, and with a strong conviction of duty. On the other hand, I was reluctant to give him any suggestion. I told him if he would see some other minister, and we two could meet him, we might give him such advice as he desired on that one point, but that on the general subject we should give none. We had systematically refrained from interposing, in any way, through any member, by any influence, to bring it up ; and from that course we should not depart.

He repeated again, before two of us, his declaration that he needed no counsel, asked no counsel, would take no counsel, concerning his general purpose and endeavor; but concerning the technical regularity of the way in which to present the charge, and to prosecute his endeavor, he did desire some advice ; which we gave him, kindly, wisely, I think, tenderly toward him, as a man oppressed with a heavy sense of great responsibility, in a spirit of perfect brotherly love and fellow-ship toward the church.

That we are responsible for the introduction of the matter into the Plymouth Church, is absolutely untrue, to the very roots, and to the topmost branch.

Now, sir, in regard to this other matter, of personal confer-ence with Mr. Beecher, I will speak for myself. I had no conference with Mr. Beecher concerning this subject; because I felt that it had been made impossible by him. I do not know that I desire, or should be willing, to add any thing beyond that, or that it is needful. I felt that, in consequence of what had previously happened, it was not within my privilege to confer with him.

Rev. Dr. RANKIN: I do not know that it is proper for Dr. Storrs to proceed any further in this direction ; but the direc-tions of our Saviour are that we go to a brother and tell him his fault, and, if we do not succeed, take another brother. It seems to me, there must be some movement toward that, before any one can say he is estopped from moving on that point. If it is not improper, I should like some further light upon it.

Rev. Professor SMYTH: I hope Dr. Storrs will not answer that question, under the feeling that the Council calls for it. That is a question which goes, simply and solely, into Dr. Storrs's personal relations with Mr. Beecher, and not to his relation with him as representing a church. We are dealing with the transactions between these churches, and between these pastors as representatives of their churches. If Dr. Storrs desires to bring before this Council his past relations, personal and pri-vate, with Mr. Beecher, I certainly ought not to interpose any difficulty in the way ; but I hope he will not answer the ques-tion simply under the feeling that the Council asks for it unanimously. I can only speak for myself. For one, I do not ask for it.

Rev. Dr. RANKIN: It strikes me that our relations to the Lord Jesus, and to our Christian brethren, are individual ; and, unless there was an attempt to make progress in that direction, it seems to me, we cannot say that we have done every thing to heal a breach before we have made it public.

The MODERATOR: We are not here to investigate the personal relations of Dr. Storrs and Mr. Beecher. We are here only to inquire concerning a certain correspondence between the inviting churches and the Plymouth Church ; and the whole raising of this issue, about what happened between the pastors of these churches before the commencement of this correspondence, seems to me to be irrelevant. I submit that to your judgment.

Rev. Dr. RANKIN : I appeal from the judgment of the Chair. I would like the judgment of the Council upon that point.

Rev. Dr. GEORGE E. ADAMS : Dr. Storrs has told us, on his honor, that he was shut out, as I understand it, from any personal approach to Mr. Beecher. That satisfies me ; and I do not see that we need to go into an investigation of the case, as to his truthfulness, or as to his good judgment in relation to it.

Rev. Dr. CHAPIN : Having raised the question, I am satisfied to leave it where Dr. Storrs has left it. My object was to get what light could be secured upon the aspect of the correspondence as it begins ; and I do not wish to press the matter into private relations at all.

Now that I am on my feet, I beg to make a suggestion in regard to this whole matter of asking questions. These matters, that are coming up here, are delicate matters ; and for one, I think — and I presume I speak also for all members of the Council, when I say it — that it is very desirable that the galleries shall not express, in any form, approval or disapproval. It is embarrassing, exceedingly ; and I hope that the intimation will be taken kindly by those who are in the galleries, and that we may depend upon their readiness to further us in arriving at a free and unbiased judgment.

The MODERATOR : I gave that suggestion to the audience in the beginning ; but I must add that if I am required to demand from them an abstinence from demonstrations of applause, I must require it also of the Council. [Laughter and applause.]

The MODERATOR : Silence!

Rev. Dr. H. M. STORRS : I would like to say a word here,—

Rev. Dr. R. S. STORRS : Mr. Moderator, I am perfectly willing to yield the floor ; but unless I get an opportunity, before

long, to reply to these questions which have been rapidly put
to me, I am afraid some of them will have passed from my
memory.

Rev. Dr. H. M. Storrs : I rise for the purpose of asking,
simply, if it would not answer the purpose of Dr. Rankin's
question to omit personal matters entirely ? He raises an inquiry as to whether there had been any communication with
Plymouth Church, on the part of the other churches, antecedent
to the published letter. That is the real thing we want to
get at. It is not the private relations of brethren, — brother
Beecher's private dealings with brothers Storrs and Budington. We are here to inquire as to the relations of churches,
not as to the private relations of pastors ; and what he evidently wanted to get at was this : whether there had been any
approaches to Plymouth Church, in any shape, antecedent to
that first letter, with such strong feeling and such settled
views as seem to be expressed by it, and to be retorted in the
letter of reply. I think that is what brother Rankin really
wants to know.

Rev. Dr. Rankin : Shall I read it, as I put it ?

Rev. Dr. R. S. Storrs : It is of no use. I shall not further
answer it.

Rev. Dr. Rankin : Dr. Storrs has said that he had been
estopped from making personal approaches to Mr. Beecher.
If I understand the decision of the chair to be that this question is out of order, I want to appeal to the Council as to
whether it be out of order.

The Moderator : What is the question ?

Rev. Dr. Rankin : This is the question : — Are these committees satisfied that in their approaches to Mr. Beecher, and
to Plymouth Church, they pursued in spirit the method recommended by our Saviour in the xviii. chapter of Matthew.

The Moderator : That is not irrelevant, if the phrase
"Mr. Beecher" signifies his official position as Pastor.

Rev. Dr. Rankin : Of course.

The Moderator : The personal relation between these
brethren and Mr. Beecher is one thing ; the official relation
of the pastors of these churches to each other is another
thing ; and so far as the question relates to official intercourse

between the bishop of one church, and the bishop of another, it is relevant. But if you come to the personal relations between these brethren, it is irrelevant.

Rev. Dr. RANKIN: Are we to suppose that in their relations as bishops of churches they have different relations to what they have as brethren in Christ?

Rev. Dr. R. S. STORRS: I should like to know if I am expected to answer that question?

Rev. Dr. RANKIN: No: that is for the Moderator.

Rev. Dr. ADAMS: I hope we may now be permitted to hear from Dr. Storrs.

THE MODERATOR: We will now hear Dr. Storrs.

Rev. Dr. R. S. STORRS: Brethren, it is simply because it seems to me altogether according to the proprieties of the occasion, and of the matter, and because I would say nothing that might seem to Mr. Beecher, or to any of his friends, as in any way, or in any degree, intended to reflect upon him, without my intending it, that I stopped with the answer which I gave when the question was suggested before. My personal relations with Mr. Beecher had been long, and intimate, and most affectionate; but at the same time, at the time when this letter was sent, I did not feel at liberty to confer with him, personally and confidentially, in regard to the matter.

As the pastor of a church Mr. Beecher is perhaps the bishop of his church, in a sense in which I am not the bishop of the Church of the Pilgrims. I observed that yesterday, in their letter, the committee of the Plymouth Church addressed the Council as " Reverend Fathers in God." Well, that is an expression which is applied in the Episcopal Church to the Episcopal bishops; but it is the first time in my life that I ever heard it applied to Congregational pastors, assembled in a Council. And it may possibly represent on the part of the Plymouth Church an idea of the dignity and authority of the pastor, which has never prevailed in the Church of the Pilgrims, and which, if I were to insist upon it there, would very likely produce a revolution. No: I am not " Reverend Father in God" to the Church of the Pilgrims; but I am an officer of that church, by its consent and acceptance, and as such have a certain degree of official responsibility, and of public as well as personal influence. But it would not have become me, in a case of this kind — I do not mean in this case merely, but in any case of the kind — to take any action as pastor of the Church of the Pilgrims which had not been specifically authorized by the church.

Suppose that any of the churches in the vicinity — any one of them — were to accept a doctrine antagonistic to the Evangelical faith, and destructive of it. My relation to them would be through the cognizance of that action, and the remonstrance against it, on the part of my church ; and I should act simply as its representative. I do not pull the church, any more than the bowsprit pulls the ship. I do not push the church. In all this matter, I have not pushed either church or committee. We have not pushed one another. We have walked abreast ; and nobody has had any more occasion or power to pull another than one blade of a propeller has to pull the rest. We have worked together, in constant harmony.

I do not know how far this Council would decide that the specific rule of discipline in the xviiith chapter of Matthew, where the offense is between individuals, applies to a case in which one church remonstrates with another. We did not treat this as a case of discipline, precisely. We did not treat it as matter of personal difference, between ourselves and Mr. Beecher. Our complaint was against a church, not against a person. We had been in fellowship with the Plymouth Church for many years, in peace, and brotherly love, and co-operation in good works ; and we saw them doing what seemed to us a fearful thing, fatal to discipline, bringing a stigma on all our churches, tending to work as a principle of mischief in every church in which it should be afterward introduced, — a principle of disease, and active as such ; a zymotic principle, fermenting as it worked. We saw that, and we felt that necessity was laid upon us to make remonstrance. It was a delicate thing to do. How did we do it ?

First, the pastors, meeting together, found that they felt precisely alike, on the subject suddenly opened before them. Secondly, they asked another pastor, wise and kind, and not connected with the incipient movement, what he thought concerning it ; and found his mind in harmony with theirs.

18*

Thirdly, they called a meeting, perfectly private, of all the officers of both their churches, taking them not as individuals, but as officers, — I mean not selecting persons by reason of any personal preference, but taking those who had been previously selected by the churches as office-bearers in the churches, — and asked them what they thought; and found that every mind among them agreed upon the dangerous nature of the action, and upon the injury to be brought on all our churches if it should go unchallenged.

Then it was brought up in the church-meeting, as a question to be discussed and decided, whether action should be taken, and to what extent, — in a church meeting regularly called; that is to say, in the Church of the Pilgrims, called precisely as every meeting which we have held for special business has been called since I have been the pastor of it, until the meeting which called this Council; called at the end of a prayer meeting,— a prayer-meeting which holds oftentimes from two to three hundred persons in it; a prayer-meeting in which the piety of the church, its intelligence, its wisdom, are supposed to be, and in point of fact are, more fully and energetically represented than in any meeting called merely for the transaction of business. At the end of such a prayer-meeting we are accustomed to do our business, when any business has arisen specially requiring to be done. At the end of the prayer-meeting in Plymouth Church, without any previous notice, they appoint delegates to Councils, by their Manual. According to their Manual, every one of you, coming together here to consider the most important question which has confronted Congregationalism in this country since Dr. Channing preached his Baltimore sermon, — every one of you would have been appointed and sent forth, to represent your churches, to represent the Congregationalism of the past and of the present, to put your hand upon the levers which are to turn the ship one way or the other for all time to come, at precisely such a meeting as we convened. You would have been sent hither thus, with this authority, in this critical emergency, — Plymouth Church itself would have sent its delegate, on precisely such an occasion, — at exactly such a meeting as we called to consider this matter.

At that meeting, it being a stormy night, there were not so many present as usual. We had not anticipated the storm. In consequence of it, if there had been one dissenting voice or face among the thirty-odd male members of the church who were present, I should have counseled delay. The moment the matter was suggested, the moment the Resolutions were read, for consideration, criticism, opposition, or assent, every voice was utterly in favor of them. The vote, when it was taken, was a vote so unanimous, so energetic, so instantaneous, that the thirty seemed multiplied by three. I never before heard so eager a vote from so many persons. The Committee of my church are here, and can be questioned as to whether their impressions agreed with mine.

After the meeting a gentleman came to me, and said: " You don't know how relieved I am. I came from a church where discipline was careful. I have enjoyed this church. I have been happy under your ministry. I have had the feeling that here I could be useful and happy for years to come. When I read the report of the proceedings of Plymouth Church, the other morning, I took it home to my wife, and said to her : 'We have made a mistake. We must get out of Congregationalism as soon as we can. Character is not safe in it. The most licentious tongue cannot be curbed. No reputation can be sure of vindication.'" That was the feeling ; not his alone, but that of many. Then we sent the letter.

Why was not the letter read ? Because it was a letter to the Plymouth Church. Because it was not a letter to the public. We desired and meant, if human skill could contrive it, to keep it private between that church and our own, and that none —

A DELEGATE [interrupting] : What you have spoken of were the Resolutions that were passed. The letter you now speak of was not read in the church-meeting?

Rev. Dr. RANKIN : How was this church-meeting called ?

Rev. Dr. R. S. STORRS : It was called at the prayer-meeting, — called as every similar meeting with us is always called, and has been from the beginning.

Mr. Moderator, if these brethren will allow me to go on now, and finish my statement, and afterward will ask me any questions, as many as they like, I will fully answer ; but these sudden interruptions break the continuity of my thought, and may delay us a good deal. I was saying that that letter was intended to be private. Therefore, and therefore only, it was not read in open church-meeting. For if it had been read in such church-meeting, instantaneously these nimble fingers [glancing toward the reporters] would have got it, and yonder unwearying types would have given it, or given an abstract of it, probably in a broken and incomplete form, in which it might have been entirely misunderstood, entirely misrepresented. If it had been published by us, in its full text, it would not have been in any sense a letter to the Plymouth Church, but a challenge to that church, before the general public, addressed to it in the newspapers. We did not mean it to be such. It was intended to be a private communication between the churches. In order to prevent its being published in a garbled form, in order to avoid the necessity of publishing it ourselves, it was not read in open church-meeting.

A Committee was appointed, under full and careful Resolutions, to which I have referred, to send such a letter, conferring with the Plymouth Church concerning this matter. We believe, in the Church of the Pilgrims, in the ancient doctrine of delegated duties, as distinguished from vested authority. Any Congregational church may delegate duties. It does so to its deacons, who are to take care of the poor, and serve at the communion. It does so to those whom it sends on Councils, like this. It does so to those whom it appoints, if it appoints them, as often it does with us, Superintendents of Sunday schools, or of mission schools. We delegate duties ; but we never vest authority in any body of men. When the duty is done, the authority is terminated ; and that is the distinction between the democratic and the aristocratic church, in our judgment. Not that all the business be done with all the brotherhood taking part in every particular. That is not necessary, though we have no objection to it ; but that all the business be done by the whole brotherhood, acting either in public assembly, or though representatives appointed for an office, appointed for a time, instructed to perform a special duty, and then to report.

That was the way which the church elected in sending this letter: to keep it private, that it might not be offensive to the Plymouth Church in the mode of its presentation. Then the letter was accepted by the Committees, was unanimously approved, unanimously signed, and sent upon its way. We did not know, of course, what the Plymouth Church would do with it. They might have taken the letter, and presented it to their Examining Committee, if they had chosen, and said: " Here is a letter the reading of which, publicly, may for the present be postponed." They had it three weeks, almost, before they read it. " We will enter into a conference with these Committees, and see if there cannot be some adjustment of this matter without publication." They might have done that, without infringing the liberty or the rights, or in any way impinging upon the dignity, of the church. We did not know what they would do.

The letter is said to have been a strong one. We meant it should be strong ; but we meant it should be kind. If we made any mistake, we most certainly apologized for that in the letter which was next sent, in which we expressly disclaimed any spirit or purpose of unkindness. We meant it to be strong, because our convictions and feelings were strong, with regard to the nature of the action they had taken, and the dangerous consequences of that action.

But the letter is overshadowed, as the sod beneath the oak is overshadowed by its branching arms and the mighty coronal of its foliage, by such words as these : " The policy is here, *as we understand it*, distinctively avowed." " It is announced as a prevailing policy of the church." Announced ! We did not say affirmed by you. " It *seems to us* to offer opportunity and positive inducement." " Such a course of action *appears to us* especially untimely." " We are *impressed with the conviction* that credit cannot properly be given." " To remain silent when a policy is avowed *which impresses us*," etc. " We do it in absolute kindness of spirit, but under the deepest convictions of duty ; *believing* that you, *however unconsciously*, are imperiling the name," etc. In one instance, where it might have been added, such an expression is omitted ; at the beginning of the last paragraph. We did not mean to say that this is an error which has been certainly adopted by the Plymouth Church. We say, "believing that you" in the preceding paragraph. And then we speak of the error itself, objectively, as "vital and vast;" understanding, ourselves, that the antecedent word "believing" qualified every thing that follows. But there might have been added the same expression, which occurs seven or eight times elsewhere.

Why did we not send a note, instead of an energetic letter? Brethren, Plymouth Church is a powerful church; a proud church, with reason; confident in its strength, with reason. It seemed to us then, it seems to me now, that a simple note of inquiry sent to that church would have been like one of last autumn's leaves dropping on the current, swift and swollen, of the unheeding brook; that, if we were to challenge any attention on their part toward this action, which seemed to us so radical in its error, and so threatening in its consequences, it must be done by a letter long enough, earnest enough, to secure the attention which we desired to command. Perhaps we made a mistake. If you think that any other course would have brought about consequences more desirable, when you are placed in the same circumstances you can try the other course, and then we can compare results.

We did the best we could, in the fear of God, in the love of that church, in the desire that our own churches should be relieved of the burden which seemed thrown upon them, and defended from the dangerous power which seemed suddenly introduced among them. Under a serious sense of our responsibility, with conference beforehand, with the approval of the wisest and most experienced men whose judgment we could get, privately, that we might not challenge them before the public, we sent a letter, long and earnest, but a letter concerning which one of the wisest and kindest of men within the circle of my acquaintance, long a minister of Christ, said, when he heard it read: "Brother, I am glad you have remembered one thing, which I always say in a case of this kind, — forbear threatening." That was his instantaneous verdict on it. That, with all the excitement under which we were, with all the vivid impressions we had of the nature and the consequences of this action which we resisted, that was our impression : that we had been self-restrained, and that the letter did not threaten. That was our intention.

This letter was sent, as I have said, without our knowing what would be done with it, what immediate disposition would be made of it. It might be treated as a matter not necessary to be spread at once before the whole brotherhood, but perhaps to be referred to some committee, and only to be made public at the end of some preceding correspondence. Possibly we might have been wholly satisfied by the result of such a correspondence, and have been ready to withdraw the letter. We didn't know. It was kept ; and after nearly three weeks had passed it was read, and the answer to it was adopted. We had kept it private until a fortnight had passed from the time when our church-meeting was held. In the interval it had been read to an assembly of many persons, — members of the church some of them, members of the society, and not of the church, some of them, — at the house of the pastor of the Plymouth Church. This was a matter of public notoriety. It had been made to be so, not by us. And then, after that, feeling that the obligation of privacy, and the responsibility for privacy, were no longer upon us, it was presented at our church-meeting, called as before, at which, in the case of my own church, more members were present ; and it was unanimously and instantaneously approved.

Brethren, if you imagine that there was any trick in getting it prepared by the Committee, and not approved at the beginning by the church, — if any representations of the Plymouth Church have made that impression upon you, — you may just as well take the impression, and carry it home with you, that I am a black man ! We did not want to heat the already warm feeling of our churches on the subject. We did not want passion, rivalry, and antagonism, to come in any sooner or faster than we could help. We wanted quietness, deliberation, a Christian judiciousness, and a Christian success; and the law of our action was in that motive.

So far, then, I have answered these questions, — what we did, and why we did it as we did. Let me now call your attention Brethren, before I finally relieve your patience, to one or two matters which I think we should consider carefully, all of us, — you on your responsibility, and we on ours.

Let me say one word, however, before I come to that, in answer to the question asked by Prof. Smyth. I said distinctly yesterday afternoon, — as I understand it, as I meant to say it, as I believe I did say it, — that the card which was published by Mr. Beecher would be accepted by sympathetic minds as a final vindication of himself from the imputations which had been cast upon him ; a truthful and complete denial of the scandalous statements which had been circulated against him. It would be accepted as such by sympathetic minds ; and they would feel that, as far as he was concerned, he had done enough. That was the argument given for not prosecuting the matter in the church, when it came up for investigation, indirectly, through the offering of these charges. Therefore I touched it, and for no other reason: to ask, for my own satisfaction and for yours, whether that vindication, to other minds, hostile to him, might not have been increased, supplemented, emphasized, re-enforced, by the distinct verdict of his own church, after investigation, with a judicial authority. I said that it seemed to us, he might thus have been shielded from certain taunts and stings which have since been flung at him.

I do not think it is necessary that I should state such in detail. A Sunday paper, published in this city in the interest of the liquor-sellers, was responsible for one of them, ten days ago. It was, simply, that he was not a man whom the matrons and maidens of Brooklyn should follow in any crusade. A Democratic paper, published in New York, was responsible for another, which happened to flash into mind as I was speaking on this point yesterday, but to which I will not further refer. I say, merely, that the answer which Plymouth Church made, — that the pastor had already vindicated himself, — in reply to our suggestion that there was an opportunity for further vindication of him by its proper action, seems to us to be met, in a measure, and replied to by the fact that here, a year and a half after the stories were first started, such flings can be still repeated ; and by the fact, which it seems to me will probably be the fact, that whenever any paper finds itself in antagonism hereafter with that eminent and powerful man, when he strikes at the Ring as he used to, when he thunders

against vice in high places as he used to, and any one desires
to fling at him a poisoned dart, this will be the dart: " Your
church did not investigate those stories!" I think the church
loved him, oh, how well! Any pastor might be proud, at the
end of fifty years, instead of twenty-five, to have such unanimous, substantial, mighty out-bursts of love and confidence
toward him. They loved him with all their hearts ; and, as I
said yesterday, I honor them for it. But I think, though they
loved him so well, they loved not wisely. To that single point
my remark about this matter had reference ; and then, beyond
that, I went on to say that to this end, of manifesting their love
with all their soul, it seemed to us that they sacrificed the whole
duty of the church in discipline : its remedial duty, if one was
guilty and could be reclaimed ; its vindicating duty toward the
innocent man, if he were unjustly accused of the offense ; its
punitive duty toward one found guilty of such offenses, if he
offered no excuse, and showed no repentance ; its vindicating
duty to itself, for the clearing of itself from any suspicion of
complicity in such wickedness ; its vindicatory duty toward
the Lord on high, who walks in garments of unblemished
brightness. We all felt this; and only in reference to that
previous point came up the remark about which this inquiry
has been made.

Now, Brethren, I beseech you to observe, before you go into
the private session, these things : that this action is corporate
action, public and formal, by the church. The question has
been asked, I suppose, of either one of us, many times : " The
pastor of the Plymouth Church is reported as having preached
so and so. Why do you not interpose there ? Why have you
not made any remonstrance about it ?" Because we have
nothing to do with that. That is for the church to take primary cognizance of ; and, as long as the creed of the church
remains evangelical, we have nothing to say. So we understand our responsibilities, and our duties. Mr. Beecher is a
man of such liberal thought, of such a far-circling mind, of
such facile and affluent utterance, that he corrects one statement by another, and the statement of one week by that of
the following ; and we have always been ready to let his statements balance and interpret one another, confident that in the
end the substance of the Gospel would therein appear.

We have never felt any right to interfere with regard to his various expressions of his opinion, so long as the church remained evangelical in its public declaration of the Faith : the church to whose creed he has expressed his assent, and does express it at every communion ; the church whose creed he has never disavowed ; the church whose creed is the public platform on which he stands every Sunday to preach.

But here is action, corporate and public, of the church itself ; an action not referring to minor matters. We have no call to interpose where a church is regulating its own affairs. It may elect deaconesses, or not ; it may let the women, in whom so largely the piety of the church resides, vote in church-meetings, or not ; it may elect its deacons for three years, or for six years, or for life, or not. All the internal arrangements of it are wholly within its own discretion. But when it touches a doctrine of the Faith, to bring which into the world the Son of God came from the throne, to interpret which in the world the Spirit of God works in the church, the maintenance and vital incorporation of which are essential to the life of God in the world, and to the coming of the Millennium, — when it touches a doctrine of the Faith, by corporate action, we have a right to interpose, as we have supposed.

This is corporate action concerning Discipline, you observe ; concerning that pure and salutary discipline which to us appears characteristic and necessary in the household of Christ. Here is a doctrine of discipline incarnated in this action, as it seems to us, which, being accepted as legitimate, and properly to be applied in any case, makes void the covenant, terminates discipline, dishonors the church, dissolves the church, and casts a stigma upon churches in connection with it, making them suspected by reason of their fellowship. It is a principle that will work, as I have said, if you give it liberty, everywhere. A church loving its ease will take it. A church following a great example will take it. Plymouth Church is powerful and prominent ; and therefore we felt that, because its influence was so wide, it was the more incumbent upon us to stand up against it, for what we hold to be the truth and purity of the Master's household.

You introduce this principle with sanction and approbation, you recognize it once and here, and it works to loosen the cement of Christian fellowship in every Congregational church, from the rock where the Plymouth Pilgrims landed to the Golden Gates of the Pacific.

Brethren, it is not a light matter. It is a matter the roots, the depth, the power of which, will appear to you more and more as you examine it. Personal considerations, one way or the other, are less than the whistle of the boy in the street against the rush of the north-east storm. Personal considerations we wholly cast aside. Here is the power, the invisible and tremendous power, of a disorganizing principle of discipline and fellowship within the church, let loose upon the air, and riding abroad upon all winds. We have breasted it as we could ; and now it is for you to do it also.

Here is a principle, also adopted, you again observe, by corporate action, in regard to the Fellowship of the churches. New and dangerous that is, as well. New? What do 'they say in their letter ? They quote their rules. They say, 'These are our immemorial rules. Plymouth Church stands where it did. Why do you interpose now ? You gave us the right hand of fellowship twenty-six or twenty-seven years ago, on the same rules as now. Why now remonstrate ?'

They *are* the same rules, but the same rules with a wholly different interpretation ; precisely the same rules that appear in the Plymouth Church Manual of 1854, in which appears this contrary interpretation : —

This independence of Congregational churches is neither discord nor isolation, as some represent. They live in close fraternal union ; often meet in Mutual Councils and Conferences ; ask and receive advice and assistance from each other ; and may admonish each other, in case of heresy, lax discipline, or any scandalous offense.

Our fellowship with them was predicated upon the rules as thus interpreted. A new interpretation makes the rule a new one. The life of it is not in the verbal form, but in the moral meaning and intent ; and the moral intent and meaning are represented by the present declaration of the mind of the church ; so that, though the rule in form continues the same, by the new interpretation it is wholly changed. What is that new interpretation ? That these rules relieve all other churches — not ours merely, every church in the city, every Congregational church in the land, every one of your churches — from responsibility for the Doctrine of that church. 'We may give up the inspiration of the Holy Scriptures, the divinity of our Lord, punishment in the life to come, the depravity of human nature, the regenerating grace of the Holy Spirit, promised by God, and realized in the human soul ; and you cannot remonstrate.' In respect to Order : 'we may become Presbyterian, Methodist, Episcopal, what we will ; and we remain in fellowship with you still, as a Congregational church.' In respect to Discipline : 'we may loosen all its bands, dissolve its covenants, and be in fellowship with you still, as a Congregational church.'

That is what the language seemed to us to mean ; and if they had gone on to say, in an equally public and authoritative way, 'therefore our relations with you henceforth are no more responsible or intimate than with a Baptist or a Methodist church :' we should have said, Amen. If the withdrawal had been complete, if they had not said in the same breath, at the same meeting, and afterward in a subsequent document, 'we are more Congregational than you are, we are Congregationalists *par eminence*,' then our path would have been cleared. We wish that church all possible success. We will utter no word, and lift no finger, to stop its triumphant marching forward. But we are not willing to be responsible for a church with which we can never remonstrate. If my neighbor lives in quietness, I live in peace with him ; but if he insists upon keeping grenades and bomb-shells in his cellar, and now and then touches one of them off, I want the party-wall made thicker.

We say, then, that this public and corporate action, first concerning Discipline, dissolves the church, practically. It leaves that church bound together by mutual sympathies, by their common attachments to a place and a service, to a pastor and to a memory ; but the same principle, of the power of dissolving covenants by a personal choice no longer to be bound by them, extends to the pastor, and to every officer ; and, carrying it out completely, the church has no more organization than a thousand sparrows, flirting and quarreling in the air. And the same action, by the principle of Fellowship which it infolds, dissolves the denomination. If a Congregational church cannot remonstrate with another, but still remains responsible for it, it is impossible that fellowship should continue to be pledged, upon such terms, and such a basis. A fellowship that may be used for remonstrance when the occasion demands it, when the necessity is great, is vital to the denomination. A fellowship that should be occupied and exercised in interfering in merely minor matters would be, of course, intolerable and tyrannous.

We have dwelt side by side with Plymouth Church all these years, and have said never a word of criticism, censure, or remonstrance, concerning any of its procedures. But when these touched what seemed to us the vital bond of the church, the covenant, and the paramount end of the church, the purification of even its erring members, the manifestation of the innocence of the upright, and the vindication of Christ's glory on the earth, — we felt bound to remonstrate, and to remonstrate earnestly.

Now, Brethren, if you say this case was exceptional, remember that Plymouth Church has never said it. Opportunity has again and again been given, and no such reply has ever been made. It might have said, " The man is a monomaniac." It might have said, " For other reasons, this case we set apart." We recognized that in our first letter, and gave the opportunity for the saying of it, if it were true. " It is not represented [we say] as a hazardous, but a seemingly necessary expedient, adopted reluctantly, in some extreme and exceptional case, the prosecution of which might be attended with peculiar embarrassments." We absolutely suggested such a reply, if such a reply could honestly be made ; and there was no response. It was announced as according to the rule ; a natural, proper application of the rule ; to be repeated fifty times a year, therefore, if fifty times a year the occasion should arise.

If you say that Plymouth Church is itself exceptional, we

admit that, to a degree: exceptional in its numbers; exceptional in the fame and power of its pastor ; exceptional in the magnificence of its income ; exceptional in the largeness of its enterprise, in various directions.   But then will you tell us at what point the exception begins to arise which relieves it from the obligations of Discipline within, and of Fellowship without ? How large must the church be ? how numerous must its membership become ? how famous and powerful must its pastor show himself ? Where is the gauge, in mental ability and mental attainment, in rising above which a man gains the right to do as he will, and remain a Congregational pastor still ?   How large must the church have become, in the expanding compass of its strength, before it becomes competent to do exactly what it chooses in respect to Doctrine, Order, and Discipline, and allow no remonstrance ?

Draw the line, Brethren.   Tell us at what point the exceptional position begins to operate for a universal freedom from the restraints which we feel binding upon us.   And if you say that such a principle of Fellowship as that is allowable, and that, in the interests of a looser discipline, a church may sever itself from all responsibility to others, and still remain a Congregational church, then, in the name of justice, in the name of reason, in the name of the gratitude we owe to the early founders of Unitarianism for their many services to letters, and morals, and liberty, and a humane religion, do not fail to carry back that principle, and say : A principle which is allowable for the giving of larger looseness in the matter of discipline, is allowable as well for the encouragement of freer speculation upon matters of doctrine ; and Unitarian societies are in fellowship with us, as Congregational churches yet !

Brethren, we are in the place where two seas meet.   Do not misunderstand the exigencies of the case.   Don't decide merely upon abstract questions.   We can argue out principles for ourselves, if we must.   We are capable of reading, each of us, and can find them in the Platform.   But give us practical advice.   Here, where the two seas come together, and the ship is in danger of being broken by the violence of the waves, we turn to you.   Here are two churches : I will not match them against Plymouth Church in numbers, in wealth, in fame in the world, though I do not know that in numbers or wealth they would not bear the comparison : but I say that they have been honest and faithful churches, to the Master, to the truth, to the order they inherit from their New England ancestors. One of them is the oldest in the city, of its order ; the other as old, within a few months, as Plymouth Church itself. There is included in these churches as fair a proportion as you will find, in any churches of the city, of those who love our Master ; who are eager to spread the tidings of his Cross through the world ; who are ready to give, of what God has given to them, liberally, gladly, continuously, for the furtherance of His work. They have done no dishonor to the Fathers' name. They compare favorably with any churches, of any order, in the city around them, for the efforts they have made for the evangelization of the heathen, and the promotion of Christian education and religion in the land. They have stood ready to help asylums and hospitals, schools and churches, and every public work, — giving of their money, and giving of their time, giving of the inmost energy of their will, of the very life of their souls, that they might build up and bless this city, now, and in the coming time.

Now you are where the two interests collide. Here are two churches ; there is one, greater, perhaps, and certainly more famous, than either or both of these. But do not think that you can cover the case between these churches by abstract propositions. Give us advice. Tell us what to do. Remember the responsibilities which are now upon you, as they have been, long and heavily, upon us. Admonish us, if you think we have erred. Direct us in our future course. Do it as mindful of Him whom we serve, and in whose presence we are every one of us to stand. And remember that you are to us the last resort !

Rev. Dr. RANKIN : May I ask if the reply of Dr. Storrs covers the action of the Clinton-avenue Church ? if that was the method adopted there ?

Rev. Dr. BUDINGTON : It was.

Rev. Dr. RANKIN : I have no present opinion. I am seeking for light and truth. We were told by Dr. Dexter that that is what we are here for. I admire the magnificent rhetoric of

Dr. Storrs as much as any one. But after all I wanted to know whether the preliminary steps that should be taken, before any thing was put upon paper, had been taken by these churches.

Rev. Dr. Post: There was one question asked, that I believe has not been answered, upon which I think an answer will be desirable: whether the construction put upon the last letter of these churches by the Plymouth Church, as declining a Mutual Council, or withdrawing their request for it, was correct, or was admitted?

Rev. Dr. Budington: In reply to the question of Dr. Post: It will be remembered that Plymouth Church asked us to state the points we had in mind to be submitted by the three churches to the Council, saying, in connection with the asking, that they would give us a prompt reply. In our letter we gave them the points, as we understood them, in frank and full answer to their question. At the same time, in another part of this letter, we affectionately and earnestly called their attention to what we understood to be the inevitable result of their Resolution of independence. We did not understand that the two things were connected together at all. We did expect a full and free answer to both; and, if either was omitted, we certainly did not expect that an answer to that part of our letter would be omitted, which was drawn forth expressly by their request, and a prompt answer to which was promised beforehand. You can understand, therefore, Brethren, how much surprised we were, when, on submitting to them the five points in our minds, they said they inferred, from the fact that we put a certain interpretation upon a certain Resolution, that therefore they were released from their promise to tell us whether those five points would be accepted, by them as by us, for common submission to a common Council.

Rev. Dr. R. S. Storrs: There is one question which I did not reply to, and one statement which I wish to make.

The question was asked, but I had forgotten it, it was so entirely unfamiliar: what power the Standing Committee has in my church? It has no power; because it does not exist, and never did exist. We have what is called an Examining Committee, whose function is expressly limited to conferring with persons desiring to enter the church, and propounding those whom they consider proper candidates ; and, further, to hearing complaints, when any complaint is made by one member against another. They have no authority whatever, beyond those two delegated duties.

The Committee which was appointed by the church to conduct this correspondence with the Plymouth Church, and which has been acting for the church in this matter ever since, —authorized to do so by successive Resolutions, empowering it to do all that was needful to bring this to its issue, and finally authorized, specifically, to issue these Letters-Missive,— is a Special Committee ; appointed for the special purpose for which the special powers have been given, and whose function terminates, absolutely, when the case is ended.

One word more : I did not see Mr. West present in the house at the moment when I made my statement in regard to the conviction on his mind which led him to make this movement in Plymouth Church, with no suggestion, with no inspiration, from us, and no previous knowledge of it on our part. I have seen him, since I ascertained that he was here, and have just asked him if he heard my statement ; and he says he did. I asked him if the statement was correct ; and he says it was.

Rev. Mr. MARTYN : Would it not have been competent for the two churches by their Committees to have asked for an explanation of these matters of common concern from the corresponding Committee of Plymouth Church ? and, if so, would not that course have been nearer to Matt. xviii. than the course that was adopted, in first sending the letter, without asking for any preliminary oral explanation ?

Rev. Dr. R. S. STORRS : Our Committees are Special Committees, as I have said, appointed for a specific duty ; their existence terminating when the duty shall be done. The Plymouth Church had no corresponding Special Committee on this subject. Our permanent Examining Committee had no authority, or privilege, to institute a movement of this kind, or to conduct it ; and we were not aware from their Manual, and never have been made aware since, that their Examining Committee had any prerogative of receiving such a communication, and reply-

15

ing to it. If they had had such an authority, it must have been given to them by the church, and for the occasion. It would have been Presbyterianism, outright, for our Examining Committee to have made a remonstrance to their Examining Committee ; for it would have concentrated the authority and power of the church in a Session, without the name. The church-membership, on our part, appointed its Special Committee to represent it. The membership of the Plymouth Church might have done the same thing, if they had chosen ; but they never did it.

Rev. Mr. MARTYN : Did you not inform us in your remarks, a few moments ago, that in your judgment it would have been competent for the Committee to have received your letter, and to have withheld it from the church for a time ? Now, if it was competent for that Committee of Plymouth Church so to act, would it not have been equally competent for that same Committee to have received from your Committee the communication to which I refer, oral, and preliminary ?

Rev. Dr. R. S. STORRS : I said that we did not know what Plymouth Church would do with our letter. A copy of it went to the Pastor, and another to the Clerk ; and they might have presented it, if they had chosen, to the Examining Committee, have taken their advice, and have got from the church, upon that advice, the authority for any Special Committee to confer with us before making the letter public. There would have been nothing un-Congregational in that. But we had no right to assume that it would be done, as in point of fact it was not done ; and we could only address our letter to the church itself, not to its Examining Committee.

Rev. Mr. BYINGTON : I would like to ask Dr. Storrs whether it is his understanding, that, in the letter of December 15, the offer of a Mutual Council, which had been made to Plymouth Church, was withdrawn ?

Rev. Dr. R. S. STORRS : No, sir. It was positively not withdrawn. We understood their Resolution to declare them practically, though not formally, outside of the circle of Congregational churches, no longer responsible to us, no longer responsible to any Council. We said then, ' It seems to us that by that action you have vacated the result of any Council of all authority or significance as concerning yourselves. We do not renew our application, lest you should take it as intimating that your recent Resolution does not mean what it says.' But we never withdrew the request, and we stated distinctly the points which we desired to submit.

Rev. Mr. WILLCOX : Dr. Storrs stated yesterday his great apprehension, and that of the Committees, to be, that so much of our time would be spent in preliminary discussions, that we should arrive at a Result only after a hasty examination of the facts before us. We have an hour before dinner, and can certainly do something in that time. But if we proceed with these questions, which we could easily do until night, we must accomplish nothing. Many of the brethren must be at home before the Sabbath. I move, therefore, that the Council be now by themselves.

Rev. C. H. EVEREST, of Brooklyn, N.Y.: I am somewhat a stranger to the brethren who are gathered here ; but I am a pastor in this city, and I know that there are many members of our churches here, and many brethren in the ministry, not members of the Council, and that we cannot give them a greater privilege than to allow them to listen to these Fathers in the Church, so eminently qualified to be their teachers. If it is not out of order, sir, I would move that the sessions of this Council, in the future, as in the past, be open.

Rev. Dr. FISKE : There is a point upon which inquiry has been made by a member of the Council, to which Dr. Budington I hope will give an answer ; as to the passage in the letter of the Plymouth Church to the parties inviting us.

Rev. Dr. BUDINGTON : As I understand it, I am inquired of whether we had reason to believe that there would be no acceptance of any further communication on our part with the Plymouth Church ; and I would say, in reply to that, that we felt that we were definitely shut out from any communication with Plymouth Church, after the reception of their last public letter, by reason of language you will find in the middle of page 49 of the pamphlet, in which they say : " We must decline to receive in any case from them " (meaning from the whole brotherhood), " or from you " (meaning the committees of the two churches), " letters containing covert insinuations

against the character of any of the members of this church."
Inasmuch as our communications respected a case of discipline, by the very necessity of the case those communications were susceptible of the interpretation of " containing
insinuations " against certain members of that church ; and
this sentence necessarily excluded us from any subsequent
communication with them.

Rev. Dr. PATTON, of Chicago, Ill. : I would like to inquire
whether any other members of the Committees of the two
churches would like to be heard.

Deacon R. P. BUCK, one of the Committee of the Church
of the Pilgrims, responded : I would say that we agree
entirely with the representations made by Drs. Storrs and
Budington, and that the Committees are united in this
thing. I would not say a word further, except for the last
question asked of Dr. Budington. It so happened, that it fell
to my lot to present the first letter to Mr. Beecher. Mr.
Beecher received us politely. The moment he opened the
letter, he asked me its contents. I told him it was a letter of
considerable length, and he had better read it at his leisure,
rather than hastily, as he would be obliged to then. He insisted, as he tore it open, on knowing its contents. I then
said to him it had relation to the action of Plymouth Church
on the 31st of October, — the lack of discipline toward a
member who had been slandering his pastor. Mr. Beecher
answered with great emphasis, and, as I thought, with some
passion : " We don't allow any one, sir, to interfere with our
matters, in this church. We don't acknowledge the right of
any body of men to interfere in any form with us." I immediately replied : " Perhaps you had better at your leisure
read the letter, before any reply is made." I merely state this
in answer to the question : that they did not allow any interference on the part of any other church, and considered it impertinent on our part that we should remonstrate with them.
I thought it proper to state this in answer to the inquiry made
of Dr. Budington about their shutting off correspondence.
The committees are perfectly satisfied with the presentation
of the case by our pastors, and agree most perfectly, I believe,
with all that has been said.

The question was stated to be on the motion that the Council be by themselves.

The MODERATOR : It has been suggested that a word of explanation is necessary. Persons who are familiar with the transaction of business in ecclesiastical Councils know that the immemorial and constant usage of a Council is to deliberate, after hearing the case presented by the parties concerned, on their Result, and to come to such Result by themselves. This is in perfect analogy with the proceedings in all similar matters. If the Council retire now, to be by themselves, not only will our friends in the galleries, and on the floor, members of these churches that have invited us, be excluded ; but the gentlemen of the press will also be excluded. They will understand that they have as little right to be present, and take note of what we say and do in this private session, as they have to be present in the jury-room when the case has been committed to the jury, or to be present at the private consultation of judges on a question of law. I make this statement for their satisfaction ; for I cannot doubt that it will be entirely satisfactory both to the gentlemen of the press, and to the members of these churches, and to the public at large. The question is : Will the Council now be by themselves?

Rev. Dr. GEORGE E. ADAMS : May I say one word in reference to this matter ? This is not a secret session. We do not go by ourselves because we have any thing to say that we are not willing the world should know, but because we can do more by ourselves, in a small room, in an hour,— where we can hear each other talk,— than we can do here in three hours, where, if we say any thing, we must make long speeches.

The question being taken, the motion was adopted, and the Council went into private session.

At twenty minutes before twelve o'clock, P.M., the Council resumed its open session. The Hon. C. I. WALKER, the Associate Moderator, was in the chair.

He said : I desire, and especially request, that there shall be no manifestations of approval or disapproval as this Result shall be read, as is becoming the order and solemnity of such an occasion. The Moderator of the Council will now read the Result, at which the Council has arrived.

The Moderator, Rev. LEONARD BACON, D.D., then read the Result, as follows : —

RESULT OF COUNCIL.

This Council has listened carefully to the Committees of the churches by which it was convened, and has received from them a clear and earnest statement of the aims and principles which have determined the action of these churches in the proceedings which they ask us to review.

We have also received from the Plymouth Church a communication declining an invitation from this Council, as well as from these two churches, to appear, by its pastor and committee, and assist in the presentation and discussion of the questions before us, but, at the same time, offering suggestions and arguments which we have carefully and candidly considered.

We cannot doubt the right of these two churches to ask advice of us concerning the regularity, and the Christian character, of what they have done in their dealing with the Plymouth Church. No church is beyond the reach of the public opinion of other churches, expressed either directly, or through an ecclesiastical Council. Any church, in its essential and inalienable independence, may, in the exercise of a reasonable discretion, consider any public action of any other church ; may, in proper methods, express its approval or disapproval ; and may make that public action the subject of friendly correspondence and remonstrance, or, if need be, the ground of a temporary or a permanent cessation of acts of inter-communion.

There has been laid before us a series of letters that have passed between these two churches and the Plymouth Church. On that correspondence it is our unquestionable right to have an opinion, and to express it, though we have no right to try the Plymouth Church, as a party before us.

We have to say, then, that the letter of remonstrance and admonition with which the correspondence began was not un-called for.

The churches throughout the United States, and the general public also, felt a painful anxiety on a question imminent and urgent in this city of Brooklyn, and involving the honor, not of the Congregational churches only, but of Christianity itself. Without any more explicit reference to that question, it will suffice to say, that, in the Plymouth Church, a complaint was brought against a member, that he had "circulated and promoted scandals, derogatory to the Christian integrity of the pastor, and injurious to the reputation of the church." The person complained of appeared in the church-meeting, and declared that, four years before that time, he had, by his own volition, terminated his connection with the church; and thereupon his name was, by a vote of the church, dropped from the catalogue of its members.

That action of the Plymouth Church was the occasion on which these two churches interposed, with remonstrance, and with a request for a friendly conference.

In this act they represented the interests of the fraternity of Congregational churches, whose principles of discipline, and whose fair Christian fame, were endangered by the course which the Plymouth Church seemed to be pursuing. For this moral heroism they deserve thanks, even should errors of judgment be traceable in some of the details of their procedure.

In our consideration of the letter then addressed to the Plymouth Church, we find that the impression made by it was in some measure different from what was intended by its authors. Written under the pressure of apprehensions and anxieties long suppressed, it seems to have impinged more painfully than was intended on the sensibilities of those to whom it was addressed.

To many the letter seems entirely unexceptionable, in matter and in manner, and entirely appropriate to the occasion ; while to others it seems unnecessarily severe in the tone of its condemnation of the proceeding complained of.

In their second letter, the complaining churches, having found what impression they had made by their remonstrance, offered an explanation, which, we trust, was not unacceptable.

Concerning the reply of the Plymouth Church to that letter, we say nothing more than that an ingenuous explanation of the reasons which had prompted the Plymouth Church to rid itself of an offending member by an exceptional method might have brought the correspondence to an early and a happy termination. We can see no sufficient reason why the request of the complaining churches for a fraternal conference should not have been granted.

In the subsequent correspondence we see, on the part of the complaining churches, an expression of their desire to unite with the Plymouth Church in referring the points of difference to the advice of a Council. We find on the part of the Plymouth Church no definite expression either of consent or of refusal. Yet, inasmuch as the Plymouth Church did not distinctly refuse to unite in a reference to a Council, we cannot but regret that the complaining churches did not urge their request, till a refusal or an evasion should have become unequivocal.

We are not invited, nor do we take it upon ourselves, to advise the Plymouth Church concerning its methods of dealing with offenders. But we are invited to advise these two churches on certain questions.

Therefore we say, distinctly, that the idea of membership in a Congregational church is the idea of a Covenant, between the individual member and the church ; that, by virtue of that Covenant, the member is responsible to the church for his conformity to the law of Christ, and the church is responsible for him ; and that this responsibility does not cease till the church, by some formal and corporate act, has declared the dissolution of the Covenant.

The Covenant may be broken by the member. He may offend, and, when duly admonished, may give no satisfactory

evidence of repentance. In that case, he is cut off from communion. The church, having given its testimony, is no longer
responsible for him ; and he can be restored only by the
removal of the censure.

Voluntary absence of a resident member from the communion of the church, and from its public worship, does not
dissolve the Covenant, but is a reasonable ground of admonition, and, if persisted in, of final censure. When a regular
complaint is made against such a member, that in some other
respect he violates the law of Christ, and especially when the
complaint is that he has "circulated and promoted scandals
derogatory to the Christian integrity of the pastor, and injurious to the reputation of the church," the consideration that
he has long ago forsaken the church is only an aggravation
of his alleged fault.

In regard to the future relations between these churches
and the Plymouth Church, we express our hope that the very
extraordinary proceeding which gave occasion for the correspondence, and for this Council, will not be a precedent for
the guidance of that church hereafter. Could we suppose
that such proceedings will be repeated, we should feel that
the disregard of the first principles involved in the idea of
church-membership, and in the idea of the fellowship of
churches with each other, would require the strongest possible protest. But the communication from the Plymouth
Church to this Council makes professions and declarations
which justify the hope that such deviation from the orderly
course of discipline will not be repeated.

The accused person in that case has not been retained in
the church, nor recommended to any other church.

We recite some of those declarations from the Plymouth
Church which encourage the hope we have expressed. "We
rejoice," says the Plymouth Church, "to live in affectionate
fellowship with all churches of the Lord Jesus, and especially with those who are in all things like-minded with us,
holding to the same faith and order, not only in things fundamental, but in things less essential, yet dear to us by
conviction or association." "We cheerfully admit, that whenever any church shall openly and avowedly change the essen-

tial conditions upon which it was publicly received into the fellowship of neighboring churches, or shall by flagrant neglect exert a pernicious and immoral influence upon the community, or upon sister churches, it is their right, either by individual action or by Council, to withdraw their fellowship. We hold that, preceding disfellowship, in all such cases, there should be such affectionate and reasonable inquiry as shall show that the evil is real ; that the causes of it are within the control of the church ; that the evil is not a transient evil, such as may befall any church, but is permanent, and tending to increase rather than diminish."

While it is not to be forgotten that this communication from the Plymouth Church is entirely subsequent to the case as it stood upon the convening of this Council, when the Plymouth Church, by its action of December 5th, had declared itself responsible for no other church, and no other church responsible for it, in respect to doctrine, order, and discipline, — which action, as interpreted by the circumstances then existing, implied a withdrawal to the ground of total Independency, — yet that church is to be fraternally judged by its latest utterance.

These professions on the part of the Plymouth Church may be accepted by other churches as indicating its intention to maintain an efficient discipline, and to regard the mutual responsibility of churches.

At the same time, the Council feels constrained to declare that these declarations seem to us inconsistent with the Resolution of interpretation adopted by the Plymouth Church, December 5th, 1873, and with other acts and statements appearing in the published documents. We think that the action of that church, as presented in these documents, if unmodified, would justify these churches in withdrawing fellowship.

Yet, inasmuch as the Plymouth Church seems to us to admit, in its communication to us, the Congregational principles of discipline and fellowship, we advise the churches convening this Council to maintain with it the relations of fellowship, as heretofore ; in the hope that the Plymouth Church may satisfy these churches of its acceptance of the principles which it has been supposed to disavow.

We also desire, in this connection, to re-affirm and emphasize the doctrine, laid down in all our platforms, of the obligation of Fellowship. This duty applies to all Christian churches. In the case of those instituted and united in accordance with the Congregational polity, it involves that more intimate communion which is exercised " in asking and giving counsel, in giving and receiving admonition," and in other acts relating to doctrine, order, and discipline.

This mutual responsibility of the Congregational churches has characterized their system from the beginning, distinguishing it from simple Independency. With the autonomy of the local church, it is one of the formative and essential principles of Congregationalism. Without it, we have no basis in our polity for that system of co-operative effort to which our churches are pledged.

We regard, therefore, the principles of fellowship which the pastors and churches convening us have so earnestly maintained, to be those which we have received from our Fathers, and the Word of God. We appreciate and honor their fidelity to these principles, under circumstances of peculiar and severe trial. And we offer our earnest prayer to the great Head of the Church, that He may bestow upon them, and upon the pastor and church with which they have been in correspondence, wisdom and grace ; that He may guide them in all their action ; and that He may quicken in all our churches, through these painful trials, a spirit of renewed fidelity to the sacred obligations of our Covenants, and our church-communion ; and we pray that He to whom all power in heaven and on earth is given, who has promised to be with His Church always, even to the end of the world, and who, under the inspiration of His spirit and His truth has joined these churches in a grand and memorable past, standing shoulder to shoulder in the great moral and spiritual battles of the age, may again unite them in the future conflicts and victories of His kingdom !

LEONARD BACON, C. I. WALKER,	*Moderators.*

A. H. QUINT, I. C. MESERVE,	*Scribes.*

When Rev. Dr. Bacon, the Moderator, had finished reading the result, he said :

This is the Result of the Council. We take pleasure in communicating it to the churches that have convened us, hoping and praying that, by means of it, they may obtain light for their guidance, and may be led in the paths of peace, unity, and righteousness.

Rev. Dr. R. S. Storrs said, in reply :

Mr. Moderator, I have only in a word, at this late hour, to express, on behalf of the Committees of the churches, and on behalf of the churches themselves which these Committees represent, our sense of indebtedness to the members of the Council, for the great patience with which they have considered the case presented to them ; for the freedom of utterance in the presentation of the case which they have allowed, on the one hand to the churches inviting them, and on the other to the Plymouth Church ; and especially for the extended and careful discussions through which these subjects have passed in the private sessions, of the details of which, of course, we know nothing, but of the extent and patience of which we are fully aware.

I believe it was Burke who said of Lord Clive, concerning his work in India, that he "forded a deep water on an unknown bottom ; but he left a bridge for his successors, across which the lame might hobble, and the blind might grope their way." We have had to deal with very extraordinary facts ; we have had to face a very extraordinary combination of antagonistic influences ; we have had to contend for principles which seemed to us vital. We are very glad that, in reviewing the past, upon the whole, we see so little to regret, and that the Council sees so little to regret, in what we have done. We rejoice that what we have done has brought into new and distinct expression, by so large a body as this, — representing the Congregational churches of all parts of the land, and, in intelligence and experience, far surpassing any similar body that was ever assembled before, — these principles, which have been with us vital and organic, for which we have contended, and which are now upborne before the land by the wisdom and the eminence of this assembly.

And as you have offered your prayer for us, that we may be kept in the paths of righteousness, and of the peace which comes with righteousness, so we offer in return our earnest prayers for you, and for the churches which you represent : that you individually may be guided and kept on your way homeward, and may find in health and in peace those whom you left there ; and that upon the churches over which you preside may come the blessing of the principles affirmed by you, in all time to come ; and the blessing of Him from whom those principles come to us ; in whose Son is our only perfect leader, in whose Spirit our only perfect guidance, and in whose Heaven our only true and everlasting home !

The following Resolution was offered :

Resolved, That the members of this Council desire to record their thanks to God for the tokens of His presence, which, during their sessions, they have enjoyed ; for the spirit of brotherhood and forbearance with which their discussions have been characterized, from first to last ; and for the signal favor which He has shown them, in guiding them toward the Result at which they have arrived. They recognize in these things the answer to the prayers which have been offered, not only by the members of the Council themselves, but by others, and by the churches whom they represent ; and they return to their several spheres of labor in the faith that the Lord hath been with us, and will bless us.

The Resolution was unanimously adopted.

The following Resolution was also offered :

Resolved, That we offer to the Pastors and the churches by whose invitation we are convened, in behalf of interests which are ours no less than theirs, the cordial and unanimous thanks of the Council, for their eminently liberal provision for our coming and entertainment, and for the thoughtful care with which they have guarded the freedom of our discussions ; and, in departing, we invoke the presence and blessing of God to abide continually in the households whose hospitality we have such reason to hold in most grateful remembrance.

The Resolution was unanimously adopted.

On motion, the Council was then dissolved, after the singing of the Doxology, and the Benediction by the Moderator.

THE FOLLOWING DOCUMENT was transmitted to the invited and accepting members of the Council, by the joint Committees of the Church of the Pilgrims, and Clinton Avenue Congregational Church, Brooklyn, N.Y., April 15, 1874.

To the Churches, and Clergymen not in the Pastoral Charge, invited to the Advisory Council, convened in Brooklyn, N.Y., March 24, 1874.

DEARLY BELOVED :— The Committees of *The Church of the Pilgrims*, and *The Clinton Avenue Congregational Church*, have been requested, by their respective churches, to send you a copy of the Report submitted by them, on the third of April, together with the Resolutions passed by the churches, at that time.

Wishing you grace, mercy, and peace, from God our Father, and the Lord Jesus Christ, we are affectionately yours, in the faith and fellowship of the Gospel : —

For the Church of the Pilgrims:	*For Clinton Avenue Congregational Church:*
RICHARD S. STORRS, *Pastor*,	WILLIAM IVES BUDINGTON, *Pastor*,
RICHARD P. BUCK, ⎫	ALFRED S. BARNES, ⎫
ARCHIBALD BAXTER, ⎪	JAMES W. ELWELL, ⎪
DWIGHT JOHNSON, ⎪	HARVEY B. SPELMAN, ⎪
JOSHUA M. VAN COTT, ⎬ *Committee.*	THOMAS S. THORP, ⎬ *Committee.*
ELI MYGATT, JUN., ⎪	AUGUSTUS F. LIBBY, ⎪
WALTER T. HATCH, ⎪	FLAMEN B. CANDLER, ⎪
LUCIEN BIRDSEYE, ⎭	CALVIN C. WOOLWORTH, ⎭

REPORT.

The Special Committee, which was requested by this church to act, on its behalf, in summoning the ADVISORY COUNCIL, called by the Letter-Missive adopted by the church, February 23d, and also in presenting to the Council, when convened, the matters to be laid before it for consideration and advice, beg leave to report:

That they have performed the offices thus intrusted to them, with the care and attention which their importance demanded, and with an earnest desire that the wishes of the church, in regard to the constitution of the Council, and to the presentation before it of the subjects to be discussed, should be fully accomplished.

The Committee, as requested by the church, after full consultation with the Committee of the Clinton Avenue Church,* designated and invited SEVENTY-NINE churches from different and distant parts of the land, with SEVENTEEN eminent divines not now in the Pastoral office ; endeavoring thus to secure a Council as impartial, as discreet, and as properly influential, as could be assembled, representing fairly the Congregational churches of the country. Of the churches invited, SEVENTY-SIX accepted the invitation ; and SEVENTY-FIVE were represented in the Council, by Pastor or Delegate, in far the larger number of instances by both. Three churches, only, declined the invitation.

Of the clergymen personally invited, a larger proportion were unable to be present. By reason of sickness, accident, absence from home, or imperative official duties, we were deprived of the aid of seven of those whose wisdom we had sought; but the remaining TEN were present and influential in the Council.

The Council was convened, in the Clinton Avenue Church, on the evening of Tuesday, March 24, and continued its sessions till midnight of Saturday, March 28, having given the most earnest, careful, patient, and intelligent attention to the important questions submitted for its advice.

The Official Report of the proceedings of the Council has not yet been forwarded to the Committee, by the officers of that body. When it is received, it will be transferred, by the Chairman of the Committee, to the Clerk of the church, unless the church shall otherwise direct, to be preserved among our files.

The Result adopted by the Council, and adopted, as we are informed, with only eight votes in the negative, has been communicated to the Committee, in advance of the full journal of the proceedings; and they herewith present it to the church. It is as follows : —

[*Vide* pp. 230-235.]

In connection with this Result of Council, the Committee offer to the church, for its consideration, and recommend for its adoption, the following Resolutions : —

Resolved, first : That this church accepts the Result of the Council, recently convened by its invitation, in connection with that of

*("Church of the Pilgrims," *as presented at Clinton Avenue Congregational Church.*

the Clinton Avenue Church, * and directs that it be entered in full on its permanent records.

Resolved, secondly : That this church is grateful to the sister churches, far and near, which responded, with such unusual readiness and unanimity, to its request for their presence and advice ; and also to the eminent clergymen who have given it the benefit of their counsel, in the peculiar circumstances in which it has been placed, and on the important questions which, in the Providence of God, have come before it.

Resolved, thirdly : That this church fully appreciates the wisdom and dignity, with the admirable spirit of kindness and candor, not toward the inviting churches only, but toward the Plymouth Church as well, which were shown by the Council in all its deliberations, and which are conspicuously manifest in its Result ; and, while recognizing thus the wisdom, impartiality, and Christian fidelity of those whose counsel it had sought, it also devoutly and gratefully recognizes the guidance and the help of God, from the inspiration of whose Spirit come all wise counsels, and all just works, and whose direction the church desires and prays ever to follow.

Resolved, fourthly : That this church welcomes the distinct recognition, by the Council, of the gravity of the occasion which called forth our earliest letter of remonstrance and admonition, and the emphatic approval expressed by it of the action in which we then " represented the interests of the fraternity of Congregational churches, whose principles of discipline, and whose fair Christian fame, were endangered ; " it is encouraged by the distinct and vigorous affirmation, given by the Council, to what this church has always regarded as essential principles in the Congregational order of government ; it is instructed and re-enforced, by the explicit declaration of the Council, that the action of the Plymouth Church, prior to the issuing of our Letters-Missive, " if unmodified, would justify these churches in withdrawing fellowship ; " and it accepts, with cordial readiness, the suggestions of the Council, or of any members of it, as to any "errors of judgment which may be traceable in some of the details of our proceedings."

Resolved, fifthly : That as this church has had but one desire and purpose in all its correspondence with the Plymouth Church, — namely, to have the true principles of discipline within the local church, and of the fellowship and mutual responsibility of Congregational churches toward each other, maintained and honored —

---

*("Church of the Pilgrims," *as presented at Clinton Avenue Congregational Church.*

and as these are judged by the Council to be now accepted and set forth by that church, with satisfactory clearness, and in a permanent form, in the declarations adopted by the Plymouth Church, March 25, and on that day presented to the Council, — which declarations constitute henceforth a part of the official records both of the Plymouth Church and of the Council, — we accept, on our part, the recommendations of the Council touching our further relations to that church. We concur in the hope expressed by the Council that the " Plymouth Church may satisfy these churches of its acceptance of the principles which it has been supposed to disavow ;" and, without memories of bitterness, or anxious anticipations, we invoke for it an ever increasing measure of Christian prosperity, and the Divine favor.

Resolved, sixthly : That the foregoing Report and Resolutions be printed, and that a copy of them be sent, by the Committee, to each of the churches, and to each of the clergymen not in the Pastoral charge, invited to the Council by our Letters-Missive.

Resolved, finally : That, after performing the duties assigned by these Resolutions, the Special Committee heretofore representing this church, in its correspondence with the Plymouth Church, and before the Council, be discharged from further duty.

For the Church of the Pilgrims ;		*For Clinton Avenue Congregational Church :*	
RICHARD S. STORRS, *Pastor,*		WILLIAM IVES BUDINGTON, *Pastor,*	
RICHARD P. BUCK,		ALFRED S. BARNES,	
ARCHIBALD BAXTER,		JAMES W. ELWELL,	
DWIGHT JOHNSON,		HARVEY B. SPELMAN,	
JOSHUA M. VAN COTT,	*Committee.*	THOMAS S. THORP,	*Committee.*
ELI MYGATT, JUN.,		AUGUSTUS F. LIBBY,	
WALTER T. HATCH,		FLAMEN B. CANDLER,	
LUCIEN BIRDSEYE,		CALVIN C. WOOLWORTH,	

BROOKLYN, N.Y., APRIL 3, 1874.

BROOKLYN, N,Y., APRIL 3, 1874.

At church-meetings, of the Church of the Pilgrims, and the Clinton Avenue Congregational Church, held this evening, the foregoing Report and Resolutions were unanimously accepted, and adopted.   Attest,

JOHN C. BARNES,
Clerk of the Church of the Pilgrims.

FLAMEN B. CANDLER,
Clerk of Clinton Avenue Congregational Church.

INDEX.

243